THE
BAD BOYS
OF
BREXIT

TALES OF MISCHIEF, MAYHEM & GUERRILLA WARFARE IN THE EU REFERENDUM CAMPAIGN

≈

ARRON BANKS

EDITED BY ISABEL OAKESHOTT

Biteback Publishing

This edition published in Great Britain in 2017 by
Biteback Publishing Ltd
Westminster Tower
3 Albert Embankment
London SE1 7SP
Copyright © Arron Banks, Isabel Oakeshott 2016, 2017

Arron Banks and Isabel Oakeshott have asserted their rights under
the Copyright, Designs and Patents Act 1988 to be identified as
the author and editor of this work.

ISBN 978-1-78590-205-5

10 9 8 7 6 5 4 3 2 1

A CIP catalogue record for this book is available from the British Library.

Set in Arno Pro by Adrian McLaughlin

Printed and bound in Great Britain by
CPI Group (UK) Ltd, Croydon CR0 4YY

To the 17.4 million

ACKNOWLEDGEMENTS

This diary covers one of the most exhausting and intense twelve-month periods of my life.

In the heat of the campaign, I never even thought about writing a book, so my records were all a bit of a jumble. Anyway, I can't imagine myself sitting down religiously every evening and writing up the day's events. So I have reconstructed what happened and what I thought at the time using emails, texts, documents, daily diaries – and my own fallible memory.

I've been careful not to give myself hindsight and have done my very best to capture exactly how I felt at the time. It is all still very vivid. I had a lot of help from Andy Wigmore, whose extraordinary memory for detail brought great colour to what is essentially a joint account.

The Leave.EU campaign was a huge collective endeavour and I want to thank those who, for one reason or another, do not receive their proper due in this book.

The team in Andy's office in London made an invaluable contribution to the wider campaign, making sure that every EU failing was put under the microscope and every Remain campaign scare story squashed.

Special thanks to Brian Monteith, the head of press in that office, who very often had to pick up the pieces after Wiggy and I decided to lob a grenade into the debate; as well as our lead writer Jack Montgomery, who managed the press effort day to day, advised on online content and helped with this book.

No less indispensable was Jordan Ryan, who had the dubious pleasure of serving as Wiggy's only adviser in the early days of the campaign and created our very best original content, often on personal initiative.

We absolutely could not have done without Victoria Hughes, who organised everything from the Grassroots Out rallies to Nigel's battle bus tour. Putting these events together while also trying to keep on top of Wiggy's whereabouts was like herding cats with rabies. She was assisted with some of this by Laura Bier-Nielsen, a keen nineteen-year-old volunteer, who delayed going to university to throw herself into the campaign.

I want to thank our backroom team in Bristol: Pierre Shepherd, Tom Brooke, Tom Price, Tony Strickland and the rest of the research and social media staff, who helped us to grow what became the biggest online campaign of the referendum. Holly Gardner managed thousands of dedicated volunteers from Land's End to the north of Scotland. Pam Palmer and the staff in our hard-pressed call centre made an invaluable contribution, particularly Rudolph, our Slovakian media darling.

Also due a special mention in Bristol are Peter Hargreaves, who really dug deep for Brexit, and his son Robert, who joined our team in Bristol towards the end and got stuck in at the coalface. Beyond our own immediate team there was also Ewen Stewart, our economic adviser, and Stuart Coster, who helped Brian organise our 'special ops' around Westminster. Alex Story and Alex Deane – thank you for your intelligence and humour.

Simon Heffer was a particular source of inspiration, always generous when sharing the benefits of his knowledge and experience with us. Raheem Kassam from Breitbart also deserves thanks for his support, strategic advice and encouragement. Chris Bruni-Lowe,

ACKNOWLEDGEMENTS

Gawain Towler, Michael Heaver, John Gill, Joe Jenkins and especially Dan Jukes, and the rest of the UKIP boys and girls, were close collaborators and always happy to co-operate. To Robin Birley, owner of 5 Hertford Street and a generous supporter of the cause, thank you for your hospitality throughout and after the campaign.

I could not have written this without the brilliant Isabel Oakeshott who lived in my head for ten weeks – I fear she will never be the same again. She has shared a big part of our adventure and I can't thank her and her editorial team enough.

Finally, thanks to all the voters who passionately supported the Leave.EU campaign and made 23 June our Independence Day.

NOTE FROM THE EDITOR

I have co-authored several high-profile books, all of which have been challenging in their own way. None quite prepared me for this project.

Arron's diary was researched and written in ten weeks, a near-impossible timeframe. I was only able to meet the deadline by drafting in several researchers who helped trawl through thousands of emails and text messages sent and received by Arron during the campaign, as well as Twitter accounts, media reports and Leave.EU's press releases.

Special thanks to Louis Trupia, a brilliant and endlessly enthusiastic Oxford undergraduate drafted in at three days' notice in the middle of his summer holiday. He provided invaluable research. Thanks also to reporter Nick Mutch and investigative journalist Margaret Crick. There were many sleepless nights but, thanks to this team, somehow we all got the job done.

Isabel Oakeshott

CONTENTS

CAST OF CHARACTERS

THE BAD BOYS

Arron Banks (Banksy): Boisterous Bristol-based insurance tycoon, diamond mine owner, philanthropist and man of the people. Leave.EU co-chairman and main funder. Mild-mannered with a hint of menace. Expelled from school for pinching lead off the roof and flogging it on the side.

Andy Wigmore (Wiggy): Banks's wingman and business associate. Described by himself as the 'worst head of communications in the world'. Former aide to senior Tory politicians, who now run a mile if he's around. Expelled from his Catholic school for pinching communion wine and flogging it on the side.

Nigel Farage: Banks's hero and Mr Brexit himself. Charismatic long-standing leader of UKIP and MEP. Disdained by the chattering classes, but led his party from the margins to victory in the 2014 European elections and delivered 3.9 million votes in the 2015 general election. Survives his eighteen-hour working days on a diet of cigarettes and alcohol. Despite the public bravado, prone to bouts of gloom.

Richard Tice (Mr Collegiate): The acceptable face of Leave.EU. The yin to Banks's yang. Public school-educated property tycoon, sportsman and ridiculously handsome winner in life. The one they'd want speaking to the police if they were all in a car and got pulled over.

James Pryor (Jimbo, the Happy Hippy): Straggly-haired former Tory Party aide infamous in Conservative Central Office for smoking cannabis while driving Margaret Thatcher's lectern around. Deserted to the Referendum Party, then went to UKIP. Also deserted from South African Special Forces. General fixer for Banks and keeps an eye on his business interests in Africa.

Honorary bad boy – Kate Hoey: Steely Labour MP from Ulster who finds herself sucked into the chaotic Banks/Wigmore operation. Pretends to disapprove of their antics but secretly enjoys the ride. One of the few Eurosceptics in her party with the guts to back Brexit, but prone to outbreaks of anxiety about appearing in too many photos with Farage.

ASSOCIATES

Liz Bilney: The responsible adult, resident human being and chief executive at Leave.EU. Life is a losing battle to bring Banks's and Wigmore's antics under control. The best she can hope is that they don't land her in prison. Super-efficient and doesn't hesitate to tear strips off the duo when required, which is frequently.

Gerry Gunster: Banks's big hire from the US as campaign strategist. Consummate Washington insider with a magic touch when it comes to referendums. Had no idea what he was getting into with Banks and Wigmore. In polite company, pretends he doesn't know them.

Katya Banks: Banks's Russian wife, daughter of a local government official and a teacher in Ekaterinburg. Speaks six languages and studied French at the Sorbonne. A larger-than-life extrovert who was caught up in a spy scandal in 2010. The number plate on the family Range Rover is X MI5 SPY.

Jack Montgomery: Scottish waiter plucked from obscurity to serve as lead writer, content adviser and sometime spokesman for Leave.EU. Spent the early days of the campaign sending furtive emails from the cutlery-polishing section of his restaurant to Banks, who decided he had an eye for a story and brought him in.

MONEY MEN

Peter Hargreaves: Billionaire co-founder of Hargreaves Lansdown financial advisers, which he started from spare bedroom in his Bristol flat. Thinks British finance industry will thrive free of Brussels straitjacket. Favourite hobby is digging vegetables; rarely bets more than a fiver at the races. Frugal lifestyle and reputation as an awkward bugger mean it will be hard for Banks to prise donations out of him, but if he does it will be worth the effort.

Jim Mellon: Banks's Isle-of-Man based friend and business partner whose deep pockets help get the campaign up and running. Said to be worth £850 million, he has a reputation for making the right call, including predicting the financial crisis, though he did once lose millions by investing in a dodgy brand of high-strength fish oil. Supposedly hates his nickname of 'the British Warren Buffett', but nobody believes him.

VOTE LEAVE

Matthew Elliott: Banks's nemesis. Smooth-talking chief executive of Vote Leave, which rivalled Leave.EU for status as the official Out campaign. Impeccably connected at Westminster, his mild manner and inscrutable expression mask a steely ambition. Plays the organ in church and (unlike Banks and Wigmore) has few obvious vices.

Dominic Cummings: Dishevelled campaign director of VL, he is Elliott's provisional wing. Hitman tendencies made Downing Street despair when he was a special adviser to Michael Gove as Education Secretary. Worked on the anti-euro campaign in the 1990s. Revels in his image as Westminster outsider, but is well in with journalists, who gleefully write him up as maverick brainbox plotter and, in one case, married him.

John Mills: Piggy in the middle in the long war of attrition between VL and Leave.EU. Chaired VL for much of the campaign, but constantly flirted with defecting to the more entertaining and Labour-friendly Banks/Wigmore operation. Very wealthy entrepreneur behind JML, the teleshopping channel, he is Labour's biggest non-union donor. Liked by all sides.

Lord (Nigel) Lawson of Blaby: Father of Nigella, replaced Mills as chairman of VL. Regarded, chiefly by Nigel Lawson, as the grandest figure and hugest intellect on the Leave side. As Chancellor under Margaret Thatcher, he fought to get Britain into the Exchange Rate Mechanism, test-bed for the single currency. Memorably resigned because he couldn't stomach her Euroscepticism and now lives in France.

Daniel Hannan: Conservative MEP with cult following on libertarian free-market wing of the Eurosceptic movement. Has a store of literary bons mots for every occasion. Douglas Carswell's brain and best chum.

GRASSROOTS OUT

Peter Bone: Dreary founder of Grassroots Out, which Banks supports. Stalwart of Eurosceptic 'bastard' tendency on the Tory back benches who senses his day may at last have come. Described as 'the voice of Michael Caine in the body of the Demon Headmaster'. Takes avuncular care of Tom Pursglove, whom he considers a future Prime Minister. He is alone in this – and many things.

Tom Pursglove: Bone's bag carrier and amanuensis. They function as a single entity, *Boneglove*. The youngest Tory MP, he makes up for lack of experience by getting up the noses of Banks and his team with his hissy fits and demands for better stage make-up. Once threatened to sack his PA for having drinks with UKIP staff.

Nick Wood: GO's florid-faced head of press, fighting constant turf war with Wigmore. Former press secretary to Tory leaders William Hague and Iain Duncan Smith, suspected by Banks's staff of being a none-too-subtle double agent for Vote Leave.

UKIP

Douglas Carswell: Arch-enemy of Farage. UKIP's only MP, representing Clacton in Essex. Defected from the Conservatives in 2014, but seen by many Kippers as a Tory plant. Member of VL board and bosom buddy of Hannan.

Chris Bruni-Lowe: Farage's energetic director of strategy and data nerd. Rules the UKIP office through brutal, laddish mockery, but spends his money on elaborate spa days for a little fluffy dog. Used to work for Carswell in the Tory Party and seen by some in UKIP as the best thing to come out of the MP's defection.

Gawain Towler: No knight more loyal at the round table of King Nigel. Farage made Gawain head of press after accosting him in a pub (where else?) in 2006. Rarely deviates from uniform of tweed jacket, corduroys and a waistcoat, even on a hot summer day.

George Cottrell (Posh George): Nigel's office fixer. Posh to the point of caricature and wilfully abrasive, but extremely generous when it comes to picking up the bar tab. Nephew of Lord Hesketh, Tory minister under Thatcher and John Major, who defected to UKIP.

MEDIA

Richard Desmond: Famously rude and off-the-wall cigar smoker and proprietor of Express newspapers. Started out as a cloakroom attendant and drummer – he still has a drum kit in his office. Made his name as publisher of top-shelf titles like *Asian Babes* and *Big Ones*. Banks's most powerful media ally.

Robbie Gibb: Put-upon, bald-headed BBC executive. All sides believe the Beeb's referendum coverage is biased and Gibb has the impossible job of keeping them all happy, so always looks anxious. Brother of Tory government minister Nick Gibb, his outward demeanour as a grey BBC bureaucrat masks a lively streak. Once amused guests at a Westminster party by getting physical with a cardboard cut-out of Margaret Thatcher.

Andrew Pierce: Veteran political columnist at the *Daily Mail* and broadcaster at LBC. Waspish, camp and good to have on your side. Always in the market for juicy gossip and loves a good-humoured bitch. Isn't afraid who he upsets, but is afraid of going bald.

Simon Heffer: Influential right-wing columnist on the *Telegraph* who likes good lunches and shooting. Banks and Wigmore cultivate him with briefings and the occasional freebie. A convinced Outer, he sees eye to eye with them on almost everything.

Lucy Fisher: Well-spoken young *Times* political reporter. Always eager for a story, becomes one of Banks's favourite media contacts after they meet at a party.

OTHERS

Lord (Michael) Ashcroft of Chichester: Self-made billionaire and international man of mystery. Lovingly cultivates Bond villain image – not entirely tongue in cheek. Wearer of many hats: businessman, author, pollster, philanthropist and irreverent tweeter. His millions kept the Conservative Party show on the road for years but he plays his political cards closer to his chest these days.

Richard North: Tireless campaigner for decades on his hobby horses of Euroscepticism and food hygiene. Formerly Farage's head of research, they fell out while sharing an office in Brussels. He and his son Peter let rip with regular tirades of abuse against Banks and Wigmore, who respond in kind.

LOCATIONS

Lysander House: Banks's HQ. A David Brent-style office block in Catbrain Lane on the outskirts of Bristol. The main local landmarks are the M5 and a Harvester restaurant. The natural home for the Leave.EU call centre.

Millbank Tower: Leave.EU's London base after Banks reluctantly decides they need an office close to the hated Westminster bubble. Hideous 1960s skyscraper on the Embankment near the Houses of Parliament. Overlooks the much smaller and uglier tower occupied by VL across the river. Formerly the nerve centre of New Labour control freakery, where Peter Mandelson masterminded the triumph of Tony Blair.

Old Down: Banks's country estate on the outskirts of Bristol, bought from musician Mike Oldfield in 2008. He restored the Victorian manor house and hires it out as a wedding venue. It's also good for wining and dining journalists, politicians and potential supporters of the cause. Banks stocked its park with llamas. Home is a house on the estate where he lives with Katya and three of his five children, Darren (16), Olivia (13) and Peter (11). Handy for Catbrain Lane.

5 Hertford Street: Private members' establishment in Mayfair opened by Robin Birley, doyen of the London club scene. Less fusty than more traditional gentlemen's clubs, but still exclusive. Perfect for a hush-hush lunch and a bit of discreet arm-twisting. Features all-important smoking terrace so Farage has no excuse to refuse invitations.

Pretoria: Banks's second home in South Africa, where he spent much of his childhood. His base when he needs to check up on his diamond mining interests in South Africa and Lesotho. Oscar Pistorius used to be a neighbour.

HOW IT BEGAN

In a way, it all started in a pub in Guernsey.

It was June 2015, and the Tories had just won the general election. The party would now have to deliver its pledge to hold an EU referendum.

The election campaign had been gruelling, and UKIP leader Nigel Farage was feeling battered. His attempt to win a parliamentary seat had ended in failure and he was unsure what the future held. When an old friend invited him to join a short business cruise for two or three dozen right-leaning industrialists on Cunard's *Queen Elizabeth*, he was glad to accept.

Also on that cruise was a political strategist named Matthew Elliott. The brains behind the influential TaxPayers' Alliance think tank, Elliott was a familiar figure in Westminster circles. He was delighted by the opportunity to network with some of the wealthiest political donors in the country. He had big plans for the year ahead.

The ship had docked for a few hours and Farage, who likes nothing better than sampling a new hostelry, had run ashore for a lunchtime pint. As he sat with a beer in St Peter Port, he spotted Elliott strolling by and beckoned him in. The discussion that followed would determine how the battle for Britain to leave the European Union would take shape.

Both men expected to play a central role. Elliott already had one successful referendum under his belt (the No to AV plebiscite on an alternative voting system in 2012) and was part of the political establishment. Respected by senior Tories and political journalists alike, over the years he had amassed a network of rich patrons who could be called upon to back his projects. By the time he and Farage met on the cruise, he had already laid the foundations for his bid to mastermind the referendum campaign by setting up a Eurosceptic pressure group called Business for Britain.

For his part, Farage had been preparing for the referendum all his political life. He had spent the best part of a quarter of a century fighting to get Britain out of the EU. Now, as the man who had done more than any other individual to bring about the referendum, he naturally expected to be at the heart of the campaign. Where did he figure in Elliott's game plan?

This is what the two men discussed that day. The tension was not just about egos – though egos certainly played a part. At heart was a fundamental difference of opinion over how the campaign should be fought and whether Farage should be at the forefront. 'I think you should leave it to the experts,' Elliott told him – by which he meant strategists like himself.

Farage was affronted. He was also worried. Years of grassroots campaigning all over Britain had taught him that immigration was a massive issue among working-class and lower-middle-class voters. When it came to Britain's relationship with Brussels, he knew that the EU's sacred open borders policy was the issue that most rankled with these groups, however queasy it made the *bien pensants* in London. Of course he recognised the importance of arguments about business and sovereignty, but he was adamant that deepening public concern about mass migration was the key to Brexit.

Elliott disagreed. He believed focusing on immigration would drag the campaign into a fatal row about racism and xenophobia.

He also believed Farage was too divisive to win over floating voters. Plus, he wanted to give Prime Minister David Cameron a chance to negotiate a better deal with Brussels – as the PM had always promised the electorate – before committing himself to an Out campaign.

There was little common ground.

A horn sounded, signalling that the *Queen Elizabeth* was preparing to leave port, and the pair hurried back to the ship. Reflecting on their conversation, Farage fell into a gloom. He now had deep misgivings about the looming campaign. On his return from the cruise, he called me. 'We're going to lose this referendum unless we do something,' he told me anxiously. I listened carefully to what Nigel had to say, and knew immediately that I wanted to help. I knew there was no greater champion of the Eurosceptic cause, and trusted his judgement implicitly. I also liked him enormously. I was ready to do whatever it took.

Our relationship had not begun well. We first met in the grand environs of the Royal Automobile Club in Pall Mall in summer 2014. Nigel, a twenty-a-day man, immediately upset staff by lighting up a cigarette. He was extremely grumpy when politely asked to desist, becoming even more bad tempered and rude when he was told he could not even smoke in the garden. He started muttering about Britain being 'a free country' and I began to have visions of my membership of the club being revoked. It did not help that we were both feeling under the weather. He seemed on edge throughout, and I left the encounter unimpressed. Nonetheless, I admired what he was doing, and indicated that I might be willing to support UKIP financially at some point in the future.

That moment came far sooner than I expected, following a remarkable upturn in UKIP's political fortunes. In the autumn of 2014, two Tory MPs – Douglas Carswell and Mark Reckless – dramatically defected, and Farage was keen to keep up the momentum.

At the time, I was still a member of the Conservatives, having been very active in the party when I was young. At the age of twenty-one, I had been vice-chairman of my local Tory association and had stood as a councillor in a Labour stronghold in Basingstoke. I was the youngest Conservative candidate in the country and received a letter from Margaret Thatcher acknowledging this special status. I failed to win the ward, however, and ended up pursuing a career in business instead.

For a long time I was too busy with my career and bringing up a young family to get actively involved in politics again. I never lost interest in politics, however, and watched with dismay as John Major blithely signed away our control over our borders via the 1992 Maastricht Treaty.

As power ebbed from Westminster, I knew it would be much harder to hold our elected representatives to account, and that this lack of accountability would lead inevitably to shoddy government and lower standards in public life. The erosion of our ability to determine our own laws and choose our way of life had only just begun. I hated it, and I couldn't understand why the party that was supposed to be more dedicated to upholding our historic constitution and hard-won democratic freedoms than any other was now palming everything off to a clique of anonymous, unelected foreign officials. It felt like a betrayal. Though I remained a member of the Tory Party, and supported my local association financially, I was becoming increasingly disillusioned by the party's weak stance on Europe.

That first meeting with Farage, unsatisfactory as it was, marked a turning point in my political allegiances. Not long afterwards, he rang rather tentatively asking whether I might consider making a donation of £100,000, which he said could be presented as another defection, albeit by a donor not an MP. I immediately agreed. My businesses in this country and overseas, where I own a number of diamond mines, were doing very well. I wanted to give something back, and help the fight to get Britain out of the EU.

My decision to give money to UKIP gave me an unpleasant taste of the way big political power players dismiss people like me who are not part of the club. On the morning the donation was made public, I was sitting in bed eating toast and honey and flicked on Sky News to see William Hague snootily dismissing me as a nobody.

A few minutes later, Farage was on the phone. 'The Foreign

Secretary is all over the television saying he doesn't know who you are, and nobody he knows has ever heard of you,' he reported.

'I know,' I replied. 'What a cheek! Let's up the donation to £1 million!'

Farage was amazed. He had been more than happy with the original amount, and didn't believe I was serious.

'I mean it,' I said firmly. 'Let's do this.'

'OK, leave it with me,' Farage replied excitably.

At which point he hotfooted it off to brief the press. Speculation was rife that more Tory MPs were going to change sides, and Nigel, somewhat disingenuously, was briefing that another defection was imminent.

Before I'd had time to gather my thoughts, hundreds of journalists and cameramen began descending on Old Down, my country estate. The scenes that followed were totally chaotic. In my fit of pique, I had forgotten that my wife and I were due to host a major fundraiser for a Belize children's charity that evening. We had invited the wife of the Prime Minister of Belize, who was staying with us, as well as half the members of the South West Conservative Party. Also joining us was as a senior figure from the Commonwealth Society with close links to the royal household, who was due to arrive early.

To his bemusement, the unfortunate Palace insider appeared at exactly the same time as the press pack were arriving. (His response to the bizarre unfolding spectacle was some most uncourtly language: *'Holy shit.'*)

Farage himself arrived in high spirits and ordered me to get out and face the cameras. As I emerged from the house and nervously surveyed the scene, I could see a ripple of disgust spread through the press pack. They had been dragged down the M4 on a false premise, and did nothing to hide their disappointment that I was not a politician.

Having come all this way, however, they were loath to waste the story, and my new donation was headline news.

When they had all buggered off, I suggested Farage spend the night at Old Down, and invited him to do the charity auction at our fundraising dinner. The Conservatives I'd invited were surprised and dismayed that their host had not only dramatically left the party but also forced them to spend an evening with Farage. It's fair to say the reaction was mixed. At least one inebriated and indignant guest had to be escorted from the premises after becoming abusive towards our special guest. Nonetheless, the evening was a roaring success and raised a lot of money for a great cause.

I was still high on adrenalin after all the guests had departed, and took it into my head to clamber onto the roof of my Land Rover to watch the sun rise.

Not long afterwards, Farage, who had stopped drinking only a little earlier and can have had no more than two hours' sleep, emerged from the house bright as a button and found me in a crumpled heap on the gravel, having rolled off the car with an ungainly thud and fallen asleep where I landed.

It marked the beginning of what has become a firm friendship.

In the months that followed, I became increasingly involved in UKIP politics. As a businessman, I was shocked and dismayed by what I learned about the inner workings of the party. It was hopelessly dysfunctional and ill-prepared for campaigning.

It was far less of a threat to the Conservatives than it appeared. Nonetheless, Farage's huge personal following frightened them. They certainly did not want him becoming an MP. As I was to discover, they were ready to go to any lengths to prevent it happening, including, apparently, breaking the law.

In this enterprise, they had a highly valuable and willing accomplice in the shape of the recently converted UKIP MP for Clacton. As one of just two Kippers in the Commons, Carswell was in a powerful position. His decision to defect must have been quite a wrench. He had been actively involved in the Tory Party for at least fifteen years, and an MP for almost a decade. The Eurosceptic Tory MEP Dan Hannan was one of his closest friends. His arrival was a huge boost for UKIP, helping to create the credibility and energy it needed to do well in 2015, but it would return to haunt Farage.

From the start, there were lingering suspicions among some

Kippers that his decision was not made on principle. Clacton is a staunchly Eurosceptic part of the country, and private polling suggested that UKIP was a serious threat to the sitting MP. Carswell was in very real danger of losing his seat.

Only he knows whether his heart was ever really in leaving the Conservative Party, but it is interesting that he went to great lengths to ensure that if his great gamble backfired, he would be well looked after. Arrangements were put in place for him to receive a considerable sum of money from UKIP if he failed to win the by-election triggered by his defection. In the event, he held onto the seat, and the compensation package proved unnecessary.

Fast forward to the general election, and Farage's own bid to enter Parliament turned South Thanet into the most bitterly contested seat in the country. In an increasingly febrile atmosphere, an array of individuals and organisations of all political hues coalesced to thwart him. It was not a fair fight. We now know that the Conservative Party had no compunction about busting legal spending limits, pouring huge sums of money and other resources into the seat. They used a variety of ruses to mask their activities. Moreover, it appears they may also have got their hands on some very useful inside information.

Carswell was one of just three individuals with access to UKIP's highly sensitive private polling on target seats. This detailed data identified specific streets and households whose support would be pivotal to win the seat. With an official role overseeing UKIP's target seat campaign, Carswell was supposed to use it to do everything in his power to propel candidates to victory – including the party leader.

As the battle for the seat intensified, Farage was surprised and concerned to find that Tory activists were targeting the exact same individuals in South Thanet. It now appears that they were doing so via a highly unethical 'push polling' operation based in the southwest London suburb of Kingston, which involved using loaded questions to plant negative ideas about Nigel in voters' minds.

How did they come to be so well informed?

We may never know. Long after polling day, however, my own forensic post-mortem examination of South Thanet revealed something quite remarkable: Carswell was routinely downloading the data and sending it to an anonymous computer server.

He did so on six separate occasions. While there were files on every target seat in the country, curiously, only the information about South Thanet was shared. Quite where the information went once it left our offices, nobody knows, but I can make an educated guess: the Tories. This private data could have made it much easier for the Tories to target floating voters in the constituency.

Farage duly lost the seat. Soon after the election, he resigned as UKIP leader.

Taken together, the excessive spending, the push polling, and the very murky 'sharing' of UKIP's private data suggest an extraordinary stitch-up by the Tories. This information is now in the hands of the police.

Farage's notorious decision to 'un-resign' was prompted by a hostile phone call from Carswell. Now UKIP's only MP (Reckless having lost his seat) and in control of £650,000 of taxpayers' money designed to support opposition parties, Carswell was more empowered than ever. During a highly unpleasant exchange, he told Farage to stay out of the referendum campaign. It was a step too far, and it backfired. Farage returned to the leadership, determined to play the campaign his own way.

Now deeply mistrustful of the Tories and elements within his own party, he asked me to consider running it. I said yes immediately.

I cared so much about the cause, and was so outraged by his treatment, that I was ready to put in several million pounds from my own fortune. In July 2015, with my friend and business associate Andy 'Wiggy' Wigmore, I began building the campaign.

Nigel had a clear vision for our role. Knowing that the Conservatives would avoid talking about immigration, he wanted us to put the issue at the forefront of our efforts. Our brief was to do what even he could not: be as provocative as required to keep immigration at the top of the agenda.

This book is the story of how we responded.

Our methods were unorthodox and often landed us in hot water. We were undoubtedly the 'bad boys' of the referendum campaign. Our belligerent approach to politicians and other people we felt were letting down the country upset the establishment and we fell out with everyone from NASA to Posh Spice. At times, even Farage thought we went too far.

Yet it worked. Through the power of social media, we were creating an extraordinary mass movement, drawing in swathes of voters neglected by the main political parties. At times our social media reach hit nearly 20 million people in a week – a third of the entire population.

We never set out to cosy up to politicians or even to influence them. Our strategy was to go direct to the people, using techniques that bypassed the mainstream media. It may have appeared chaotic, but the thinking behind it was very clear. In America, Donald Trump, the ultimate political outsider, is doing similar things.

For all the larks, we took our efforts to persuade the Electoral Commission to designate us as the official Leave campaign extremely seriously. In the end, we failed. In hindsight, it's not surprising. We were rank outsiders, and could be loose cannons. In any case, it turned out to be a good thing. So far from giving up, we proceeded to run a parallel operation to the official campaign run by Elliott. While we were constrained by legal spending limits, we were otherwise gloriously unaccountable.

Ours became the guerrilla war. It was not for the faint-hearted, but we enjoyed almost every minute. I believe it was pivotal to the outcome of the referendum.

This is my diary of our adventures.

Arron Banks,
September 2016

PART 1:
JULY–SEPTEMBER 2015

JULY 2015

1 JULY

A summer break with Farage

We're off. After far too long pounding the streets of South Thanet with our fellow fruitcakes and loonies, Nigel and I are doing a runner from reality and flying to the sunnier climes of Belize.

He's exhausted and needs a change of scene. The drama of his resignation from the UKIP leadership followed by his now-infamous un-resignation was mentally and physically draining.

His adviser Raheem Kassam, a young right-wing firebrand, used to have him in the sauna every other day sweating buckets, so he wouldn't look all damp-faced and shifty – the dreaded 'Nixon lip' – at hustings. On at least one occasion this led to a half-conscious Farage having to avert his eyes as Kassam engaged in a sweaty naked wrestling match with a local idiot who was trying to snap a sly picture of the UKIP leader's tackle for BuzzFeed. It was like a scene from *Borat*.

We'll be travelling with Andy 'Wiggy' Wigmore, my business

associate and one of my best friends. As far as I can tell, his life's been one long adventure. He has anecdotes about everything, from nearly getting blown to pieces by a piano stuffed with semtex in Zululand to lodging with a retired Ronald Reagan at his ranch in California.

He comes from a long line of fugitive pirates and buccaneers who landed up in Belize after outrunning the hangman's noose. Supposedly, he's descended from Blackbeard himself, which seems less implausible than it first sounds once you've spent any amount of time with him. Somehow he's acquired a sufficient veneer of respectability to have a role as the Belize government's trade rep to the UK, giving him diplomatic status.

The three of us have spent the past few months traipsing around the country on the campaign trail, which at least fine-tuned our ability to have fun in unpromising places. We spent one particularly memorable afternoon canvassing on a council estate in Ramsgate, winding up in a sticky-floored pub where we lost a pile of money playing darts with the locals.

For all the larks, though, Nigel is a workhorse, and it was quite an effort to persuade him he deserves a break. One draw was the fishing: Belize is a great place to go out on the water. It's a far cry from his usual sea angling off North Shields with the locals, but it has its compensations, not least staying at Francis Ford Coppola's hotel on Placencia beach.

He would never have agreed to come without a work-related lure, so we've fixed up a meeting with Michael Ashcroft, who grew up in Belize and considers it home. His wealth, political influence and Eurosceptic leanings all mean he could be a useful ally for the EU referendum. We're keen to sound him out.

That campaign has to be our focus now. We've spent enough time crying into our beer over what happened at the general election. It's criminal – probably literally – that UKIP didn't gain a single seat, and what happened to Nigel in South Thanet was scandalous. We ran an honest campaign and toiled our guts out to help him win the seat, only to see the Tories cheat their way to victory.

But we need to move on.

What matters is that Nigel achieved his bigger goal: forcing David Cameron to have a referendum. There's no way the PM can escape. Most people don't seem to think it will happen for at least eighteen months, but Nigel is convinced Cameron will want to get it out of the way and insists there's no time to waste.

I'm ready to do whatever it takes. Wiggy's also in. It's a high-risk strategy, but we're going to run this show together. His propensity for high jinks and my inability to resist saying exactly what I think mean there will probably be a few hairy moments, but at least it won't be boring.

I've put him on notice that he'll be head of press. He's hopelessly disorganised and can't spell, but he can charm anyone and has friends and contacts everywhere from Basutoland to Buckingham Palace. As political outsiders, we'll need all the support we can get.

I'm clear how we can help win the referendum: by acting as the provisional wing of the Brexit campaign, doing and saying the things that, as leader of Britain's third biggest political party, Nigel can't. I've told him my priority will be to put immigration at the heart of the debate and engage millions of voters who dislike and distrust the political classes.

'Let's shake this up,' I said cheerfully. 'The more outrageous we are, the more attention we'll get; the more attention we get, the more outrageous we'll be.'

He looked a little unconvinced by this strategy.

'Only time will tell if you and Wigmore are geniuses or complete idiots,' he said.

The Turtle Inn will be the perfect place to relax – and plot. It's right by the beach and the accommodation is beautiful: Balinese-style cottages with glossy dark-wood interiors and verandas on the sand. There are aquamarine plunge pools, tropical flowers, turtles and terrapins everywhere, and the food's incredible.

All in all, the perfect place to forget our ordeal on the Kent coast and figure out our next move.

2 JULY

Airborne

We met Nigel at Heathrow. He still seemed in reflective mood. He can't stop beating himself up about whether he could have done more to win the seat.

He soon snapped out of it though, as people started coming up to him in the departures lounge, commiserating and telling him what a great bloke he is. Several actually apologised for voting Conservative, saying they wanted him to win but they were scared by the prospect of letting Ed Miliband and the SNP in by the back door.

Nigel got more of the hero treatment when we boarded the plane. The captain had seen his name on the flight manifest and came out of the cockpit to meet him. 'Thank you for everything you're doing for the country,' he enthused, pumping Nigel's hand.

Minutes later, we were all armed with glasses of champagne and Nigel was looking more relaxed.

This is going to do him the world of good.

3 JULY

Chillaxing

The problem with Belize is that it takes bloody ages to get here, and after multiple flights and transfers, I didn't have the energy to do much today except chill out by the pool.

True to form, Nigel was up at the crack of dawn, itching to get out on a boat. His ability to get by on a few hours' sleep, even after his usual heavy nights, never ceases to amaze. Wiggy put a brave face on the jetlag and the pair of them set off at some uncivilised hour, armed with a box of beer and sandwiches, leaving me to put my feet up with a novel and a rum punch cocktail like a proper people's army soldier.

Their plan was to spend the day in a small boat on a crocodile-infested swamp. Apparently there are good things to catch, but eight hours on a millpond in 90-degree heat and humidity was a temptation I found easy to resist.

They returned late afternoon looking sweaty but pleased with themselves. Turned out their Rastafarian fishing guide was an Anglophile and had seen Nigel on YouTube giving Jean-Claude Juncker and his faceless Eurocrat mates the hairdryer treatment. Cue lots of excited backslapping and selfies.

This evening we took their haul (mostly snook) to a breezy gastro bar in Placencia, overlooking a cricket pitch. Called Rumfish y Vino, it's famous for having the best wine list in Belize, so it seemed only polite to sample as many of their best bottles as we could. You can bring your own fish, which they gut and cook. Delicious.

For once, we didn't talk politics. Nigel seems happier already.

4 JULY

Politicians and sharks

Another blissful day without anyone bending my ear. Farage and Wiggy set off early for another day's fishing, this time on the open water. They headed for Silk Caye, about twenty nautical miles from Placencia, where there are two picture-postcard desert islands, all palm trees and crystalline waters by a barrier reef.

The idea was to catch barracuda, but they ended up landing more than they'd reckoned for after hooking a yellow tuna. Just as they were reeling it in, something much bigger grabbed it and also got stuck. It was a shark. It was quite an impressive specimen and Wiggy took a great picture of Nigel grappling with his catch. Sharks are protected under conservation laws, so of course he let it go and it swam off happily enough.

We're on for Ashcroft tomorrow. I've never met him and am curious to see if he lives up to his fearsome reputation. I had hoped Wiggy could pull some strings to get me an introduction when I was first sucked into frontline politics a year or so ago, but he snubbed me.

Apparently, he wasn't impressed by a little spat I had with William Hague when I made my first big donation to UKIP. 'Hague's my mate,' was the message that came back. Seems he's put that behind him now.

What Nigel doesn't know is that getting to Ashcroft's lair means island-hopping on very small aircraft. After his plane crash in 2010, he's not too keen on flying, especially not on tiny planes like the one he was in when the accident happened. Wiggy and I decided not to tell him till morning. No point giving him a sleepless night.

5 JULY

Interrogated by Ashcroft

Say what you like about Farage, but he has guts. It took us five short hops on a wobbly little plane to get to San Pedro, a small fishing town on the southern part of Ambergris Caye where we were meeting Ashcroft, and he didn't complain. He just went a bit quiet.

Ashcroft, who's a big deal in this neck of the woods ('the uncrowned king of Belize', as Wiggy puts it) was waiting to meet us at the airport, grinning like a crocodile. Sharp as a tack, he immediately spotted that Farage was looking a bit peaky.

'Enjoy the flight, Nigel? Nice day for a bit of island-hopping,' he teased. 'Let's get a drink into you.' He and his son Andrew took us to a fancy place on a pier with amazing views and we had a quick drink before checking into our hotel. It's another eye-popper, right on the edge of the Belize Barrier Reef. Two nights here is nowhere near enough!

After we'd dumped our stuff, we sauntered down the beach to one of Ashcroft's favourite haunts, a shack where he likes to have breakfast and tweet pictures of beautiful women in bikinis in an attempt to make his followers jealous.

As soon as we sat down he started taking the piss out of Nigel. 'Seen much of Liz Hurley lately?' he asked mischievously. Nigel blushed. She's a Eurosceptic, and they've met. Warming to his theme, Ashcroft promptly tweeted a scantily clad picture of Hugh Grant's old flame with Nigel's Twitter handle suggestively attached. Nigel pretended to be cross but I could see he was pleased. It doesn't do his image any harm.

Ashy and I were in danger of getting off on the wrong foot when he started grilling me about my big donation to UKIP in 2014.

I'd only planned to give them £100,000 – until our old flop of a Foreign Secretary Hague declared he didn't know who I was. There was only one way to reply, which was to up the donation to a million, which made a bit of a splash at the time. 'They said I was a nobody,' the press reported me saying. 'They know who I am now.'

Ashcroft didn't see the funny side. 'Bit of a waste of money, wasn't it?' he asked, rather aggressively, I thought.

I don't see it that way. It was Nigel's growing popularity that forced the Tories to promise a referendum, and that pledge, combined with a huge UKIP surge among Labour's traditional working-class supporters, killed Miliband in the marginals and gave Cameron his unexpected majority.

I was taken aback at the mini-inquisition, but soon realised it's just his lordship's way.

'So what are you going to do next?' Ashcroft asked Nigel after the main course (and a fair few Belkin beers. The local brew is very good.).

'I'm going to win the referendum,' Nigel replied.

Now it was our turn to wind Ashcroft up, asking him if he was going to join the fight, perhaps even put a bit of money into the pot. He played his cards close to his chest. We parted ways very merry, but none the wiser, though he told us to keep in touch. I am sure he's an Outer at heart, but he doesn't want to commit himself yet.

We whiled away the rest of the day in a dodgy bar, where Nigel let rip. Perhaps it was the combination of sun and alcohol, or just jet-lag, but he really was paralytic. Wiggy and I wanted to call it a day but, try as we might, we couldn't prise him away. His stamina was unbelievable.

Suddenly he remembered he'd promised to write an op-ed for the *Telegraph*.

'Christ!' he spluttered, muttering something about bloody press officers.

He grabbed his phone and stumbled outside. It looked bad, but just a few minutes later, I could hear him, cool, calm and collected, dictating flowing prose on the fly. He was as lucid and precise as if his belly were full of nothing but lemonade. God knows how he does it.

7 JULY

Catbrain Lane – mission control

It's time to get back to work and real life, half a world away from the Turtle Inn. That means a building on an industrial estate on the edge of Bristol. In the next few weeks, I am going to transform it into the nerve centre of the referendum campaign.

I took a long lease on the place about fifteen years ago when I was building my company, mostly because it's really handy to get to from my house at Old Down. It's located at a real beauty spot just off Junction 17 of the M5. The offices come with a made-up sounding address – Catbrain Lane – and the sort of views that are not going to distract anyone from their computer screens. Over the road is Topps Tiles and the nearest boozer is a Harvester. There's another one, the Farmhouse Inn, just by the car park. It seems to manage a brisk trade with its £4.75 'daily fresh carvery'.

Visitors from London always say our HQ looks like the setting for *The Office*, and I suppose there's more than a passing likeness to David Brent's paper merchant's office in Slough. But I like to think I'm a bit more formidable than Ricky Gervais's famous character. As for Wiggy, I can't see him trading in his dapper little pocket squares for a clip-on tie and a read-through of health and safety briefings by the photocopier.

Nobody's pretending it's glamorous here, but I don't need anything fancy. Today I dined in true Cribbs Causeway luxury: white plastic sandwiches, a packet of crisps and a glass of tap water. Tea if I'm lucky. Not exactly gourmet, but I'm busy getting on with it.

After recharging my batteries in Belize, I'm ready to hit the ground running. Our job is to excite people about this referendum, hold the establishment's feet to the fire, and well and truly burst the Westminster bubble. Nobody knows who we are, so we'll need sharp elbows to push our way past the clapped-out Eurosceptic aristocracy, who have been trotting out the same self-serving after-dinner speeches for years. The cravats-and-blazers brigade might lap it up, but we need to engage the wider public. We are going to be blunt, edgy and controversial, Donald Trump-style. If BBC producers aren't spluttering organic muesli over their breakfast tables every morning, we won't be doing our job.

I've put Liz Bilney, my CEO, in charge of day-to-day operations. She's super smart, knows what I'm like, and isn't afraid to kick arse to get the job done right.

We've already signed up a Soho-based advertising company called The Minimart. Their slogan is 'Fierce Thinking' and I want them to live up to it. We need to take risks, not the safe route. We've been using them for a while to pump out stuff for UKIP, some of which has gone viral.

They've already come up with some branding. We're going to call our campaign "The Know'. The idea's simple: the referendum question is expected to be: 'Do you want Britain to stay in the European Union?' with a choice of Yes or No.

If we're going to persuade undecideds to vote No, they'll need to be 'in the know' about Brussels. I want to get ahead of the game with a soft launch this week while lazy Westminster types are still on their sun loungers. I get the impression MPs aren't planning to get their finger out until at least September, which is far too late. I want to set a pace that blows their minds.

8 JULY

Let's get cracking

Thanked Ashcroft for his hospitality in Belize. He may give us some help developing simple messages for the campaign: 'Don't sleepwalk into the euro by voting Yes' – that type of thing.

The campaign mustn't be monopolised by politicians or it won't get any traction beyond the M25. The last thing we want is some self-congratulatory Tory operation from central London, crashing bores talking to crashing bores, and preachers preaching to the converted. My plan is to have supporters from every walk of life, led by brand ambassadors from a range of fields: sports, entertainment, business, medicine, science, education.

Finding the right people will be hard work, so I'm going on a schmooze-fest. It won't do much for my waistline, but the diet can wait. Lunching with Express boss Richard Desmond on Monday followed by Peter Hargreaves, the founder of Hargreaves Lansdown, a big financial services company, on Wednesday. They're both going to be very valuable supporters.

I'm also hatching a plan for a £250,000 competition for the best essay on post-Brexit Britain. Toby Blackwell of the Blackwell book-shops family says he'll fund it. It's a hell of a prize, and that kind of money should attract some serious thinkers.

Wiggy kicked off our online campaign today by tweeting about The Know. He attached a tile (a kind of social media advert) tagged 'Coming soon, The Know, theknow.eu'. It won't trouble Reuters, but it's a start.

Today's big running story was Osborne's plan to abolish permanent non-dom status. I'm not offshore myself, but kept my head down. Doesn't do to be sticking up for the super-rich. Unfortunately, Wiggy rather distracted from our message by wading into the debate. 'Thanks a bunch,' was his Twitter reaction to Osborne's announcement. It rather suggested he's taken advantage of the non-dom thing himself and doesn't exactly burnish our 'everyman' credentials.

Cue a predictable torrent of Twitter abuse about him being a rich git. Told him he needs to engage his brain before he types if we're going to get this campaign past first base.

Sky's just called asking if anyone's available for an interview tomorrow. They want to talk about The Know. There's no way I'm doing it even though I'd like to – I've got an ear infection and am on antibiotics. So I volunteered Wiggy.

He seemed reluctant, which was a bit of a surprise. He's not exactly shy. He needs to find his feet quickly if he's going to be our frontman, so I gave him a motivational speech – 'Don't fuck it up, get a bloody haircut' – and sent him on his way.

He does have his uses, though. He's got hold of a rare silk-bound copy of Rudyard Kipling's *Rewards and Fairies* for me. It includes the great poem 'If'. Worth its £2,750 price tag. I think I'll give it to Ashcroft as a thank-you for meeting up.

9 JULY

Sexy spinner

We've been looking for someone to help Wiggy with our PR.

Jim Pickard, the *Financial Times* journalist, has suggested a few names. It was nice of him to help. I doubt we're going to see eye to eye with him as the campaign hots up. The *FT* is shamelessly Europhile and the way its editor Lionel Barber's going, we'll be doing well to keep relations as cordial as this.

I ran Pickard's suggestions through Google and was a little disappointed.

'For Christ's sake, find someone presentable,' I told Wiggy.

He looked delighted at this task, and trotted off. I heard him murmuring appreciatively in the next room as he trawled the websites of likely-sounding think tanks for candidates who fitted the bill. Before long, he reappeared, triumphantly brandishing his iPad.

'How about her?' he asked, pointing at an image of a foxy brunette from the Institute of Economic Affairs. I suspect the picture was not from the IEA website, however, as she was in a kind of lipstick-lesbian pose with a girl force-feeding her tequilas. 'Found her in the staff section of their website. Checked her out online.'

Told him to get a grip.

13 JULY

Top-shelf tips

Lunch with Richard Desmond, who built his publishing empire on various top-shelf titles. I banned Wiggy from joining us on the basis that he'd only derail the serious discussions by asking for recommendations.

Desmond's great company and we had fun. Sorry to say I ended up giving in to a cigar, which won't please my doctor.

The *FT*, meanwhile, has surprised me by agreeing to run a piece about the Brexit essay competition. It'll be *Apprentice*-style, with job offers for the top five winners from a shortlist of ten. We'll have three judges – one of them will be Jim Mellon, who made a fortune in fund management and is now backing us. We'll also have a Eurosceptic and a pro-EU judge. One more piece of encouraging news: the Bruges Group, a think tank once headed by Lady Thatcher herself, has been in touch saying they love our idea of a non-political campaign and will help our efforts to set up a united front. A great start.

14 JULY

The big plan

Followed up lunch with Desmond with an email describing my vision for the campaign. I also thanked him for helping persuade

Nigel that UKIP's got to change. The party's a shambles, and needs root-and-branch reform. I'd kick half of them out if I had my way, starting with that Tory turncoat Douglas Carswell.

We were all delighted when he defected from the Conservatives, but it's become increasingly obvious he only did it because he knew he was going to lose the seat. He made sure his arse was well covered by demanding a hefty sum in compensation from the party if his little gamble didn't pay off, with a guarantee that his family would be 'looked after'. He's been nothing but a pain in the backside since.

Cameron wasn't wrong when he said UKIP has more than its fair share of fruitcakes and loonies, far too many of whom have wormed their way to the top. I was shocked by how disorganised they were during the election campaign. There's only so much one man (Nigel) can do to keep the show on the road. If it wasn't for his energy and charisma, they wouldn't be anywhere.

Told Desmond: 'I fully endorse your comments on UKIP and unforced errors, we need to radically overhaul the back office … The unfortunate fact is we were very disorganised at the election and this must improve.'

The Know will be a very different operation: ruthlessly efficient, like my businesses. My plan is a media blitz in late September (full-page ads in national newspapers, TV, online media etc.) to set out what we think David Cameron's so-called renegotiation of Britain's EU membership should deliver.

Right now, the PM's being hopelessly vague. Nobody knows what he hopes to achieve and I am sure he'd like it to stay that way. We'll invite him to play the hero and bat for Britain (for a change). He should really be aiming for associate membership that leaves us with free trade but no political or economic integration with the Eurozone – in other words, what people voted for back in 1975.

I'm not holding my breath, but we need to raise people's expectations of what an acceptable deal would look like, so that Cameron's inevitable empty repackaging of the existing terms will be seen for the sham it is.

I told Desmond we've been looking at how Obama and the

Italian Five Star movement have exploited social media. I think we can achieve similar success once we've primed the pump.

I signed off by reminding Desmond how important Farage is to all this, even if his party is a dog's breakfast. Told him:

> In terms of UKIP, it's a separate campaign but in due course it might provide the building blocks and infrastructure for something very interesting.
> Best
> Arron
>
> PS. Nigel is a top bloke and cares about his country – UKIP may not be perfect but he has single-handedly changed the country by forcing the agenda.

Thinking about it, we'll have to have a base at Westminster. I've no desire to run this show from the dreaded London SW1 – the whole point is that Wiggy and I are outside the political bubble. But we have to be realistic about how much can be done from Catbrain Lane.

I'm in the process of recruiting the right people to make this fly. I'm going to exploit all the data I can find and use hundreds of call centre staff to convert as many as 10,000 people a day to the cause. Got to think big. We'll back it up with a massive ad campaign. I'm also looking to extend the campaign around the world, especially the US. Cameron will be calling in favours from the global elites and we need sympathisers abroad too. Wiggy and I are watching how Trump's playing this. The rise of outsider politics is not just a UK thing.

15 JULY

Stale Kippers

Been bogged down all day with more UKIP grumbles. It's so bloody dysfunctional.

Jamie Huntman, a big cheese in the party hierarchy, is hopping mad about an email sent out to members by some dunderhead at HQ which finishes with the rallying cry 'Remember the Battle of Britain, let's get airborne'. Christ. What year do they think this is – 1940?

He emailed me complaining that these are the same people who (in his words) 'cocked up' the general election campaign. As he pointed out, the party's membership is slipping; our vote share is going down in by-elections and yet they're still sticking with the same broken formula, churning out press releases and emails that conveniently omit to mention their single greatest asset: Nigel. Some in the party want to erase the leader.

'If this was a business, the shareholders would demand change,' Huntman concluded. 'We need once and for all to remove the "fruit-cakes" tag. If this does not happen soon we are toast.'

Couldn't have put it better myself.

~

Failed my life insurance check this morning because I've been smoking. I blame the cigar I had after that lunch with Desmond. They've hiked up my premiums by 50 per cent – an extra £600 a month. Bloody expensive lunch in retrospect. Emailed Desmond and Nigel, who are both serious tobacco-heads, to tell them the price I've paid for their company.

I stuck in a plug for my foundation, Love Saves the Day, which crowdfunds grants for development projects around the world, especially the Commonwealth. Charity's a big part of my life these days. I am going to use the connections we make during the referendum to drum up support for other good causes. I've made all the money I need, and while I won't deny I enjoy making more, I don't need yachts and private planes.

17 JULY

Embarrassed myself this morning by forgetting I was supposed to be having breakfast with the *Telegraph*'s Christopher Hope. He sat in the Corinthia Hotel for an hour reading the *Daily Mail* and wondering where the fuck I was. Cock-up, no excuse. I'm usually good at keeping to my diary.

Texted him apologising profusely and he was understanding. I told him I'm meeting his proprietors, the Barclay brothers, next week, to talk business and Brexit.

Good news for our international networking efforts though – a right-wing think tank in the States called the Heritage Foundation has promised to find us a couple of 'red-hot interns from the Republican Party'. Wiggy will be pleased, but they need top-notch brains. I've got no time for airheads.

I'm currently drafting a letter to potential donors. Some of the high-net-worth individuals I'm targeting have never been interested in politics. I'm hoping we can enthuse them with a positive vision of a global future for Britain, contrasted with the depressing prospects of the EU.

18 JULY

The *FT*'s covered our Brexit prize plan. I told Wiggy to punt out a press release. We have to set a brisk pace, even at this early stage. He'd be the first to say he's not the ideal head of comms. He's dyslexic, which he does a good job of hiding, but when he's not concentrating, he can barely spell his own name. As for his grammar, my Russian wife Katya has a better grasp.

Right now, though, he's the best we've got. And he's doing it for free. Once we've got a few staffers in, they can take over the hard graft and he can concentrate on doing what he does best – annoying our opponents and charming those we need to win over.

20 JULY

Farage's guard dogs

Wiggy and I have a complicated relationship with Farage. We're like loyal guard dogs that are more than a little feral and unpredictable when off the lead. He loves us and we love him, but occasionally we bite him on the backside and he responds with a sharp kick.

We can tell how much trouble we're in by the number of missed calls we get from him on our mobiles. If it's one, he's happy; two; something's up; three or more means we're in the soup and it's best to lie low until he's returned to room temperature.

Part of our job is to protect him – not just by taking the flak on some of our punchier messages, but also quite literally. We pay for a few heavies to watch his back. The politics of the supposedly compassionate left is pretty ugly and he has been harassed not just on the campaign trail but when he's out with his family. A particularly nasty incident while he was having Sunday lunch in his local pub with his young daughters was the final straw. They had to hide behind the bar and call the police after the place was invaded by a baying mob.

22 JULY

Best in the business

I'm trying to poach Lynton Crosby. I know he doesn't like the EU and I'm convinced this referendum is winnable if we get the finest minds on board.

Crosby's a serious operator, and if we could swipe him from under Cameron's nose it would be sweet. He's the Aussie election wizard who masterminded the Conservative victory this year and helped Boris Johnson land the London mayoralty not once but twice. I like his style. When BoJo was being flaky at the beginning of the mayoral campaign in 2008, Crosby famously told him: 'Don't let us down or we'll cut your fucking knees off.' That's what you get for twenty grand a month.

I have a good in with his business partner Mark Fullbrook, who is a former head of campaigns for the Conservatives. Way back when I was a Tory candidate, he was my agent. We've kept in touch ever since.

Wiggy and I met him today at a hotel near their offices in Park Lane and asked if he could coax Crosby into working for us. We made a few noises about offering him a couple of million, but we know it's a long shot. Fullbrook was surprisingly encouraging. He reckons we can win. 'Yours to lose,' was how he put it. He said he'd go away and think about our offer.

Sizing up my rival

Pleasant enough lunch with political strategist and lobbyist Matthew Elliott, who runs an outfit called Business for Britain. It's Eurosceptic, but is grovellingly determined to give the PM a chance to get a better deal from Brussels. Too namby-pamby for me.

Elliott's been working the backstairs of Westminster for years and has his sights on running the Brexit campaign. He knows everyone there is to know and probably thinks he'll get a free run. In reality, it's up to the Electoral Commission to decide who gets official designation if there's more than one Out campaign, but that's a long way off.

We met at my club, 5 Hertford Street. It's run by Robin Birley, elder statesman of the London private club scene. It is one of my favourite places, though it seems to attract a lot of expensive-looking middle-aged women with leathery tans. It has a fantastic dining terrace where Wiggy and Nigel can smoke.

It was good to get things out in the open. I told Matthew straight up that he can't move as fast as we can and that I think his 'we must give the PM a chance' line (yawn) is lame. There's no way we can sit around waiting for the PM to set the timetable for this campaign. We have to get on with a politician-free campaign to galvanise ordinary folk beyond the Westminster village.

He was polite, but distant: we're not on the same page. I suspect there will have to be parallel campaigns: his bland Tory operation (when it gets off the ground) and our hard-hitting one.

Maybe we should embrace the good Thatcherite principle of letting the market decide. I can't see why both campaigns shouldn't run side by side for a while. The competition should force us both to up our game.

The In campaign, meanwhile, is clearly going to be lazy and complacent. It will be a dumping ground for washed-up politicians like Nick Clegg to find something to do and a place for the children and godchildren of the political classes to 'cut their teeth'.

But I'm open to a joint effort, and suggested Matthew's sidekick Dominic Cummings come and run The Know. It might prepare the ground for a full merger when the time's right. Cummings isn't a people pleaser and seems to have fallen out with half the Tory Party over the years, which to be fair is probably a mark of good taste. I'd be happy to hire him and pay him a good whack. Elliott was predictably non-committal and I'm not holding my breath.

A model of corporate rectitude

If anyone can smooth-talk Cummings, it's Richard Tice.

He's cut from very different cloth to Wiggy and me. He's upright and corporate, never says the wrong thing and likes to talk about business plans and things being minuted. His favourite word is 'collegiate'.

At first Wiggy didn't actually know what the word meant but was too embarrassed to admit it. Eventually he looked it up in the dictionary and realised it's definitely not representative of our approach. We prefer flying by the seat of our pants, and neither of us has ever written a business plan in our life.

All the same, Tice is an asset to any cause. He's had a fine public school education and looks like something out of a Swiss watch advert. He's 6ft 2in., nauseatingly handsome, and everything about him oozes success.

We started talking to him about the referendum back in February over a few drinks at Claridge's, my favourite London hotel. He's on the board of a Eurosceptic business group called Global Britain, and we were keen to put a face to a name. At first it was all a bit awkward because he's so buttoned up. We were drinking, he wasn't; we were cracking jokes and taking the piss out of everyone; he wasn't. We were being very politically incorrect; he pursed his lips and kept a poker face. Even Wiggy, who charms everyone, failed to break down his barriers.

However, we knew we needed someone serious and sensible on board, so we stuck with it. At least we could bond with him over the cause. At the end of the meeting, he leaned across the table and said – with a slightly terrifying Robocop-style intensity – 'I'm in, I'm in. Whatever. Needs. To. Be. Done. I'm in.'

Wiggy and I couldn't look at each other for fear of laughing. You couldn't miss his passion, but he just sounded so repressed. Since then, he's begun to loosen up. A few more months with us and he'll be a new man. I gave him a call tonight and told him to speak to Cummings.

Worth a try.

23 JULY

The Indy's run a story about Jim Mellon putting £100,000 into the campaign, noting that he has made £850 million in property and finance. They tried to imply that he's a bit dodgy by saying he's a 'tax exile' on the Isle of Man.

We're still new to this game and, while it's only *The Independent* (who reads that anyway?), it's advance warning that we need to be ready for some flak. The leftie media is waking up to our existence, and I sense sharpening of the hatchets.

The article wasn't entirely unhelpful: it pointed out that we're not politicians, and that we want to present a relentlessly positive story about what life will be like outside the EU. But I'm under no illusions about what lies ahead.

24 JULY

Crosby's turned us down. Says he's honour-bound not to take Cameron on. What a wuss. We'll have to look elsewhere.

We're lining up guests for a dinner on HMS *Victory* in September. We'll be eating in Nelson's cabin. Can't get a more patriotic venue than that. We'll helicopter guests in from London and encourage them to cough up for the cause.

I'm hoping we'll be able to persuade General Sir David Richards, former head of the armed forces, to come along. He is a firm, though very discreet, friend to the cause.

I reassured Nigel, who knows the General well, that I am not going to hassle him. Apparently he's quite twitchy about being publicly associated with one side or another in the referendum campaign and prefers not to have to deal with political bollocks. Can't say I blame him.

I do have reservations about this event, though. We'll need to think about whether we should be laying on a party for the great and the good – we're the people's campaign, after all.

≈

Sent Channel 4 reporter Gary Gibbon a text congratulating him on a superb report on TV tonight which got the dynamic of the campaign just right. Told him: 'The Westminster bubble has no idea what's coming down the tracks at them.'

25 JULY

The Happy Hippy

Things are starting to move. Donations are beginning to filter in. Mellon is off to Silicon Valley and is going to sniff out some online fundraising experts. The Bristol centre is up and running. I have asked the team to put together a list of 100,000 people with incomes of £100,000 or more for a mailshot.

I'd like to say it's all very professional but the banter at HQ is shamefully lowbrow. Tice would be appalled. Wiggy seems to have spent most of today trading insults with Jimbo Pryor – my fixer in Africa – whom he considers a 'lazy hippy arse'. It's par for the course, I'm afraid. Yesterday it was 'rancid chubby hippy'. 'Blubber guts' and 'c***'. It's pathetic, but it seems to keep them amused.

The pair of them go back a long way. Back in the late '80s, they both used to work for the Tory Party. Jimbo was a long-haired, pot-smoking South African Special Forces deserter called James Pryor.

Young James used to look after Maggie's lectern and speaking notes at No. 10, doing the set-up for keynote addresses and the like. We know him as 'the Happy Hippy'. He got his nickname from some of Downing Street's close protection officers on account of the billowing clouds of dope that would surround the van he used to transport Thatcher's rostrum. Wiggy says he revelled in the fact that he was basically unarrestable. The two of them used to harass the snooty young Oxbridge advisers who swaggered around Central Office, a fresh-faced Cameron among them. Not much has changed, though the straggly hippy locks are greyer than they were.

26 JULY

Planning a trip to South Africa soon to check up on the mines. I grew up in Durban, where my dad was in the sugar industry. A few years ago I bought several old De Beers mines: two in South Africa and two in Lesotho. I go out two or three times a year to check on production, usually with the Happy Hippy. He's in Africa most of the time and texts me when they find big stones or anything with a unique colour. Blue and violet shades are particularly prized.

I've also got a jewellery manufacturing business in Pretoria, where we take the diamonds and turn them into beautiful pieces to sell online. Last year I bought Parsons, Britain's oldest jewellery store. It's been going for 306 years, and I'm busy turning it into a brand.

28 JULY

Cocktails for the cause

Had a fun lunch at 5 Hertford Street with Nigel's mate Jim Davidson of *The Generation Game* fame.

Jim likes a few drinks, and I needed no encouragement, so it may not have been entirely wise to spend what remained of the afternoon drinking piña coladas with Andrew Pierce from the *Daily Mail*.

'Appalling piece of time management,' was Nigel's response when I told him.

Nothing to do with the booze. He hates the *Mail* and says I should be seeing Charles Moore and Simon Heffer from the *Telegraph* instead.

I've been reflecting that politicos need to know who we are, even if we'd rather not know them. Might be an idea to take a stand at the annual party conferences this autumn. Have told Wiggy to get onto it.

29 JULY

My 'time management' may be lousy but the piña coladas with Pierce were worth it. He emailed to say his boss, legendary *Daily Mail* editor Paul Dacre, wants a chat. I hope he's not bullshitting. Piercey's a wily fox and has made a career out of telling people what they want to hear.

30 JULY

The Guardian has run a ridiculous article describing us as a UKIP 'front' with Farage as puppet master. What a joke. Wiggy, Nigel and I are thick as thieves, but nobody pulls my strings. Sam Coates at *The Times* emailed describing the piece as 'ludicrous'. Quite. Wiggy's so useless at his job as our chief spin doctor that I suspect it's his fault. He probably gave them some half-baked briefing which they used to stitch us up.

I emailed him asking if he had anything to declare.

'As Director of Communications, I take NO responsibility,' he replied huffily.

I have been thinking about the role the Electoral Commission will play in the months ahead. I'm worried. They will be overseeing the legalities of the referendum campaign, which puts them in a very powerful position. I looked up their team on the web tonight and they're a bunch of dreary-looking mandarins and local government types. Do they know what they're doing? I've written to them asking if they think politicians are more important than other professionals such as doctors, scientists, nurses etc. when it comes to who should run this campaign. I want to mark their card.

AUGUST 2015

1 AUGUST

Trouble at t'mill

The day got off to a bad start when I received a complaint from one of our supporters about a recent email we sent out. He claimed the font's so small he needed a bloody microscope to read it. Emailed Liz telling her to sort it out.

'It's a shame we can't organise anything. Please call this guy,' I said.

Admittedly my opening line was a bit spiky. Sure enough, I got a sniffy reply, pointing out that there 'will always be people with opinions on how things should be done. I will however contact him. FYI the font was normal. Size 12. Used in emails every day.'

Couldn't believe we were arguing the toss about font sizes. This is a historic national campaign – or is at least it's trying to be. Anyway, it's not just that. I sense some of her people in the Bristol office are swinging the lead. Told her I was 'appalled' by the lazy pace and that I want daily reports on number of registrations, donations and site usage as well as a weekly newsletter.

Actually I agree with the bloke who complained.

As I told Liz:

> The email looked shit – I don't expect to have to write them as well as design the look and feel – we agreed on the wording. You lot just cut and pasted my version, with no spell check or editing and sent it out in small font?
>
> I will speak next week but I expect to see a massive improvement in attitude and performance with these people.
>
> A

She sent me a long snore-athon about how they're all working their backsides off, going grey with stress and exhaustion and haven't seen their grannies/goldfish/pet hamsters for weeks.

I didn't give an inch. Eventually she threw a massive strop and threatened to quit.

> I'm tired of this constant kicking. Find someone else then to do a better job! Over and out.

Realised I'd gone too far (frankly, everything will crumble without her) but I was blowed if I was going to show any weakness.

'Fine,' I replied. 'I don't have time for sensitive people.'

I suggested she went for a run and a shower and then come back and get a grip.

I'm trying to focus on signing up wealthy donors. Sorting out the admin should the easy bit. Eventually, Liz cooled off and emailed saying she'd drunk a pint of 'suckitup' (her words) and was getting on with the job. She must have caught the un-resigning bug from Farage. I could have done without the drama. What does she think this is – a docu-soap?

Heading to the States tomorrow, supposedly on holiday but there won't be any downtime at this rate. Made a note to contact Hugh Whittow, the *Daily Express* editor, about our next stage of development. He's been very positive about our planned advertising, as has Dacre at the *Daily Mail*. Hopefully, if we spend big bucks with these papers, we'll get coverage to match. (The *Express* needs the cash.)

4 AUGUST

We're binning the HMS *Victory* donors' event. This needs to be about people power, not millionaires in helicopters.

5 AUGUST

I'm in a trailer on a campsite – my PA booked it for me instead of a house. Liz is a bit surprised as she thought I was drinking limoncello in the Hamptons. I don't go there till next week. Meanwhile, Tice has owned up to being a Facebook virgin. Wiggy told him it's better than Tinder. How does he know?

'Everyone knows about Tinder. I take a purely academic interest,' he sniffed.

6 AUGUST

We've still not got our act together with the website. Being thousands of miles away when I know people back in the office are screwing things up does bad things to my blood pressure. Rattled off some belligerent emails to the team, making it clear that Facebook 'likes' need to be translated into emails and donations. I want to see a strategy in place. Told Liz to put a rocket under it. I don't care how much it costs – we're doing this properly.

⸺

Australia's batting collapse in the Ashes Test match has prompted some quality piss-take of Nigel's proposal for an Australian-style points-based immigration system. Apparently he has just called for an Australian cricket-based system – all out in two hours. I think we should post it on Facebook. The public will appreciate us doing some leg-pulling of our own side.

7 AUGUST

Loving watching Donald Trump blow up the election in the States. He's just had a massive row with Megyn Kelly at Fox and retweeted a message from a supporter calling her a bimbo. Great drama. The lofty British commentariat delight in competitive virtue-signalling about The Donald, dismissing him as stupid and dangerous, but I think they're missing a trick. All over the world people are fed up with professional politicians. Outsiders are making the running. He represents a new kind of politics, and I think it's coming here.

8 AUGUST

Just sort it

Now in sunny Maine but not letting my attention wander.
There's been another complaint from a punter about not being

able to donate through the website. Am at boiling point with this. The plan is to campaign like Obama, not Benny fucking Hill.

I've spent nearly a million in a month laying down the infrastructure, website, call centre, social media strategy and so on. Our Facebook posts are good. But we are missing open goals. For example, we're telling folk the EU costs £12 billion a year, without giving it any context. Let's relate it to things like the NHS and the number of teachers. The figures are huge. We need to get our message across in a way that actually means something to voters.

9 AUGUST

Tice has been explaining his plans for what he calls (corporate speak alert) a 'combined campaign'. He's talking about an 'alliance of skills' that excludes politicians and big business as far as possible. Shoot me now! He's right, though – everyone knows MPs aren't trusted by voters.

I'll be interviewing possible campaign directors in New York before I go to stay at the Hamptons in the last two weeks of August – I want to hire early next month.

16 AUGUST

Cards on the table

Lovely out here in the Hamptons. Sat by the pool last night and watched our neighbours have an amazing firework display. Still waiting to be invited to one of their parties.

I emailed Elliott dropping in a line about my beautiful surroundings and telling him Business for Britain needs to clarify its position about the renegotiation and also about working with us.

We're campaigning for Out. Simple as that. If the PM's renegotiation results in something really impressive, we could be converted, but in my view it's academic: it's obvious Cameron's not planning to ask for much, and the issue I think people care about most – immigration – just can't be resolved while Merkel, Hollande etc. cling to their precious principle of free movement of people.

Tensions are rising across Europe and the grand EU project is holed below the waterline. Jim Mellon and I (who jointly run the only independent bank on the Isle of Man) both think the euro is going to break up under pressure from north and south like all currency unions do. The only thing we can't predict is when and how. It's time Elliott got off the fence.

The economic news from China, where Jim does a lot of business, is worrying, and currency wars are back on the agenda. I told Elliott that the reason I joined UKIP was the Tories' wrongheaded responses to the big global challenges – allowing unlimited immigration and helping to keep wages down, doubling the national debt and printing £375 billion in quantitative easing and (criminally, in my view) taking interest rates to zero. This has pumped up ridiculous asset bubbles in housing, the stock market and bonds without any real economic recovery. As the Greeks have learned to their cost, you can only get away with suspending the laws of economics for a while until they whack you in the face. Britain will find this out soon enough, which is why I am stockpiling gold.

Signed off my email saying I was sure we can figure out a way of working together if he's willing to be a bit less Tory.

Got a nice reply:

Hi Arron,

It sounds marvellous out there – I'm very envious! My wife's family have a property on the beachfront on the Outer Banks, North Carolina, which we love to visit.

When we win the referendum, we'll both have invitations piling up (and people saying they were with us all along, knew it would happen etc. – such is life!)

Your position is exactly the same as ours – not a cigarette paper's difference between them. The only real difference is that you've gone public, and we'll be going public before conference. You're right to say that it's academic though – all the signals are that they want to pretend there's been a change, without actually delivering a change.

Your insights into China are very interesting – I didn't realise things were so bad out there. Also interesting you're buying gold (is the price starting to go up again?)

… Winning our country back is exactly what I'm in this for – we're completely on the same page. As for being political, I've always steered clear of political parties. Issue-based politics is my gig (and always will be!). Thank you for the compliment though. I've always had a soft spot for serial entrepreneurs too :)

From an overcast London…

Best,

Matthew

He needs to understand that this government will be the most reviled ever once its economic policies unravel, and he should not be afraid to strike out from under the shadow of his pet Tory donors. Plenty of money from other sources out there.

18 AUGUST

Game of Thrones

Back in the UK and just had the weirdest day. I got a call from a prominent UKIP supporter inviting me for a 'beneficial chat' about the referendum at his headquarters on Great Queen Street in London. Something about his tone struck me as odd, and when I looked up his address, I discovered that it was the UK headquarters of the Freemasons. Wiggy and I were both intrigued, and arranged to meet him at the pub opposite the building. This was an unnerving experience in itself: the other customers were in black-and-white costumes and were giving us funny looks.

We made nervous small talk until a dapper gentleman glided over and introduced himself as our man. 'Let's go over the road where we can talk privately,' he suggested. Relieved to get out of the pub, we trotted behind him as he led us into Freemasons' Hall, the headquarters of the United Grand Lodge of England. After passing through grand public areas, we arrived at what he called a 'meeting room', at one end of which were three impressive-looking thrones. The room had six identical internal doors with knockers, and a number of upside-down clocks. Wiggy and I did our best to act as if all this was very normal.

Our host drew us towards the thrones, and I was just about to sit myself down when he yelped at me to stop. 'They're reserved for Masters!' he barked. He motioned to us to stand, while he took up position on the middle throne, which was flanked by two ornate wands.

The conversation began fairly conventionally, with some run-of-the-mill chit-chat about UKIP. Before too long, however, he began veering into conspiracy theories.

Wiggy and I exchanged desperate glances.

'He's mad!' Wiggy mouthed.

I rolled my eyes.

'Let's go,' I mouthed.

This was easier said than done. For a start, I couldn't remember which of the six doors was the exit. Meanwhile, our host was only just warming up. We hovered uncomfortably while he rattled on about 9/11 being a CIA plot and other such rubbish. I could tell Wiggy was getting impatient. The novelty of our situation was wearing off. Without warning, he lunged towards one of the thrones.

'Can I sit next to you?' he asked brightly.

Without waiting for an answer, he plonked himself down.

Mr Mason blanched.

'Get off that!' he yelled.

Alarmed, Wiggy leapt to his feet, kicking over one of the antique wands in his haste.

Time stood still as the stick toppled over, and the silver dove on its handle smashed on the floor.

'That's 300 years old!' exclaimed Mr Mason. 'Time you left!'

We needed no further encouragement.

Muttering our apologies, and trying desperately not to laugh, we bolted for what we hoped was a door that opened, leaving one very angry Freemason literally picking up the pieces.

'Fuck me,' said Wiggy. 'That was nuts.'

I don't suppose we'll be invited back for another 'beneficial chat'.

~

Suzanne Evans, one of Carswell's groupies, has decided she wants to run for London Mayor. What a joke. Nobody's ever heard of her. She's one of the plotters who tried to oust Nigel after the general election. The BBC are happy to make room on their studio couches for her as they know she stirs the pot. But she's a ditzy double-crosser who couldn't win even 15 per cent of the vote in Shropshire when she tried to get a seat in 2015. She'll sink like a latticework canoe in London.

Given the way she's behaved over the past few months trying to undermine Nigel, a councillor spot in Clacton might be more appropriate. Nigel messaged saying her self-belief is way beyond her ability. That sums it up.

22 AUGUST

Shadow boxing

Time to start throwing a few experimental punches. I've suggested we put out a contentious tweet contrasting the way in which Iraqi translators who risked their lives working for British forces are barred from coming to the UK, while any number of jobless EU migrants can come here.

General Richards thinks the treatment of these translators is a travesty. Let's kick up a row. I don't mind taking a bit of flak. Have told the team that from now on all posts must be cleared by me or Wiggy before going live. We need to get the political content right.

Today's market collapse in New York kept me busy. Being short on the major indexes and long on gold has paid off big time – probably best week ever, with some big wins. Maybe I should stay here the way things are going. Back at home, the UK is about to hit the reverse button back towards recession with all the monetary bullets fired.

23 AUGUST

Gloves off

The *Sunday Times* has run an article which might as well have been a free advert for Elliott. Apparently he's appointed himself CEO of the No campaign and has £6 million of backing. He and Cummings are boasting that they've lined up seven Cabinet ministers. Like that's going to excite the average voter on the left. I don't believe the £6 million boast.

The article pissed me off: our friendly tango is over. Let the fun begin. Dispatched a lofty email to Cummings informing him we're interviewing for campaign director. He replied with a patronising message saying they're 'just getting on with it'. I thought he was supposed to be some kind of mad genius. So far, not seen any evidence of either madness or genius. He's just boring. Am sure he thinks Wiggy and I are just businessmen with more money than sense. Told him I'm happy to be underestimated.

'I don't see things in antagonistic terms,' he replied snottily. 'I have watched the Eurosceptic world for 15 years. It has largely gone nowhere with the brief exception of 1999–2002 partly because of infighting. I wish you well.'

If it weren't for his first sentence I might have taken him a bit more seriously. I may not know much about Westminster, but I do know that when he worked for Michael Gove (who was Education

Secretary at the time) he made a career out of seeing *everything* in antagonistic terms. What a shyster.

The *Sunday Times* article was clearly designed to shake the tree. I had journalists texting me all morning. They want a good dust-up – and I'm happy to oblige. I know Elliott and Cummings are briefing against me and I'm not letting it go unchallenged. Cummings needs reminding that the 'Eurosceptic world', as he puts it, does not stop at his front door. UKIP achieved 3.9 million votes at the last election and forced Cameron to have the referendum.

Been cultivating Christopher Hope on the *Telegraph*. He reckons Elliott may be panicking at the unexpected competition. Thinks he may struggle to raise the £7 million that designation permits. I doubt he's even got 70k, unless his big backer Peter Cruddas is bailing him out. I could put £7 million of my own money into this tomorrow if I had to, but the point is that the cash should come from a wide variety of sources.

Told Hope that if he wants to run anything by me, he should let me know. Elliott thinks he's got a monopoly on lobby journalists, but I'm building my own network.

25 AUGUST

Two former UKIP strategists have approached us offering their services. I told Liz not to touch them with a bargepole. If they were involved in running UKIP's campaign, I don't want to know. The whole thing was a shambles.

The big question Remainers will ask is what Britain will 'look like' outside the EU. We need an answer. One concept doing the rounds is called Flexcit. It's a stupid name but it's had real thought put into it. The bloke behind the idea is called Richard North, who has been around the Eurosceptic world for ever. Essentially, his view is that Britain should leave the EU gradually, first leaving the political institutions and re-joining the EEA, and then finally decoupling from the bloc altogether. By phasing the leaving process out, there is less chance of a sharp economic hit from suddenly abandoning all trading relationships at once. He thinks voters will always be wary of taking the plunge. He doesn't seem to like UKIP much, but he's an interesting thinker. Perhaps we should get him on board.

27 AUGUST

King Arthur and brain control

Just had one of the most bizarre and enjoyable conversations of my life with a bloke called John Mappin, of the Mappin & Webb family. He's been in touch offering support. I called him back and he's a total fruit loop.

He told me he's trying to launch a super-powered brain-control system that requires delivery facilities in fifty languages in every major city. He says the European HQ will be his country pile in Cornwall, Camelot Castle, which he also runs as a hotel. He's a big Trump fan and somehow tied up with Scientology. He's also a UKIP supporter and used to be friends with Jonathan Aitken. Frankly, I had no idea what he was talking about, but he sounds like David Cameron's dream UKIP supporter. He has everything but the black armband.

Needless to say it will be a business requirement for Wiggy, Jimbo and I to travel to Camelot Castle, see the nerve centre and sit round a version of King Arthur's round table in the hall. What a wonderful eccentric.

28 AUGUST

Banned

The Tories have banned us from their party conference. Wiggy got a pompous email from a sales director called Lizzy McDowell, who didn't pretend they're doing it for any reason apart from politics.

'I am sorry to have to inform you, but the party has declined the-know.eu attendance and exhibition space based on political reasons. I am not at liberty to, nor do I have, any further information, regarding this,' she wrote.

I'm no grammar expert, but stringing a sentence together is obviously not a Tory skill these days. I take our exclusion as a compliment. What are they afraid of?

Still in the Hamptons. I've updated everyone on progress: we signed 50,000 people to the campaign in August alone and that's before the website is launched. We're piling on 1,500 new members a day via Facebook. Our office on Millbank – just along the road from Parliament, by the Thames – is up and running and we have forty staff in the Bristol call centre. We aim to expand this to 200 by early October, signing up 10,000 people a day. At the moment, it's mainly a mix of Tories and Kippers with some Labour supporters thrown in, people who are worried about the TTIP trade deal between Europe and the US.

Liz says we've had a £50 donation from a fourteen-year-old in Lancaster, who told us to 'just get on with it'. It shows that we're getting real reach. We'll need a huge grassroots campaign to win. I want lots more teenagers getting involved. Jim Mellon reckons Jeremy Corbyn will be Labour leader when the referendum takes place. Ah, Corbyn and Cameron, political titans for our age. I hope he's right. Everyone knows Corbyn's a Eurosceptic.

Not all been positive today, though. Richard North's son Pete, who's also a Eurosceptic boffin, has been slagging us off, accusing us of running a 'cringeworthy' campaign. Apparently we are 'preaching to the converted with the same tired old Eurosceptic memes' and 'grunting about foreigners'. Thinks we should 'shape up or shut up'.

I responded by giving him both barrels on our achievements so far – 50,000 supporters and so on. Pointed out that I'm a simple businessman who has built and sold three insurance businesses, owns a bank, a major diamond group in Kimberley and a major leisure business in the south-west. I finished off by wishing him a good bank holiday. What a knob. Maybe if we get his dad on board he'll shut up.

Kate Hoey, a Eurosceptic Labour MP we've been talking to for a while, has been in touch wanting an update on the campaign. I told her about the attacks from North.

'I wouldn't worry about the knockers!' she replied.

> That particular guy is just so anti UKIP he can't think of anything else. We all will have to work together if we want to win and politicians certainly can't do it without people like you and the business community.
> Best wishes
> Kate

I assured her I can handle it.

> Thanks Kate.
> I'm a big boy! But thanks for the best wishes -- if nothing else it's getting people on the move.
> Best
> Arron

> PS – I saw Frank Field the other day and reflecting there was something he said I liked. About loving one's country wasn't the preserve of the Tories or the right. I want to run it past someone else – if you are around it would be good to discuss.

Kate replied that Frank is 'sound' but not keen to go public yet.

> He will though eventually. Important the referendum is not seen as the preserve of one particular party – that would be a disaster.
> Kate

She's one of the few MPs who seem to get it.

Have made a further effort to reach out to Elliott and Cummings.

Told Cummings I'd pay him £200,000 for the year and maybe a victory bonus too if he'd like to come and be our campaign director. I mentioned that we might have found a US election strategist.

Jimbo's been going on about a company called Goddard Gunster, which specialises in referendums in the States. They have a great reputation and are big on Obama-style social media stuff. Cummings actually sounded quite receptive and we've agreed to meet for a coffee.

SEPTEMBER 2015

1 SEPTEMBER

A dream is born

Wiggy and I have had a stroke of inspiration. How about a Brexit concert, like Rock the Vote in the States?

It won't be our first joint musical venture, though our last effort never quite got off the ground. It was about this time last year, and everyone was kicking off about a calypso record backed by UKIP. It was embarrassingly bad, featuring former Radio 1 DJ Mike Read warbling about illegal immigrants in a faux-Caribbean accent. Of course it was immediately decried as racist, and Nigel's appeal to voters to help get the song to No. 1 was swiftly undermined by Read himself getting cold feet and declaring that the song should be withdrawn.

Wiggy and I thought it would be fun to make a more authentic version, and the perfect opportunity presented itself a few weeks later when Wiggy was on holiday in Jamaica. Strolling along the beach, he came across a very stoned local, who, in exchange for a crisp US $10 note, agreed to provide some sample vocals.

I was in the office when my phone bleeped with a video of a Rastafarian slumped on a decrepit deckchair.

'Hello, my name is Richard,' he drawled, sounding as if he was off his head.

'Perfect,' I texted Wiggy. 'Get him to do a proper recording.'

I don't quite know what happened, but for one reason or another, it never materialised.

Anyway, this is a much better opportunity: not just a silly stunt, but a musical extravaganza.

We were having a couple of drinks at 5 Hertford Street and the more G&Ts we had the more excited we got. We could have a big piss-up, A-list headliners and get Nigel to speak to a crowd of tens of thousands of people. It will look great on social media, and is an opportunity to challenge people's perceptions of the campaign.

'This will be expensive – a few hundred grand easily,' Wiggy warned.

'So what?' I replied excitedly. 'We'll only get this chance once…
We know the right people to talk to. Could be a massive hit. Call it BRock around the Clock, or BPops or something like that… We could get Mick Jagger, or Roger Daltrey… Some really great people who back Brexit would love a chance to get involved like this.'

It could also help if we end up having to compete with Elliott for the designation – show we're really down with the kids.

A referendum wizard

Have wasted a lot of money and smashed my mobile phone, but all in all, a bloody good day.

The Electoral Commission has announced the wording of the referendum question: 'Should the United Kingdom remain a member of the European Union or leave the European Union.'

Bang goes The Know! All our branding will have to be binned, because people aren't going to be asked to choose between Yes and No. Minimart's furious and there are a few unhappy folks in our office. I thought it merited a symbolic gesture to show I felt their pain and I theatrically threw my phone against the wall, but secretly I was pleased. Nigel's also happy. He thinks it's the best question we could get and that it's a sign the Electoral Commission is willing to kick back against Cameron's attempts to rig the referendum.

Jimbo and I had a preliminary meeting with some strategists from Goddard Gunster at the Conrad St James's Hotel today. They're going to put together a detailed pitch before we meet Gerry Gunster, the big cheese. Gunster's won thirty-three out of thirty-six referendum campaigns he has fought – quite a record. He defeated Hillary Clinton's Hillarycare health programme when Bill was President and nixed a plan for a sugar tax on soft drinks in California. Could be a very exciting development.

2 SEPTEMBER

Met up with Christopher Hope from the *Telegraph*. He's an ally, but he wound me up. He told me people still see us as a 'UKIP front'. Don't they realise Elliott and Cummings are funded by UKIP peer Malcolm Pearson and the party's old treasurer Stuart Wheeler? Bloody cheek. Told Chris we're a serious operation – way more professional than UKIP – and we're ahead of the game. Business for Britain has four staff and we have thirty in Bristol and a few in Millbank before we have even properly launched. Threw in the Gunster Goddard link-up. Hope he was suitably impressed.

6 SEPTEMBER

Scurrilous

The *Mail on Sunday*'s printed some absolute bollocks about me being on the Ashley Madison database for married people who want affairs. If I wanted a bit on the side I wouldn't join some poxy dating agency. I have no idea how my name got mixed up in this, and didn't take it very seriously when their reporter rang me for a comment yesterday. Told them it was rubbish and thought they'd drop it, but I woke up this morning to a barrage of texts and emails saying I was all over the paper. Hotfooted it down to the local newsagent and bought a copy.

'TOP UKIP DONOR CRIES "DIRTY TRICKS" AFTER HIS NAME IS FOUND IN HACKED DATABASE OF ASHLEY MADISON USERS'!

Never let the truth get in the way of a good story, eh? Briefly considered desperado measures like buying the entire stack of papers, but then thought, 'Fuck it.' It's not true, so what have I got to hide?

Ever full of tea and sympathy, Andy compounded my humiliation by tweeting a link to the article with a characteristically supportive comment: 'U filthy pervert.'

With friends like him...

7 SEPTEMBER

We've been banned by the TUC. For perhaps the only time in their history, the brothers are taking their cue from the Tories and won't give us a stand at their conference. Thought it'd make a decent diary item for the *Mail* and emailed Pierce to tip him off.

'You're getting noticed, dear heart,' he replied.

8 SEPTEMBER

Cold feet

Some resistance to our pop concert idea from the lads in the London office.

Jack Montgomery, one of our young PR guys, told Wiggy it'll be a disaster. Apparently Rock the Vote isn't cool any more – or perhaps never was. He gave Wiggy a lecture about how it was 'conformist, left-leaning and didn't do the Republicans any favours in terms of the voters it brought in'. He reckons there's no point targeting a registration drive at a demographic that seems likely to vote against us.

He's particularly exercised by our plan to get Farage up on stage. He told Wiggy he can just see some luvvie musician finishing his set with a rousing call to arms against UKIP: 'Thank you, Birmingham, and good night! Before we go, I just want to say that we're voting Remain and Nigel Farage is a racist t***.'

Wiggy told him he's overreacting. We've got a great idea for a stunt involving Kate Hoey driving Michael Caine onto the stage in a specially designed Mini while The Who blasts 'We're not gonna take it any more'. Aim high.

Speaking of Kate, I emailed her saying we've now got more than 100,000 supporters and sixty people working in Bristol. I want Westminster types to know this is a heavyweight operation, which I'm resourcing to the max. Social media is exploding with more than 3,000 new Facebook followers every day. Left-wing voters are going to be crucial. Very keen to talk to Kate about what more we can do.

9 SEPTEMBER

My security guys have told me I have a private investigator on my tail!

One of the team discovered that my computer had been hacked, so we ran a counter surveillance operation, which revealed that I'm being followed. WTF?!

I have been running through all my enemies and can't think of anyone who'd do this except perhaps Elliott.

Sent him a passive-aggressive email warning him to watch his back.

> Thought I would drop you a line. I'm aware that I have a personal investigator on my tail. The heat is obviously rising in the kitchen!! You might want to watch out – I have a business that specialises in personal security and counter intelligence and if you're in need of any help, just shout.
>
> It's called precisionriskintelligence.com. We have ex mi5 and SAS operatives who specialise in counter surveillance.

It's almost certainly going to be a dirty war so shout if you need help.
Arron

Ps I hope you are thinking about coming together because together we are stronger!

10 SEPTEMBER

Met Toby Blackwell today. Told him that if he'd write an article in the *Mail* endorsing us, this would help more than cash. On the money side, I outlined my idea for bonds. It would mean he can keep a low profile if he wants to. I told him we are playing to win.
Very good feedback afterwards:

> Arron,
> Terrific meeting. I now understand and am very seriously impressed.
> ...
> I've kicked the tyres and am now lighting the fires.
> Standby,
> Toby

It's interesting that Penguin Books was founded in his garden under the apple tree.

11 SEPTEMBER

We've been flogging Brussels-bashing T-shirts on our website. A hundred and fifty orders for our 'Love Europe, Leave the EU' design on the first day. Our off-the-peg offerings won't be troubling anyone at London Fashion Week, but it all helps get the message out.
I've had to blow out my old friend Andrew Umbers (investment

banker who used to be chairman of Leeds United). He invited me grouse shooting on his family's moor in Yorkshire tomorrow but I'm just too busy.

The migrant crisis has put rocket boosters under the campaign and I've had hundreds of calls and emails. I can't be gallivanting around the countryside. Also, the Labour leadership contest ends this weekend and it's going to be Corbynmania. I told the team it's time to get topical. I want a post on whether he's an Outer. Told them to rake through everything he's said about the EU in the past.

Cameron's helped the cause by handing £1.7 billion extra to the EU this week. Brussels had upped the bill because our economy's bigger than we previously thought. That's partly because the government added in the value of sexual services and illegal drugs to the estimates to 'harmonise' with the EU. Tells you all you need to know about their priorities that they think this is a legitimate part of the economy – and another good reason to stay off the coke and hookers.

If people understood how much it costs being in the EU, we'd have the public on our side faster than a pack of greyhounds chasing a rocket-powered rabbit.

I have sent Pierce some copies of our EU cartoons by Gary Barker – including a choice one of a British border guard having a kip as shady types troop through customs. Slightly concerned that Barker's cartoon of Mario Draghi, the dodgy governor of the European Central Bank, makes him look a bit too much like Nigel, right down to the trilby and the velvet collar on his overcoat. Hopefully nobody will notice.

Wiggy's suggested a meeting with Cummings and his press officer Robert Oxley to discuss co-ordinating our messages. Tice agreed and wants regular 'theme of the moment' meetings. Groan.

I told the pair of them they're wasting their breath. These guys are political to the core and don't give a flying fuck about anyone who doesn't hang out at the Cinnamon Club, that fancy curry house in Westminster. We should not let them drag us down. Let's show them how business can outshine them with a proper campaign.

But, to illustrate just how 'collegiate' I am, I rattled off an email to Cummings asking if he's looking forward to spending the next few months whiling away the afternoons working out what colour pens to use. I reckon that's what working with Elliott's like.

No reply so far.

Just off the phone to a journalist who gave me chapter and verse on the latest briefing against us from their side. Emailed Elliott warning I'm onto him.

> I spent an hour on the phone to a journalist who had been briefed against us by one of your people. I'm going on the front foot now (v pissed off) – either pack it in or we will properly go at it.

Underestimating me is a big mistake.

12 SEPTEMBER

Corbyn's been elected leader with a massive mandate. He won with almost 60 per cent of first-round votes. That's more than Tony Blair got when he stood. He's an old-fashioned sort of leftist, not exactly patriotic or likely to command the confidence of anyone with a mortgage, but genuinely believes in what he is saying. People already like his authenticity, but I can't see them trusting him to run the country. He's a Labour Eurosceptic of the old school, like Tony Benn or Michael Foot.

I've been heartened to find out that there is already a Eurosceptic Labour group. It's been around since 2013 and is very low-profile at the moment but could have huge potential.

13 SEPTEMBER

Wiggy's very taken by an article in the *Express* which quotes Boris Johnson saying Britain 'can't leave Europe'. He stresses the difference between the EU as a political construct compared with the reality of being geographically part of Europe and culturally part of the same civilisation.

Elliott's equally impressed and has written a follow-up complaining about people using the terms 'Europe' and 'EU' interchangeably.

Wiggy thinks Elliott's piece is 'excellent' – and tweeted so. Credit where it's due.

14 SEPTEMBER

Peter got smashed up playing rugby yesterday and has been sent home from school. He is very groggy and under the weather so I stayed at home. I was quite a good rugby player myself, and know what it's like when you've been knocked about. However busy this campaign gets, I'm going to do my very best not to break my routine of spending Wednesday afternoons with the kids, either at home or watching them play sport. I love this time with them.

15 SEPTEMBER

Pierce the pussy cat

We're producing a pack of cards featuring the fifty-two 'most wanted' Europhiles. Pierce has sent us some ideas. Among others he suggested Nicky Morgan (a 'frumpy old housewife'), Danny Alexander ('ginger rodent') and Roland Rudd, brother of earnest Amber, the Energy Secretary.

Pierce said Rudd is 'losing his hair and is desperately upset about it'. Meow. Bit rich coming from someone who's written articles for the *Daily Mail* about how devastated he is to find his own hair thinning! Piercey got so desperate he used to hang upside down on the bars at his gym in the hope of making it grow back by creating a rush of blood to his scalp. He ended up spending a fortune injecting 'vitamins and minerals' into his scalp and having some daft hot water bottle strapped to his head. What a ponce.

He's lined up an interview with Toby Blackwell, who is endearingly anxious about it and wants my advice. He wrote to me saying:

Dear Arron

No apologies for the length of this email as this is very serious business.

If I am faced with a serious interview I do a lot of homework so,

Who is this guy? I have just got Wikipedia on him. Good Tory but handle like eggs.

What do we want out of the interview?

To put across that we are different, we are working from the bottom up,

We deliberately have no politicians or celebs up front, etc. as I wrote about us.

OK? Help me here.

What does Andrew want out of the interview?

Usually, he only has a ¼ page piece.

But in today's Mail he has a full page in which he factually, unemotionally crucifies John McDonnell in authoritative detail.

He will smell out and expose even the smallest piece of bullshit.

He is as frightening as his reputation.

If he comes to Osse Field should I take him out to lunch at the White Hart?

What does he like to drink and how much?

When I took Richard Littlejohn out to lunch I gave the landlord a bottle of Grey Goose Vodka because I found out that it was Richard's favourite starter.

Andy can, I'm sure, find this out.

I plan how I will dress, for Andrew definitely not with a university tie.

I will have to do homework on things like the UK's trade with the EU if we exit.

I like to start 'I thought that was a very incisive piece you did on so and so...'

If I do get an interview, I will give it my very best shot, but help please.

Toby

Bless. Told him Pierce is a friend and he has nothing to worry about.

I will do a full briefing for you and rest assured he will be a pussy cat!!

He replied sweetly describing himself as 'the man with no ego'. Phew, that's a relief.

It's the campaign that matters not me. And that ain't bullshit.

Toby

What a gent.

≈

Almost forgot to mention I've joined Twitter. Reckon I'll be good at conveying peace, love and charity in 140 characters when I get the hang of it. Annoyingly, there are loads of other people out there called Arron Banks, including a hoodie from Brooklyn with nineteen followers and a bloke whose avatar is a motorbike and hasn't tweeted since joining in 2014. I had to use an underscore to distinguish myself from the competition.

So far I've got two followers – Wiggy and Tice. I'm sure I'll soon have a cult following.

Wonder if I can turn myself into a mass movement?

That's all for tonight!

@Arron_banks

16 SEPTEMBER

All sorts of people are now backing our campaign, including – intriguingly – a chicken sexer. How on earth do you sex a chicken? The mind boggles.

We also have doctors, scientists, housewives, builders, plumbers, policemen, nurses. The plan is to create a panel of twelve people to act as a jury on our failed political classes. They'll act as spokespeople for the campaign and will come from all walks of life and political views. I've always said we need to bypass politicians and let ordinary people speak. We'll select the panel and give them proper media training.

I'm feeling much happier about progress generally. We have a CEO, a website, fifty people on the phones, social media's motoring, donations from the public starting to flow in. The supporter base has exceeded 120,000 in five weeks. We've had the presentation in from Gunster Goddard, and it's impressive.

Now we need to recruit some bright young things who want to cut their teeth on what's shaping up to be the biggest event in British political history since WWII – especially since the Labour Party has gone doolally and much of the left is unexpectedly swinging towards Out. We've been offered the domain name 'leave.eu', which is worth snapping up now the Electoral Commission's changed the question. All to play for.

Getting hammered with the hacks

Wiggy and I braved a party at Westminster tonight: leaving drinks for a political journalist from *The Times* called Laura Pitel. I don't think she's written anything nice about us, but we like her anyway and it seemed a good networking opportunity, dipping our toes into the lobby journalists' piranha pool.

It took me an age to get into London from Bristol and I was still miles away when Wiggy arrived. Being stuck on the M4 for hours put me in a bad mood. As I sat in the gridlock, I remembered that

Nigel once suggested immigration might have something to do with the huge tailbacks on our groaning road network. Everyone went nuts. I thought he had a point.

I finally arrived at some random boozer near Laura's office called the Faucet Inn, where I discovered Wiggy making polite small talk.

The place was packed and the pair of us wandered around not really knowing anyone.

It was all a bit dull till we got talking to a scruffy Tory MP called Therese Coffey. Let's just say they didn't invent the phrase 'wake up and smell the coffee' with this lady in mind. She started rambling on about how the PM is going to get an incredible deal from Europe in his renegotiation; it's all going to be so amazing and no one in their right mind would vote Out.

So I gave her a few economics lessons and told her she must have swallowed the playbook of Conservative Scientology whole if she believed this rubbish. She took umbrage at my tone and lumbered off in a huff, then spent the rest of the evening glaring at me and Wiggy from the other side of the room.

By this time I was getting a bit squiffy and was starting to enjoy myself. There's nothing I like more than a verbal punch-up when I know I'm going to come out on top. I thought I'd see who else I could wind up, and wandered round happily introducing myself to people and sizing them up. I tried to pique their interest by dropping a few indiscretions about UKIP into the conversation. I saw Gawain Towler, who knows all the hacks, glowering at me but I wasn't going to stop. He thinks I'm a loose cannon, but he knows I have his boss's backing.

Watching me work the room in my inimitable style, Wiggy was beginning to look nervous. He wandered off for a fag, muttering, 'No good can come of this.'

'Time to leave, Banksy. Let's quit while we're ahead,' he said when he came back.

But I was just warming up.

'Just one more drink,' I replied. Which of course turned into five.

The rest of the evening is rather a blur, to be honest. I think I made some new friends though.

17 SEPTEMBER

Woke up to a seriously sore head and a text from Lucy Fisher, a political correspondent from *The Times* we met last night. She overheard my set-to with Therese and wants to get to know us better. She suggested 'a proper fucking lunch, to quote the UKIP lingo'. Once I've recovered from this hangover, I'll happily oblige.

18 SEPTEMBER

Have suggested lunch with Lucy on Monday. She says it will need to be speedy, which is fine, because I've already bust my alcohol quota for the month.

Our security boys say I still have a private investigator following me. I would love to know who's paying him. I think I'll put a tail on Elliott to see if it's him. Might turn up something interesting.

19 SEPTEMBER

We're definitely hiring Gerry Gunster. I've not met him yet but his record speaks for itself and his pitch is great. We'll send him the signed contract on Monday and wire him the first twenty grand.

He may be American but he appreciates the magnitude of this thing. He says his team is excited at the prospect of making history. They love the heat of a tough campaign.

I told him we've signed up Hargreaves, who is worth a few billion, and that we've bought the domain name leave.eu. Tipped Lucy Fisher off about Gunster. Keen to get out the word that we have a top operator.

22 SEPTEMBER

Euro-chumps

Our '52 most wanted' Europhile Top Chumps cards have arrived. They include 'Pro-EU Yes vote architect and Prince of Darkness' Peter Mandelson, the ace of spades, and Chris Huhne, the knave of clubs, wearing a ball and chain in tribute to his convict past. Angela Merkel, the queen of clubs, is wielding a whip and she's 'German Chancellor and EU queen dominatrix'.

We took our inspiration from the playing cards the Americans put out during the Iraq War, featuring Saddam Hussein and all his henchmen. Someone may have a go at us for being tasteless but nothing's done more damage to the credibility of the political class in recent years than the Iraq War. Most of the Brussels lovers were for it. Nigel was staunchly opposed.

The economic news is bad and the markets are selling. This will all play a part in the campaign.

Carry on up the charts

Liz has been contacted by a singer-songwriter who wants to make a Brexit hit.

Her name's Antonia Suñer and nobody I know has ever heard of her, but she claims her godmother was Diana Dors, who's just the kind of 1950s sex symbol Kippers get misty-eyed over. Liz reckons if we market it right, it could be the Christmas No. 1.

The plan is to produce a cover version of Carly Simon's big hit, 'Let the River Run'.

I suppose the EU has its own official anthem, Beethoven's 'Ode to Joy' – so why shouldn't we have a Brexit theme tune? At a stretch, I can just about imagine the lyrics referring to getting out of the EU. 'Let all the dreamers / wake the nation / come, the New Jerusalem… we the great and small / stand on a star / and blaze a trail of desire / through the dark'ning dawn.'

Hmm, maybe. I'm not sure this one's going to fly. Suñer doesn't bear any resemblance to Diana Dors and when I looked her up on YouTube, all I could find was a Spanish video of a woman with the same name teaching folk how to cook gluten-free pizza.

But by the time I'd had a chance to intervene, it was too late. Liz was already fantasising about knocking Justin Bieber off the top spot and had said yes.

23 SEPTEMBER

Pierce has junked the Toby Blackwell interview on the pretext of some 'special project'. Sounds like bullshit. 'Fucking journalists,' I told Wiggy, cc-ing Pierce. 'He would be round in a shot if it was a pig head story.'

We're off to Doncaster Racecourse tomorrow for UKIP's annual conference. I'm looking forward to it. It's bound to be the usual circus. There's a lot of tension between Nigel and Carswell at the moment, and it will probably end in tears.

Nigel has told us he'll officially back Leave.EU, but that Carswell hasn't declared his hand. Apparently he's planning to throw in his lot with Elliott. What a tosser. Just proves he's a Tory at heart.

The Carswell v. Farage saga is hardly news, but the media is beginning to pick up on their differences over which Leave campaign to back. *The Guardian* rang to quiz me. Gave what I thought was a fairly neutral answer, knowing Nigel will bollock us if we stir things up. I told him that it will be hard for the Electoral Commission to go against whichever campaign Nigel decides to endorse. After all, he leads the UK Independence Party. The clue's in the name. I added that Carswell will either have to leave the party or fall into line.

Not sure what *The Guardian* will write, but it should make a nice scene-setter.

25 SEPTEMBER

Ding-dong in Doncaster

Up in Doncaster. Great to get out of London. I'm spending far too much time there. Texted the Happy Hippy the other day to say I fancy a break in Wales, trudging up Mount Snowdon with just a tent and thirty quid in my back pocket.

There is a press mob up here and I was asked onto the *Today* programme this morning. Justin Webb, the presenter, went straight for the jugular, trying to suggest I've been exaggerating how many groups support us. Happily, I was on solid ground on this one. If I'm heartened by one thing it's the extent to which many other Eurosceptic organisations share our concerns about Elliott and co. We've already got backing from all sorts: the Bruges Group, Democracy movement, CIB, People's Pledge, Global Britain and so on.

'You say you have united all the groups, but here are ten that aren't supporting you,' Webb said craftily. He started rattling off names.

Luckily for me, he ballsed up the second example.

'I'll stop you right there – those guys are actually supporting us,' I said confidently. This took the wind right out of his sails. Round one to Banks.

He moved swiftly on, asking if it's true that we approached Crosby and offered him £2 million to run the Out campaign.

'Yes, but Lynton's the Prime Minister's adviser, so I would be pretty surprised if he backed anyone other than the Prime Minister,' I replied – which killed the question.

I was sorely tempted to mention Gerry Gunster, but for once I kept my mouth zipped. Apparently we have to tread a bit carefully with our new hire. Some of his clients are Europhiles and he would not have been best pleased if I'd suddenly announced his appointment.

By this point Webb was beginning to sound a bit despondent.

He'd shot his bolt on his two main lines of attack and run out of hostile things to ask. I left the studio feeling pleased with myself, but the Happy Hippy was not impressed. He'd already had a furious text from Fullbrook asking what the fuck was going on. Apparently he assumed our discussions were confidential and wants to know how it got out. I love Mark, but seriously? This is politics. He and Lynton of all people know how the game is played.

This afternoon Wiggy and I made our way to the auditorium for Nigel's big set-piece.

Michael Crick from Channel 4 parked himself next to us and we had a banter. Naturally, the speech was a blinder. Farage let fly about 'toxic Tory toffs from Tufton Street' (Elliott's office address. It went straight over most of the audience's heads but sounded suitably unpleasant and made me and Wiggy laugh).

After the speech we trooped off to the media room to do a bit of briefing or at least find someone bearable to talk to. To our dismay, practically the first person we bumped into was Carswell.

He'd been prancing around like a right prat all day, telling anyone who'd listen that he's UKIP's 'only MP' and trying to make out that he's the biggest show in town. We spotted him in the spin room, yammering away to Lucy Fisher. Suddenly he swivelled an eye towards us in that disconcerting way of his. Before we could get out of there, he marched over to us, face contorted with anger. Conscious people might be watching, I decided to be polite.

'Hello, Douglas. How are you?' I asked sweetly, keeping my voice down.

'Who do you think you are?' he yelled, jabbing a finger in my direction. 'What was that article all about?'

He looked half-crazed and for a moment I was quite alarmed by this uncharacteristic display of alpha-male behaviour. Evidently Michael White had run my comment saying he should be deselected, a suggestion he obviously didn't welcome. His eyes were boggling and he was hopping from foot to foot, ranting about me damaging the party, not knowing my place etc.

I decided the best approach was to shrug it off.

'Stay classy, San Diego,' I replied casually, or words to that effect, and Wiggy and I slunk off, firmly on the moral high ground.

That might have been the end of the matter, but unfortunately we'd been overheard by a few people.

'What was that all about?' said Owen Bennett from the Huffington Post.

There was only so far I was willing to go with the non-confrontation strategy. I told him it was just Carswell being Carswell.

'He's autistic with a touch of mental illness,' I added breezily.

'Is that on the record?' Bennett asked eagerly.

'Yes,' I replied.

'No,' Wiggy interjected hurriedly. But I'm sick of Nigel constantly being stabbed in the back and decided I didn't give a shit if people got upset.

'Nah, leave that bit on the record,' I countered.

Wiggy looked alarmed, but it was too late. Bennett had already hurried off to file. It was red meat to the press pack, whose experience of total immersion in Kipper company had created a near-fatal outbreak of collective boredom.

ITV, BBC and Sky leapt on it, saying the conference had descended into a fracas. I was rather enjoying the drama.

Frankly, I'm sure the man is on the spectrum, and I was just telling it how I see it. However, our little contretemps immediately knocked Nigel off the top of the news bulletins, and he was not pleased. The second we were alone, he started laying into me.

'What the fuck have you done?!' he boomed. 'I might as well not have given my speech. Your comments are all anyone's talking about. You've got to put out an apology. There's no upside to this sort of comment. No upside!'

'No upside' is his favourite phrase, and I'm quite used to hearing it. He usually simmers down if you leave it a while.

By now the press pack was in full cry, and it was looking like Wiggy and I would have to do a runner. It was building into a proper shit-storm, with everyone piling in: indignant autism charities, sanctimonious politicians who've supposedly devoted their careers to campaigning for the mentally disabled, etc. Surveying the 'breaking news' ticker tape on a nearby TV screen, even I could see we had a problem.

'OK, OK, I'll say sorry,' I told Nigel reluctantly. So Wiggy and I cobbled together a rather grudging statement, saying Carswell had been 'appallingly rude and provocative' towards me, but adding that his behaviour did not justify my comments, 'for which I apologise'.

It's the first time I've had to say sorry for one of these things, but I should probably start getting used to it as I don't plan to edit myself in this campaign. Of course, I was sure to make it clear that it was an apology to people with autism for comparing them to Douglas Carswell, not the other way round.

Nigel was still really angry and was striding around the conference centre with his anxious-looking entourage scuttling behind him, trying to keep pace. As he made his way through the throng, he was accosted by a reporter from Sky News who wanted to talk to him about Corbyn's leadership victory. After the combined stress of his speech and my screw-up, he offered a rather more colourful response than was perhaps wise, dismissing the new Labour leader as a bicycle-riding, muesli-munching vegan. For good measure, he added that UKIP has probably lost the pedalling, lentil-stewing vegan vote now.

'I thought you told me not to say anything insulting?' I teased, when we were safely out of carshot.

'It's OK for me, just not for you,' he replied grumpily. But I could tell he was in a better mood.

~

Arron Banks, campaigner, insurance tycoon, gambler, diamond miner – and agony aunt. In the dead of night, I received a string of heartrending text messages, which began: 'I'm so heartbroken.' Then a whole load of stuff like 'I don't think you get it', 'I have to walk away', 'You have left me feeling so exposed and vulnerable … I feel deeply cynical about you and life. Which basically has killed me.'

Crikey. Dramatic stuff. For a split second I wondered if I might be the object of someone's unrequited love. Then I saw who the messages were from: a journalist, who was clearly having a domestic crisis.

I wasn't quite sure what to do, but felt she needed to know that her messages had ended up in the wrong place.

So I hesitantly replied: '??? I am assuming this is for someone else. Arron PS only comment, no one else can make you happy, start loving yourself first x'.

My late-night messenger, appalled at confusing me with her misbehaving other half, replied, 'Gulp' and 'So sorry', to which, now getting used to my role, I said: 'No worries. I was just a little worried about you'. Then from the other end: 'You are now my confidant x'. Job interview passed. If this campaign all goes belly-up, maybe I should take up counselling.

26 SEPTEMBER

Banned from Twitter on Farage's orders

Nigel rang Andy today begging him to ban me from Twitter. 'You've got to get him off. He's out of control,' he instructed.

It didn't take me long to figure out how the system works, and I've been quite enjoying a few virtual bust-ups.

It's true I've been getting increasingly pugnacious, especially about Carswell and a *Spectator* blogger called Sebastian Payne who gets up my nose. The little twerp used the magazine's Coffee House blog to run a hatchet job on me, saying I'd been going round bragging that I have Nigel 'by the short and curlies financially'. It's true that the party needs my money, but nobody tells Nigel what to do.

I tweeted that I didn't give a fuck what *The Spectator* thinks because only one person in north London ever reads it. That upset Andrew Neil, who as well as being a formidable BBC presenter is also the magazine's chairman. He also has gazillions of Twitter followers. He fired back, claiming *The Spectator* has 200,000 readers and 2 million website users and all the rest of it. 'Carry on insulting,' he sniffed.

Neil's probably right that it's unwise to slag off a magazine that's as solidly Eurosceptic as his but sometimes I can't stop myself.

'Seb Payne's an idiot,' I tweeted back cheerily.

I'd forgotten all about it till Wiggy told me Nigel had been on the blower. 'Nigel's serious about this,' Wiggy said. 'You've got to stop. You're getting people's backs up. We don't want you becoming the story.' Help. I have created a monster. Andy thinks he's Alastair bloody Campbell.

Still, looking over my tweets, I could see his point, so I've reluctantly agreed to give it a rest. I fired off a final missive to my swelling army of followers, sorrowfully announcing my premature retirement. 'Twitter's above my pay grade. Cheerio!'

Probably best for all concerned.

27 SEPTEMBER

Simon Heffer has written a great piece about us in the *Telegraph*, for which I've thanked him. He credited me and Tice with creating a united Eurosceptic front. Not entirely sure what he's talking about (thanks to Elliott, Cummings, Carswell et al., it's hardly united) but it means we've had a surge in people visiting the website and donating a few quid.

On the flip side, our website still doesn't always work. People are trying to give us money and the system keeps crashing. I buy online the whole time and never have these problems, so why is our website so crap? I don't want recriminations; I just want it sorted.

Apparently Carswell and Suzanne Evans are definitely backing Elliott. Jamie Huntman sent me a supportive email, saying how angry he is. 'Is it so difficult to back the Party instead of the Westminster bubble that Douglas professes to attack but is inherently part of?' he asked.

Spot on. I'd throw the pair of them out of the party for gross disloyalty. Sadly there are boring things called rules and procedures. Nigel's wife Kirsten has been discouraging him from taking the nuclear option. She thinks it 'would be called fascism' (which seems a bit over the top), but she may have a point about how it would look. In her view, they're too high-profile to expel, and if we push things that far, it will backfire.

Bring it on, I'd say. It's nothing Nigel can't handle.

28 SEPTEMBER

Jim Pickard has run a story suggesting Elliott's lot are 'expected' to get the official designation. WTF? Expected by Elliott, he means. This really pisses me off. It's just a lazy assumption, based on nothing more than the fact that he and Cummings are big swinging dicks at Westminster and well in with the Tory crowd.

I bashed out an email to Pickard asking what he was on about. I told him that we've raised the funds, we've now got 160k supporters, we're backed by UKIP and all the major Eurosceptic groups, and we've hired the top referendum firm in the US to run the campaign. So why does the press assume Elliott has it all sewn up?

He and Cummings are setting up a new office south of the river. Perhaps they think a bit of water between their lazy backsides and the Palace of Westminster means they're technically outside the bubble? If so, they're wrong. The bubble isn't a geographical location; it's a state of mind.

29 SEPTEMBER

Wigmore gets sensible

Wiggy's written a long report for our supporters following the events of the last few days. The publicity's been a bit mixed since my Doncaster clash with Carswell and he's fretting about our image. He thinks we're still seen as too close to Nigel, and a bit of distance wouldn't do any harm.

I am not going to apologise for getting on well with Nigel, but I can see his point. He's suggested I do one last interview with the *Telegraph* and then withdraw to being a diligent boardroom boy and allow other people to speak for us.

I'm happy to go along with it for the time being. The campaign's more important than the personalities and we don't want to alienate potential supporters at this stage.

Tice agrees with Andy's proposal but is worried that I'm not taking my little 'demotion' seriously. He knows me too well.

30 SEPTEMBER

Gerry's getting twitchy about his association with us. He had a 'minor confrontation' (his words) with a client in the States who wants him to keep his public profile 'in check'. Gerry says he wants a balance so that the clients don't have to defend their use of Goddard Gunster, which would be embarrassing for all concerned. If they let him go, it wouldn't look great for our campaign. I've advised him to do a few things with us then vanish. Told Gerry that if he pulls this one off and we end up leaving the EU, it will be his epitaph. Though he told me he likes the heat in the kitchen. Well, this will be the test.

PART 2:
OCTOBER–
DECEMBER 2015

OCTOBER 2015

1 OCTOBER

Grave-digging

Lord Lawson, the former Europhile who tried to con us into the single currency and betrayed Thatcher when she spoke out against Brussels, has emerged from whatever dusty crypt the French have preserved him in to declare himself leader of the campaign to take us out of the EU.

In reality, he's just a figurehead for an organisation nobody's ever heard of called Conservatives for Britain. According to today's *Times*, Lawson's outfit will be backing Elliott. Yawn.

Nigella's old man may play well with the deluded clique of Tory fanboys who've convinced themselves they can resurrect him as the hero who will lead us out of the EU, but what are younger voters supposed to make of the Brexit campaign with this waxwork as its public face?

He says he wants to take charge of the campaign to keep out 'less moderate, xenophobic voices' – by which he means us. I've always found the idea that we have some sort of pathological fear of Europeans bizarre, given that Farage is married to a German. It's just another lazy way to denigrate anyone worried about uncontrolled immigration.

Lawson says he won't share a platform with us, though he has generously proclaimed that all may 'rally to his banner'.

Wiggy and I banged out a press release saying he should get back in his box. It would be better if decrepit old Tories like Lawson stayed in the background. They alienate people who hate the Conservative Party – in other words, the voters we need to win this campaign.

We ran our statement past Simon Heffer.

'Excellent, but do get Andy to clean up the punctuation!' he replied.

He helpfully attached a more literate version of our release. Sadly we'd already pushed the button on it, iffy grammar and all. In his haste, Wiggy omitted to clear it with Tice, which was unfortunate given it went out in his name.

I suspect he knew Tice wouldn't sign it off. The language wasn't exactly 'collegiate' – the phrase 'Labour-minded voters will find the sight of the grisly spectre of the Ghost of Thatcherism Past on the airwaves about as welcome as a pork pie at a bar mitzvah' may have been used – and I suspect Wiggy thought he would just chance his arm.

Naturally, Tice went ballistic, but by then it was too late.

3 OCTOBER

Domestics

We've landed Toby Blackwell in the proverbial with his missus after being a little over-enthusiastic. The *Telegraph* ran a breathless article today revealing that he'll be giving Leave.EU 'full 100% support'. It included some punchy quotes from Toby about us being the 'people's campaign' and the only group that can deliver Brexit. Bang on message!

'When the pilots took off from Biggin Hill for the Battle of Britain, they did not worry about the money. This is our generation's Battle for Britain,' declared Sir Winston Blackwell. Cue stirring music, as a great army of patriots from all walks of life rise up to take back our country.

So far, so good. What pissed off his wife was the suggestion that he's going to bankroll the campaign with millions of pounds.

Truth is, I stuck that bit in myself. I did call Toby, who's worth £300 million or so, to check it was OK. He was a bit squiffy and feeling bullish, assenting with a casual, 'Yeah, no problem!'

Mrs Blackwell went ape, and so did he when he sobered up and realised we'd signed him up for a seven-figure donation. Nice day's work from yours truly.

A Tory MP called Bernard Jenkin, one of Elliott's crowd, has been in touch with Andy suggesting we meet up. Not sure what he's playing at, but I suppose we might as well hear him out.

4 OCTOBER

Furious with the BBC. I caught the back end of the *Marr* show, which proclaimed Business for Britain the official Out campaign. How did they figure that one out?

Right now there are two campaigns, and only one of them – ours – is backed by UKIP and every major Eurosceptic group, including the Conservative Bow Group. We now have 200,000 supporters and thousands of members of the public sending in donations.

It's no surprise that the BBC would rather their precious EU was up against the rabble of unlovable Tories with whom they've been sharing studio couches for years, but we've got to nip this in the bud. It sounds drastic but I think we need to issue legal proceedings.

I told our barrister Francis Hoar to produce the toughest letter he could and bang it over to the BBC, *Sunday Times*, *Times* and *FT*. Today! I want to hit them hard. Told Wiggy to warn them that if they persist, we'll seek an injunction. Hopefully it will result in an edict to their reporters and presenters to think before they open their mouths.

6 OCTOBER

Been asked to do Radio 4 *Any Questions?* on 27 November in Manchester. Ready for a good scrap!

When they first met me, Nigel's spin doctors tried to stop me doing press because I hadn't had media training. I ignored them and followed a simple rule: say exactly what you think. It seems to work – after my first big interview, Nigel's strategist Chris Bruni-Lowe described me as a 'natural' – but I can't pretend I don't get a bit nervous. As Wiggy likes to remind me when I get too cocky, 'Even you are capable of making a tit of yourself when you set your mind to it, Banksy!'

7 OCTOBER

Tice's media moment

I'm not the only one in demand on the airwaves: Tice has also been getting requests. He's been invited on *Marr* this weekend, and is very anxious to look his best. I tried not to chuckle at the thought of our handsome, clean-cut talisman fretting over how he'll come across.

'What's your advice?' he asked eagerly.

This was catnip to Wiggy.

'Right, Richard, I hate to say this but you need a haircut,' he replied gravely, gesturing at the long and far-too-lovingly groomed locks framing his own perma-tanned mug.

'Oh,' said our impeccably turned-out corporate beast, sounding crestfallen.

'I'm sure you know this already, but you've a good side and a bad side,' Wiggy added.

Tice looked dismayed and suddenly self-conscious. Which side was his bad side? I suppressed a laugh.

Wiggy then mimed a sort of half-sitting, half-standing contortion.

'And, Richard, when you sit on the *Marr Show* couch you must keep really rigid as everyone wants to see your profile. Make sure you can look at the interviewer, but don't move your head, as that profile is what everyone wants to see.'

'Oh, really, OK, I see,' Ticey agreed, clearly not seeing at all.

By now he was quite worried. His malfunctioning humour circuits mean he struggles to detect jokes.

'Plus, you've got to wear the right suit,' added Wiggy gleefully. 'We want to see your sex appeal. Right now you look as if you've just come from the City. We want people to like you, so nothing too buttoned up. Straightforward colours, nice tie, nice shirt, got it?'

Tice should have known it was a wind-up: Wiggy has a style of his own, and was delivering this lecture wearing a pair of brown suede loafers and bright yellow socks, but Gok Wan he is not.

I was tempted to mention the 1970s pornstar clobber he once bought for us in Lesotho when we were short of suitable attire for an unexpected invitation to visit the King, of all people, but I was enjoying the joke and thought it might put him off his stride.

Tice was swallowing the whole thing hook, line and sinker as surely as that shark Nigel caught in Belize.

'What about make-up?' he asked anxiously. Andy put him right: 'I don't want to disappoint, but they do that for you at the studio. And your hair,' he said. Can't wait to watch.

~

Met Stuart Wheeler, the venerable, multi-millionaire card sharp who pretty much invented spread betting. We were at a party thrown by a mutual friend and he loped over to say hello, peering at me quizzically through his square-rimmed glasses. Under any other circumstances, we'd get on brilliantly. He loves bridge, and when I was growing up, cards were all round the house as my grandparents were world-class players of the game. (That's why I never really took it up. Led to too much… ill-feeling.)

I suggested a game of solo instead and said I'd declare a misère hand – that's when you say you are going to lose every trick and put your cards on the table to prove it.

Although he's UKIP's old treasurer, and should be on our side, he's in Elliott's gang. A pity, but at least he wants to connect. We've fixed lunch later this week.

8 OCTOBER

Lunch with a gambler

Met Wheeler at his club, the Army and Navy in Pall Mall. What a gent!

Unlike many of the hangers-on who are members of the A&N, he's the real deal, doing his National Service as an officer in the Welsh Guards. At university, he was nicknamed Bullets on account of somehow accidentally shooting himself in the face. Whoever patched him up did a good job – the only sign of it is a little scar above his lip. He went on to marry a society beauty and his daughter Jacquetta is a model.

On the face of it, he has the same ultra-establishment credentials as Cameron – Eton, Oxford, the Bullingdon Club – but his backstory is more interesting. Born in the 1930s, he's the son of a single mother who gave him up at birth. He was adopted by wealthy Americans and didn't track down his blood relatives until his seventies. By then his real mum was dead, but a TV company found some old footage of her walking bolt upright with her hands behind her back – just like her son.

Turns out she was also a big bridge player.

Wheeler told me how he'd made his fortune inventing spread

betting on the stock market in the early 1970s with a company called IG Index. In 2000, he floated it and earned £90 million in shares, though he likes to pretend he's on his uppers because of the maintenance bill for his Jacobean castle in Kent. He's still a massive gambler and heads out to Vegas every year for the World Poker Championships.

I thought I'd better try to match his anecdotes, so I casually mentioned that I once shut down a South African casino. They literally had to come and throw a cloth over the blackjack table after I cleaned them out of chips.

He looked a bit sceptical, but I think he enjoyed the lunch, particularly after a few glasses of red. He toddled off half-cut, still saying Elliott was the best thing since sliced bread. Not exactly the result I was hoping for, but it's a start.

9 OCTOBER

Let the games begin. Elliott has officially launched his Brexit campaign group, which he's calling Vote Leave. Its establishment line-up is clearly designed to impress the Electoral Commission, but the website is dreadful: Voteleavetakecontrol.org.

How depressing. We may be rivals for the official designation, but we both want to win this thing. He's killing the campaign before it's even started, botching the job just so we don't steal too much of a march on them.

Emailed Kate Hoey, feeling very gloomy. On this showing, we don't stand a chance.

> I'm annoyed because I want to win [the referendum] and frankly shocked at the level of incompetence displayed here. The In campaign is being run with advice from industry (WPP), I can see that. They have done a smashing job... For me this is about winning... I have been at this full time for three months. This is not about personalities but a winning

mind set. I am annoyed because I know the other side will have resources, talent from business and flair. This reflects V badly all round...

Kate replied saying none of us should waste any more time attacking each other, and telling me off for being negative about MPs. 'You do seem to think politicians are dreadful people. I can assure you that I am in this because I do also care hugely about the issue,' she said.

Reassured her she's one of a handful of MPs I do respect.

I was still fizzing about it when I got home from work and bashed out an email to Elliott giving him both barrels.

> The website is awful, the Facebook page worse. I am at a total loss on the name, the cardinal rule of marketing is keep it simple. You may know politics, but have ABSOLUTELY no clue how to reach out to a wider audience or how to market. The In campaign has been put together professionally and by experts (WPP etc.), they mean business... I know MPs don't live in the real world but surely someone ran it past someone!

Half an hour later, I still hadn't got it out of my system.

> If the campaign means so little to you that [you] produce work like this, it's a good job someone is giving 100%. I'm doing this because I care, not because it's a job...
> Having lunch with the whole of Westminster does not qualify you to run a campaign.
> Really
> Arron

That's quite enough for tonight. The team think I'm overreacting and they're probably right. Taking Katya to Venice tomorrow. Will do me good to get out.

10 OCTOBER

Been war-gaming the campaign from the legendary Harry's Bar off St Mark's Square in Venice. Yours truly excepted, the place has a very glamorous clientele. When they first opened their doors back in the 1930s, they served lunch to King Alfonso XIII of Spain, Queen Wilhelmina of Holland, King Paul of Greece and King Peter of Yugoslavia, all on the same day. W Somerset Maugham, Noël Coward, Charlie Chaplin, Truman Capote, Orson Welles and Ernest Hemingway all liked a tipple there.

Pierce texted to suggest I head to the Cipriani Hotel for cocktails in the garden. Nice idea, but I've tried most of them already and am quite happy where I am.

Sky News rang asking if we'd like to put anyone up to go head to head with someone from Remain tomorrow. I said yes right away. It's their official launch and we need to be all over it. It's one for Liz – she's young, she's pretty, and she sounds like a normal human being. She'll be great.

I rang her with the happy news.

'You're going on Sky tomorrow!' I told her cheerfully. 'You're going up against someone from Remain.'

I told her it would probably be *Apprentice* star and Tory business-woman Karren Brady. There was a brief silence.

'What?' she said eventually. 'I've never been on TV. I haven't had media training. I don't want to do it.'

I calmed her down. 'Don't worry about it!' I cried. 'You're a natural. It will be fine.'

I promised to make some crib notes for her and said we'd talk it through in the morning. 'No point discussing it now. You'll just forget it all,' I said breezily.

She still sounded angsty, but I think she'll be great.

11 OCTOBER

Liz goes down in flames

In the doghouse with Liz. She bombed on Sky. The trouble was I got waylaid this morning – in a boat at the Trieste regatta to be precise – and by the time I was clear, it was too late to talk her through the interview before she went on air. When I looked at my phone, I had about eighteen missed calls. I rang her back, excited to hear how it went.

'Well? Did you enjoy it?' I asked eagerly.

'It was a total nightmare!' she snapped. 'I crashed and burned. I can't believe you just made me do that. I quit. It's not my job to be on TV. I've been trying to call you all morning and you never picked up the bloody phone. I had no idea it was live. I didn't have a clue what I was doing. I was so rubbish that the producers actually had to interrupt the interview to tell me to stop looking at the floor.'

'What?' I replied, taken aback. 'I'm sure it's not as bad as you're making out?'

'It definitely is,' she replied. 'Watch it. It was horrendous. Worst moment of my life.'

I was sure she was exaggerating, but when I checked it out she really was terrible. She looked like someone had spiked her drink. At one point she completely dried up. Half the time her eyes were boggling like Nemo and the other half she looked like she was falling asleep.

'That's because they had a bloody TV monitor on the floor, and I could see myself on the screen. It was virtually impossible not to keep looking down,' she explained.

Thank God she wasn't up against Karren Brady or it would have been even more excruciating. Her opponent was some totally forgettable Mr Blobby character from the Open Europe think tank. All the same, I don't think I'll subject anyone to that again any time soon.

'You're right. You were awful,' I conceded. 'You're benched.'

'Good,' she said huffily.

Tice goes on Marr – and soars

Some you win, some you lose. It was also Tice's big day on TV and, unlike Liz, he was a big hit.

Andy and I had been feeling a tiny bit guilty about our wind-up the other day, as it had consequences. He thought our media advice was serious and went off and blew three grand on 'bespoke media training' for his debut on *Marr*. It seemed to work because, when I texted him first thing this morning, he sounded very confident.

Wiggy went with him to the studio at New Broadcasting House on Portland Place and gave him a pep talk.

'Right, Richard, do you know what they're likely to ask you and have you thought about what you're going to say?' he asked.

To which Richard pulled out a huge stack of notes and said yes, he thought he'd covered everything.

'Look, mate, did you read the papers this morning?' Wiggy pressed.

Tice replied that he'd glanced at the headlines. 'That's what they are going to ask you about!' Wiggy exclaimed.

'Oh right,' replied Tice, crestfallen again.

'Bin those!' Wiggy instructed, gesturing at Tice's stack of crib notes. 'Forget all of it. Just read the papers.'

By now Tice was getting agitated.

'Oh, ah, can't I take my notes on? In media training they said I had to prepare very clear notes?'

'Yes, mate, but on half the back of an envelope, not fucking *War and Peace!*' Wiggy chided. Seeing Tice's deflated expression, he decided to row back a bit. After all, we wanted him to do well.

'You're going to be excellent, Richard,' he soothed, as Tice frantically leafed through the Sunday papers.

I called him just before he went on air to give my tuppenny's worth, as did Nigel, who instructed him to be honest, stick to his points, repeat those points and, crucially, if Marr asked him a difficult question, just ignore it. (The politician speaks!)

Well, what do you know? After all that, Tice went and pulled off a commanding performance. He swaggered off set all puffed up, his trouser leg vibrating as the plaudits came buzzing in on his phone.

Wiggy still hadn't finished winding him up.

'How do you think I did, Andy?' Tice asked him breathlessly.

'Not good at all, Richard,' replied Wiggy gravely. 'Have you seen yourself? What did I tell you about sitting still! You were bobbing up and down like a fucking chicken!' Darkening his voice further, he told Tice to call me.

'Speak to Banksy. See what he thinks about you doing more of these gigs.'

Tice was flattened.

'Really? I was that crap? Oh Christ, oh Christ,' he replied miserably.

Just then, one of the show's producers, Libby Jukes, sailed past.

'Thanks for that, Richard! You were great. Hope you'll come on again,' she praised.

Suddenly the scales fell from his eyes, and he realised it had all been a giant wind-up.

'Fucking hell, Wigmore! Fucking hell!' he shouted.

'You were brilliant!' Andy confirmed.

Soon Nigel was on the blower.

'Richard, that was fantastic,' he enthused.

'Oh!' said Tice modestly, wilting under all this unexpected praise. 'Do you really think so…? Do you think so? Did I keep my head in the right place?'

This afternoon, everyone seemed to want a slice of Tice: journalists seeking comments, producers inviting him onto shows. Apparently Mrs Tice (an elusive figure he keeps well out of our way, probably wisely) was thrilled.

'Perhaps I'll start getting recognised?' Tice mused as he and Wiggy trooped out of the BBC building.

Wouldn't be surprised.

12 OCTOBER

A big day for Remain. They launched their campaign under the banner 'Britain Stronger in Europe'. I thought Vote Leave was mediocre, but BSE (!) takes it to a whole new level.

It's being headed up by Lord Rose, the former M&S boss who presided over one of the crappest periods in that fine company's history. Hopefully he can work the same magic on BSE. He had the audacity at the launch to brand people who want out of the EU 'quitters'. I suspect we're going to be hearing a lot of this sound bite. Bring it on! There's nothing clever about refusing to quit a sinking ship.

So far, I'm underwhelmed by their campaign. They've posted a fancy-schmancy launch video that supposedly features loads of celebs, but other than Karren Brady I've no idea who any of them are. With totally topsy turvy logic, Rose has been trying to appeal to people's patriotism to stay in the EU. He claims the patriotic course for Britain is 'not retreat'.

It's a fundamentally flawed position – Leave is the campaign that says Britain will succeed running its own affairs, while Remain is the campaign that says Britain will fall to pieces without Eurocrats to make our decisions for us.

Meanwhile, our own operation is attracting international attention. Alexander Yakovenko, the Russian ambassador, has invited me, Wiggy and Katya to lunch on 6 November. He wants to know what we're up to. Intriguing!

13 OCTOBER

Been mulling over renewing my bridge-building efforts with Elliott by getting together with Labour donor John Mills and his sidekick Alan Halsall, who co-chair Business for Britain, the precursor to Vote Leave. They both seem reasonable people. It's a question of finding the right moment: no point doing it now.

Andrew Neil's asked me to speak at an event for the Addison

Club, his very elite private dining society, on 3 November. He seems to have forgotten our Twitter spat. He's emailed saying he thinks I'll 'find a fair few in our membership sympathetic to your case and even a few with chequebooks'. I agreed, and asked him to chair an event to introduce Gerry to the press on 18 November. I still haven't met Gerry myself, and will have to make sure we get together before we 'unveil' him to journalists. Better check he hasn't got two heads.

Gerry's going to be working closely with an election analyst called Ian Warren who correctly predicted the outcomes of the last two US presidential elections, with a 100 per cent record in every state. Crack team!

Got a reply from Neil saying he wouldn't do it unless there were Remain people on the panel as well. Er, no – not on this occasion, Andrew. But I'll give him credit for maintaining his BBC impartiality.

Have told Liz I want her to focus on making stuff happen in the office this week. We need to turn it into a really proactive sales hub and start driving donations. She's done a spreadsheet of roles and responsibilities, which helps us all focus on who needs a kick up the backside for what.

Wiggy's come up with a stunt to take the piss out of Cameron's renegotiation with Brussels. Everyone knows it's going to be a fudge. So let's make a stack of the stuff and send him some. We'll call it the Great British Fudge-Off.

It reminds me of the time I gave him a kitchen sink. It was the Rochester and Strood by-election in 2014, following Tory MP Mark Reckless's defection to UKIP. He had a healthy majority and we were confident. The Tories were in a sweat, and had dispatched all their big names to the constituency to try to save the seat. Cameron did one of his embarrassing 'that pumps me up!' speeches where he doesn't wear a jacket or tie and rolls up his sleeves. I read somewhere that Crosby thinks it makes him look 'passionate', but I always think he looks as if he's about to shove his arm up a cow's arse.

During that speech, he declared that his party would 'throw the kitchen sink at it' to make sure they won. A week out, and our private polling was looking good. While Tory ministers grumbled about having to traipse to Kent, our volunteers saw it as a great day out. They poured in from all over the country – 350 of them! So many people wanted to come to our election night bash that we had to find a bigger venue.

When the polls closed, I put £7,000 behind the bar and soon the place was heaving. Everyone wanted a pint with Nigel. Reckless held onto his seat – and Dave's sink missed its target by a country mile.

I left halfway through the party to go to the Tory offices, which they'd hastily abandoned. I left a kitchen sink on the doorstep with a note to Cameron.

'Thought I'd return this. Best, Arron.'

Still makes Wiggy laugh.

15 OCTOBER

Tice has started getting fan mail! Following his outing on *Marr*, we've had some letters from admirers. I suspect Wiggy is jealous.

'This one's from a woman called Beryl, and this is from a Doris,' he said, slightly sourly, I thought.

He probably thinks he'd get fan mail from an army of sexy Sophias if I let him loose on TV.

This afternoon he and Tice had a pow-wow with Robbie Gibb, the BBC executive who is overseeing the Corporation's referendum coverage. They met for coffee in Millbank to discuss our concerns about the Beeb's bias. Gibb was very professional and seemed to take our points seriously. Here's hoping they stop acting as if Vote Leave's the only show in town.

16 OCTOBER

Peter Hargreaves, our richest supporter, has added his voice to the peacenik party: he wants Leave.EU and Vote Leave to stop slagging each other off. Says we all need to work together after the designation. I know, I know, but has he ever tried dealing with these people?

Meanwhile, are we ever going to get this fricking website sorted? First it was the complaints about people not being able to donate online, now my inbox is jammed with messages from people who can't register. This is basic stuff. I'm seriously unimpressed with the people who built the site. Liz will have to have words – again.

18 OCTOBER

Gerry's up for the press conference on 18 November. I'm hoping to hold it somewhere around Westminster.

I've suggested he meet me and Wiggy in Bermuda at the end of the month. We're heading out there on business and he might as well join us for a night. He told me he woke up this morning and had to remove ice from his car, so a blast of sunshine should be just the ticket. He's arriving at 1.35 p.m. on the Friday and will probably stay at our favourite hotel, Tucker's Point. He has to leave early Saturday so it will be a flying visit.

19 OCTOBER

Grovelling

Wiggy's phone practically melted after we tweeted a tile emblazoned with the words 'BBC Lies'. I'm always telling the team I want them to get punchy, so when they heard yet another reporter talking about 'leaving Europe' as opposed to leaving the EU, they swung into action. It is impossible for us to leave Europe: what we want to leave is a political construct, and our social media people know I'm sick of the media conflating the two.

I'm all for holding the BBC's feet to the fire, but our timing was dreadful. Wiggy and Tice only met Robbie a few days ago and in recent weeks he's been making a real effort to get us airtime.

He went nuts and sent Wiggy a furious text: 'I am personally deeply offended. I took the trouble of meeting up with you guys; briefed you on how to get good BBC coverage; put Richard on Marr, and then in less than a week I'm called a liar.'

The last thing we want to do is alienate him. I told Wiggy to do some very rapid back-pedalling, apologise and say we'll change the graphic.

Wiggy texted me later, unusually chastened.

'We are liabilities – boo hoo,' he admitted.

None of this changes my basic view that being confrontational and provocative is the way ahead. We'll take some flak, but it will get people talking, engaging them in the campaign.

20 OCTOBER

Still worrying about Gibb. Thought a personal apology was in order, so I emailed him admitting we'd mishandled this one. Made it clear that our intention was to highlight an issue our supporters feel strongly about: we asked them for their view, and 10,000 of them signed a letter to the BBC which we penned and attached to our posting.

Told him I was the first to shout about perceived BBC errors and therefore must be the first to apologise for ours.

Got a nice letter back, saying it was 'good of me to write' and that he appreciated the apology:

> Since you and Andy Wigmore first got in touch I believe
> we have responded positively to all the points you made
> in your email. For example, I contacted BBC editors and
> political correspondents before the launch of Vote Leave
> to ensure it was made clear the decision had still not been

made by the EC as to which group would be the official 'out'
campaign. I also invited Richard to appear on the Andrew
Marr Show on the following Sunday to debate with the
'In' campaign (which also appeared on the 10 o'clock news
that evening).

I met up with Richard and Andy in the hope we could
build a positive relationship going forward (this is going to
be a long campaign!)...

Hopefully we've got away with it this time but we need to be more
careful.

Our efforts to win friends and influence people are proving more
successful with trade unions. We've been trying to get them on board
via an outfit called Trade Unionists Against the EU (TUAEU).

Nigel knows some folk at the RMT transport union and has
introduced us. After a lot of delicate diplomacy, they seem to trust
us. We're giving TUAEU £25,000 to help their campaign. Feel I have
much more in common with some of these guys than I do with
Tories these days. Up the revolution!

22 OCTOBER

We've hired Cambridge Analytica, an American company that uses
'big data and advanced psychographics' to influence people.

Inspired by Obama-style data analytics and social media campaigns, they've worked on dozens of political campaigns in the
States. At the moment they are on the payroll of Ted Cruz and Ben
Carson, who are challenging Trump for the Republican Party nomination. Their role will be to develop messages for target voters. They
devise psychological profiles of the electorate, using thousands of
pieces of data to filter the population into 150 personality types.
With this information, you can tailor campaign material to particular groups to vote. It may sound a bit creepy, but these days it's how
most big political parties work.

25 OCTOBER

Cummings has been shooting his mouth off about having two referendums. The idea is that a vote to leave would be a stronger mandate to renegotiate (again), with the public getting a second referendum on whatever new terms come out of that. Dangerous stuff. I think it muddies the waters and suggests Vote Leave don't think Brexit can win support on its own merits. If people think there's going to be a series of referendums they won't bother to vote. They need to know that this is a once-in-a-lifetime chance to get out of the EU. Need to knock this on the head.

I've been discussing it with Jim Mellon. He agrees it's a bad idea. He thinks Elliott and Cummings may be stooges set up to fail, though he pointed out that at least the two-refs bollocks suggests they think the first one is winnable. He shares my fear that if the idea gets legs, businesses will be in limbo for years, not knowing if we're in or out. It's classic Cummings, trying to be clever, and risks diluting the whole idea of leaving. Tice texted to say he'd bumped into Nigel at the rugby at Twickenham. They're both very worried.

We put out a press release with some strident quotes from Gerry expressing our concern. Unfortunately, Wiggy omitted to tell him and he wasn't happy. He sent me a stiff email making it clear that in future he has to clear everything attributed to him. Wiggy apologised but he's on the naughty step. On a positive note, Gerry described Wiggy as 'world-class'. Not sure what world he's referring to. Sui generis, more like.

I'm fired up and eager for Cameron to set the referendum date. Meanwhile, I can't afford to get too distracted from the day job. Campaigns on this scale don't pay for themselves. We head out to Bermuda tomorrow.

27 OCTOBER

Someone in the Westminster village is putting it about that the decision over who runs the official Brexit campaign will be made by MPs.

I suspect Elliott and Cummings have a hand in this so I emailed them telling them to pack it in.

> Andy and myself have been fielding dozens of calls from the press saying that they have been briefed that the final decision on designation will be taken out of the hands of the EC and made by MPs. This is not true. One of the journalists told me off the record it was by Vote Leave.
>
> We will accordingly be writing to the EC to clarify the matter and will publish the letter and the response. I also intend to tell the EC the source of the concern. Our lawyer will draft the letter today. This will create more tension between the out camps – it's very distracting for all concerned.

For good measure I told him (in so many words) to stop being such a loser.

> Maybe this how you do it in Westminster but it's very tiresome for the rest of us. (although instructive)
> Arron
>
> PS following up from signing up 1,300 councillors of all political colours, we will announce shortly a huge number of SME owners joining up. Our social media numbers are cruising upwards. Why don't you roll up your sleeves and do some work rather than sniping the whole time?

I soon got a sniffy reply from Cummings.

> Whoever has told you that is talking total balls. The EC decision is set in law. The MPs couldn't take over if they wanted to.

We would never claim such a thing as the media would think we've gone mad.

You are the victim of bullshit gossip.

My advice is to ignore it, not discuss it with hacks – it is an old trick of hacks to get you to do what they want for their purposes of causing trouble.

The source of your crossness remains a mystery to me but if you do as you suggest below you will undermine your credibility with the media for no gain.

We won't comment if asked.

Best wishes

D

Wiggy's texted telling me to stop emailing them. I should be making the most of this amazing weather, instead of getting sucked back into all this crap and making things worse.

28 OCTOBER

Told Andrew Neil I'm going to have to blow him out for the event on 3 November as I'll still be in Bermuda. My first takeover for five years is taking longer than planned and 'regretfully' I'm stuck out here for a few more days. Offered him Tice instead. 'Groan,' he replied. Doesn't he know that Tice has a cult following, at least with the ladies?

Brillo wasn't impressed, bleating that he'd 'invited sixty-five high net worth, very busy and important people to hear you at a hugely influential and exclusive Club dinner'.

The crafty bugger told me Elliott had offered himself up as a substitute. That sealed it. I said I would spare his blushes and agreed to come back early for his dinner – on condition that Sebastian Payne, his awful metropolitan pipsqueak of a columnist, is served up on the menu as 'stuffed guttersnipe'.

Neil replied that Payne can't be on the menu as they have 'sold him to the *FT*". Good. He will feel much more at home at that Brussels propaganda rag. Must have been a cheap transfer.

When I get back, I also need a meeting with Tim Clyde from Minimart about the website and where we go from here. We bought an all-singing, all-dancing site and got presented with something my kids could have knocked together for a few quid in the garden shed.

29 OCTOBER

Immigration, immigration, immigration

We've commissioned an interesting new poll on immigration, which I'm still convinced is the key to this referendum. It may not be a fashionable subject in the leafier parts of London, but it's a huge issue across the rest of the country, especially in deprived areas.

Our poll shows Theresa May would be the figure most trusted to deliver on the message that 'leaving is the only way we can control our own borders and set our own immigration policy'. It's no surprise that David 'I'll bring net migration down to the tens of thousands' Cameron doesn't have any credibility.

It seems voters were impressed by May's speech to the Tory Party conference this month when she pledged to come down hard on illegal immigrants and declared that mass migration from Europe is also unsustainable.

Wiggy reckons she'd be the best person to front the Leave campaign. 'Basically, May for leader!' was his response. I'm not so sure. She's been responsible for border control for the past five years. If the numbers are out of control, it's at least partly down to her.

BPop, not just a pipe dream

The Brexit concert is beginning to take shape. We've been talking to a company called This Is Metropolis about how to take it forward. One of their guys, a producer named Louis Brown, has emailed saying they can arrange it all: artists, video production, social media teams, event promotion; the lot. We'll fork out the cash and bring Nigel, Kate and maybe Liam Fox. Looks like it will cost at least £200k for three top acts. Money well spent.

It doesn't even have to be a Brexit-only event. We could have campaigners and artists of all political stripes and none, as long as the keynote speakers stress the importance of getting out the vote and getting young people to register. Maybe we could link up with that campaign group that tries to get young people to vote – Bite the Ballot?

Timing's a bit tricky as we still don't know the referendum date, so we've agreed to talk specifics later on. Can't wait.

31 OCTOBER

Going bananas in Bermuda

Wiggy arrived in Bermuda yesterday, and since then it's all been a bit of a mess.

He and I like drinking as much as we like business but, unlike Nigel, we're not very good at it. After a few pints we were a little light-headed. The deal we were doing was important, and to put it charitably we were so consumed by it (and our celebratory drinks) that we forgot Gerry was coming. When we woke up this morning, we couldn't really think beyond the rum we were sweating out, and took an executive decision not to move from the pool.

Suddenly Wiggy remembered the date. 'Shit, Banksy! We're supposed to be meeting Gerry!'

'Cancel him,' I said wearily. 'I've got a really sore head.'

'We bloody well can't! The poor man's flown all the way from the States to see us!' Wiggy replied, not unreasonably.

'Seriously, I'm not sure I can even muster the energy for lunch. Cancel him,' I groaned, unreasonably.

Wiggy rang the Happy Hippy and spun a yarn about how we had to fly back to Blighty early. The Hippy was aghast. 'You can't fuck this guy off! He's a real big shot in the States. Didn't you read the emails I sent you? It's too late!' he snapped. I could hear him from my sun lounger, and it wasn't helping my hangover. 'I've worked my arse off to persuade this guy to see you. For Christ's sake, sober up!' At this point we thought we'd better face facts: one or both of us was going to have to leave the pool, tank up on coffee and get business-like.

Naturally, Wiggy hadn't read Jimbo's email with all the detail. Somehow he'd got it into his head that the meeting was due to take place at 11 a.m., when in fact it was not till afternoon. The upshot was that we had a hair-of-the-dog at midday, and then several more, while we sat in the hotel lobby at the Rosewood, Tucker's Point, endlessly scanning the horizon for our hotshot adviser.

We had at least dressed the part. I was sporting orange Bermuda shorts with red socks – a horrible clash – while Wiggy had even baggier shorts in that dodgy light blue that Cameron used for the Conservative logo when he changed it from the old flaming torch to an eco-friendly tree. To complete the colonial look, he was wearing knee-high turquoise socks. We spent most of the afternoon carousing around the lobby, mojitos in hand, hailing every stranger with 'Are you Gerry?' which, after a few cocktails, seemed very funny.

Finally, a neat-looking gentleman appeared, a vision of corporate America, immaculately dressed in a dark-blue suit, crisp white shirt, summoning all his professionalism to maintain a fixed smile as he surveyed the scene. Or at least Wiggy thought it was him. I had no idea and wasn't really concentrating.

'Come on, let's pack it in. I think the Hippy must have cancelled him,' I said. But the stranger was indeed our man! And from what I could tell through the alcoholic fug, he was pissed off.

'Go and charm him,' I urged. 'Give him your poshest English accent. That always seems to work with Yanks.'

Summoning remarkable reserves of willpower, Wiggy staggered up, collected himself, and fixed our guest with one of his brightest smiles. 'You must be Mr Gunster?' he asked briskly, and proceeded to greet him like a long-lost friend.

It turned out that we'd neglected to tell Gerry where to meet us, and the poor man had been wandering around, unable to raise us on the mobile. He looked tired and hot. 'Why don't you go over the road and buy yourself some Bermuda shorts?' I suggested helpfully. 'You'll feel better once you're out of that suit.' Relieved to get out of his shirt and tie, or just eager for our business, he trotted off, returning a few minutes later wearing some suitably silly shorts.

It quickly became apparent that this was a man with whom we could do business. It wasn't that we had much in common – he seemed so polite and mild-mannered – but he was game for a laugh and soon got stuck into the drinks.

By 3 a.m., we were done. It was at this point that we realised we hadn't even got him a room. He was still sitting there with his suitcase.

Fortunately, Wiggy declared that he had 'a minor local difficulty' to attend to in Belize, and should get a dawn flight.

'You can have my room,' he offered.

'Thanks. Is everything OK? Some emergency?' Gerry replied gratefully.

It was and it wasn't. Wiggy explained that, in his capacity as a representative of the Belize government, there was a certain character he had to see in connection with the drugs trade, to try to persuade this individual to remain on the right side of the law.

There ensued a very serious discussion between the two of them about something called the 'Kingpin Act' and its attendant designation, with which Gerry seemed familiar, at least from a US point of view.

In 2015 there were only three drug barons in the whole world designated 'Kingpins' and, for entirely proper reasons, namely that this Kingpin designation was in danger of disrupting Belize's banana trade, Wiggy was off to see one of the trio.

'Ah,' said Gerry, sounding understanding but hesitant.

Wiggy continued. There was a general election on in Belize, and the designated Kingpin owned a 10,000-acre banana plantation. In addition to supporting the livelihoods of some 10,000 locals, this also effectively accounts for 4–5 per cent of the Belizean economy.

With the Kingpin Act preventing US nationals from doing any kind of business with the company in question, Belize was suffering from all kinds of serious financial and diplomatic complications, not least that 2,000 jobs were on the line.

A safe pair of hands was what was needed – someone with a mix of British charm and local nous. Wiggy explained that in his capacity as trade envoy he'd been sent to sort it out, and so, after polishing off his ninth mojito and leaving his Bermuda shorts on the bathroom floor, he departed, diplomatic passport in hand.

Our American friend absorbed all this. It was certainly a colourful tale and Wiggy was picture-perfect as a kind of late-Edwardian gentleman rogue – louche, frightfully British and off to the frontier to parlay with the local warlords – but it was all rather unorthodox. I noticed that Gerry was looking a bit pale.

Anxious not to lose our star player before he'd entered the pitch, I reassured him that Wiggy was on the side of the angels. 'Things just work a bit differently in Belize,' I said airily, and swiftly moved onto something more humdrum.

Let's hope we haven't freaked him out.

Launching the singing señorita

Liz's 'pop star' Antonia Suñer launched the Brexit song at an obscure private members' club in Hove tonight. Last time UKIP held a public event in that neck of the woods there was a public protest, so she decided we needed to keep it under wraps.

I think she was trying to replicate the fever-pitch excitement that grips Radio 1 audiences before stars like Adele release tickets for their sell-out tours. If so, it didn't work. The Hove Club isn't the O2 and the sorry truth is we could barely have filled a working men's club.

Nigel ducked out, making some lame excuse about being on the *Marr Show* tomorrow, and unfortunately Wiggy and I were both otherwise engaged in various parts of the Caribbean.

Apparently the song is already rocketing up the Amazon chart (not).

NOVEMBER 2015

1 NOVEMBER

Theresa May dodges the question

Back in Blighty. Switched on my phone to discover a rather worrying message from Gerry. He has informed me that in the light of our recent conversations, he feels he needs to consult his team about whether to press ahead with the contract.

Shit! Wiggy better not have screwed this up for us with his mad dogs and Englishmen routine.

Our immigration poll is still running on the news. I caught the tail end of *Marr* and was pleased to see Theresa May coming under pressure to say if she'll be fronting the Leave campaign. She's still sitting on the fence. The Happy Hippy knows one of her people from his Tory days and rang them to make sure it's on her radar.

I told the team to put out a simple statement saying we'd be delighted to have her aboard the campaign for Britain to leave the EU. But Nigel thinks it will backfire and gave us a bollocking. He thinks she'll run a mile from us if it looks like we're campaigning for her to replace Cameron. Are we that toxic?

Wiggy's still in Belize on his secret mission. With a patchy mobile signal, he kept ringing in with updates from his Land Rover in some forbidding stretch of banana plantation near the Guatemalan border, where he was navigating a dirt track under the glare of the occasional gun-toting henchman.

Eventually he arrived at a luxurious hacienda, where he did his best to play the starched British diplomat in the searing heat and humidity. His target turned out to be a most interesting fellow, named by the US Treasury as being one the biggest players in Central American drug cartels.

Andy's mission was to convince him to sell his plantation to a more salubrious buyer and so unfreeze this crucial sector of the economy.

'Do you know why I am here?' he asked the drug lord.

'Yes, what do you want?' the Kingpin Designate replied suspiciously.

Wiggy told him he had two options: sell his banana plantation to get the economy moving again and save 2,000 jobs, or he's fucked. Wiggy had a buyer if he was interested.

At this point the Kingpin Designate started spinning some sob story about his miserable childhood.

'Do you know my story?' he implored. 'My mother was Honduran, my father Palestinian. My father died when I was a very young, and yes, it is true, I went off the rails a little bit, and yes, it is true I got involved with drugs and spent years in a Guatemalan prison. When I come back, I do bananas. These days I am helping the authorities, and my Kingpin designation is under review. Look, here are my legal papers that the US government has.'

Now, this obviously changed things: it appeared the Kingpin had been helping the US and was thus now a force for good!

'Do the press know?' Wiggy asked.

'I told no one. Who do I need to tell?' he asked. Wiggy responded that he needed to tell everyone; jobs were at stake – and bananas!

'Get me the Prime Minister; get me the American ambassador; get me the British High Commissioner,' our friend replied obligingly. So Wiggy got on the blower to his contacts and was able to tell his Kingpin that various officials would soon be converging on the scene.

By now they were both inside the hacienda, our man having quickly concluded that Wiggy was no great threat and not an MI6 agent. It was at this point that Wiggy made a rather inconvenient discovery.

Belize is a small place, and it transpired that the drug lord's mother was, in fact, a distant relative of his grandmother. This put a rather different complexion on matters.

Feeling that it was only right to disclose this slight conflict of interest, he rang the offices of the Belizean PM and the British High Commission in Belize, soberly informing them that he had just discovered he was a blood relative of the Kingpin Designate (albeit a designate under review).

'Oh fuck, Andy, now you are really in the shit,' was the gist of their response.

And there the matter rests.

4 NOVEMBER

Good news. Gerry's got back to me saying it's all OK. Thank goodness.

I've been contacted by a journalist from the *Express* who says Boris isn't ruling out leading the campaign to leave the EU. I hope this is true. He'd be an amazing asset.

Tice fired off a statement saying 'we would be thrilled to have the support and leadership skills of Boris, who would be a Churchillian figure in the fight to save our country'.

I went along to Andrew Neil's dinner tonight. The evening consisted of drinks at old-school gents' club Boodles in St James's, followed by a very tasty sit-down dinner at Brown's in Mayfair. After the meal, Neil said a few words and I gave my speech.

My guest was my old chum Kobus Coetzee, a former South African spook. Was worried my inexperience at this kind of thing showed, but Neil emailed tonight saying I had done well.

'I fear it is going to be unpleasant as the debate progresses,' he added ominously.

We're ready for it.

6 NOVEMBER

Sampling Stalin's vodka

Wiggy's back, apparently none the worse for wear after his adventures. He rocked up at the office brandishing a bottle of rum from

Belize: a gift for Alexander Yakovenko, the Russian ambassador, with whom we were due to have lunch.

Katya decided not to come, which was a shame as they could have had some good Russian banter. We've been married for fifteen years and you can count on the fingers of one hand the number of Russian words I know. Katya, on the other hand, speaks five languages in addition to her mother tongue: English, French, German, Italian and Spanish. Her French is so good the people think she's a native.

We set off for the ambassador's private residence on Kensington Palace Gardens feeling a little nervous. We'd been invited by a shady character called Oleg we'd met in Doncaster at UKIP's conference. He was introduced to us as the First Secretary at the Embassy – in other words, the KGB's man in London. We approached him with due caution. It was a one-hour appointment, but we hit it off from the word go.

Wiggy started regaling Alexander with tales of his father's work with the Soviets at the Berlin Air Safety Centre in the 1980s, and we were off. One hour swiftly turned into two, and then four, and finally more like six. It was everything you'd hope for in a meeting with the Russians.

Our host wanted the inside track on the Brexit campaign and grilled us on the potential implications of an Out vote for Europe. We chose our words carefully but we didn't mind telling him we think everyone's in for a shock.

The conversation was rattling along nicely and diplomatic relations only improved when our new friend produced a special surprise. It was a bottle of vodka which he claimed was 'one of only three in a batch made for Stalin personally'.

'Try it!' he urged. 'Only because I'm enjoying your company so much!'

We needed no encouragement, and in a trice two shot glasses appeared. Whatever its provenance, it was bloody good. 'Wow. Can I have another?' I asked eagerly.

This was a faux pas.

'Absolutely not. There are only three bottles and there is not much left in this one. But I have lovely brandy,' Alexander said helpfully. 'By the way, you're sitting in the same chair Churchill used when he came to see the Russian ambassador!'

I looked suitably impressed, secretly wondering whether he uses the same lines – perhaps even the same vodka – on every guest.

By mid-afternoon, everyone was quite merry and diplomatic protocols were rapidly falling by the wayside. It transpired that Alexander had recently had a discussion with the Foreign Secretary which had left him deeply unimpressed. 'We talked about Syria,' he growled. 'I asked if he has a Plan B. You know what his answer was?'

We didn't.

'He just said, "No." Niet!' he spluttered indignantly.

Eventually, it was time to leave. We shook hands and promised to meet again. As we made our way out, our host had one final flourish. 'Unique ambassador's blend. Only for very special guests!' he said, thrusting a box of tea into my hand.

I hope it's not radioactive.

8 NOVEMBER

Poppy day panic

Bit of a shit-storm today after Wiggy posted a Remembrance Sunday-themed tweet suggesting that voting for Brexit would honour Britain's war dead.

'Freedom and democracy. Let's not give up values for which our ancestors paid the ultimate sacrifice' was his message of the day. We'd posted it along with a picture of an old Chelsea Pensioner whose views, I admit, we had no idea about. At least Wiggy had the sense to wait until after the two minutes' silence, but predictably, everyone kicked off anyway, accusing us of 'shameful opportunism' etc.

Naturally, Britain Stronger in Europe lost no time leaping into the pulpit, issuing a sanctimonious statement to the effect that we should be 'reflecting and honouring the fallen, not making crass political points'. Meanwhile, the usual gobshites started kicking off on Twitter. 'Glad my relatives fought for your right to talk utter shite,' was how one indignant bloke put it.

Wiggy had a brief stint in the forces, so I'm sure he knew it was going to cause trouble, but even he seemed a bit taken aback by the scale of the outcry. Naturally, Tice (who hadn't been consulted) was very cross. 'Bit fucking stupid. Not your best. Who authorised it?' he demanded. Wiggy confessed it was him. 'Not presenting us in a good light,' Tice sniffed.

Nigel gave us an even more vehement rendition of his usual 'no upside' lecture. A little later that afternoon, when I gingerly logged onto Twitter to see if the storm had abated, I saw the offending message had gone!

'What happened to it?' I asked.

'I took it down,' Andy replied quietly. He looked a bit wan, which is saying something for a man with a perma-tan. He told me sheepishly that he'd apologised 'unreservedly', which is not in the playbook, unless we're doing it tongue in cheek. Said he'd tried to hose down the *Daily Mail*, who were threatening to turn us over.

'What did you do that for? Put it back up!' I instructed. We were getting a load of supportive emails from ex-servicemen.

So he did. That made three stories for the price of one. First for the original tweet; then a story about how we'd taken it down in shame; and then another story about how we'd brazenly put it back up again.

OK, it was probably all a bit crass, but I stand by the sentiments of the message, and we got loads of publicity. We're slowly beginning to understand how the media works.

9 NOVEMBER

We're still getting grief about the tweet. The awful Pete North asked if we are 'going to have to spend the entire campaign in damage control mode or will you do something sensible like sack Wigmore? At what point does your operation get its act together?'

The Happy Hippy reverted to Tory mode, sending me an email accusing us of screwing up. 'You still don't get it, do you??? The campaign fucked up – take it on the chin and move on.'

Political types like him get way too fussed by minor hiccups! Why not rail about Tony Blair, who started all those wars? Or have a pop at the chief of the defence staff, who blasted Corbyn on Remembrance Day? Or Cameron laying a wreath while showing what he thinks of the forces by sacking thousands of them and refusing to give the rest a pay rise, while saying the EU guarantees our security?

Anyway, we constantly get letters from people who fought for their country and feel we've sold out to the EU. With all the controversy, our Facebook feed has skyrocketed and we've been inundated with messages of support. The outrage has helped us pull in more people and we can start talking to them about other stuff. Wiggy's been monitoring readers' comments on the *Daily Mail* website and they're massively on our side. Tice is still grumbling, but I have no regrets.

Moral high ground

Cameron has given a big speech to the CBI, the 'upside' of which (as Nigel would say) was that it furnished us with a rare opportunity to take the moral high ground.

He was busy pontificating to business leaders about the importance of the EU; his long-term economic plan, blah blah, when two students suddenly leapt up from the crowd, brandishing a banner saying 'CBI: Voice of Brussels'. They began to heckle about the audience being EU stooges.

Now, Cameron hasn't got where he is today by allowing himself to get flustered by oiks sounding off from the cheap seats, and calmly told them to sit down and stop making fools of themselves.

It was a rare bit of drama for a Remain snoozefest, and the media lapped it up. Within hours they discovered that the two 'students' were in fact plants from Vote Leave who'd registered under a shell company called Lyon Sheppard Web Solutions.

Quite a surprise from that prim and proper lot! Predictably, they got an absolute pasting: Stronger In piled in with a sanctimonious statement calling it a grubby little tactic; *The Guardian* mounted its high horse and moaned that it was the perfect way to spoil a half-decent point with a silly stunt; and we told anyone who asked that we wouldn't dream of doing such a thing.

I don't suppose anyone believed us, but it was fun while it lasted.

10 NOVEMBER

Two Tories give a lecture

One thing I've learned so far is that every Tory politician assumes they have the right to tell everyone how to do everything all of the time.

So I wasn't entirely surprised when Peter Bone and Tom Pursglove – who belong to a very exclusive band of Conservative MPs who like us – invited us to Millbank to lecture us on how to handle the press.

Bone is a veteran member of the backbench Tory awkward squad who resembles the Demon Headmaster. The much younger Pursglove resembles an overgrown foetus.

Old Drearybones and his curious little sidekick gravely informed me that I am a hopeless novice and must take my cue from seasoned navigators of the choppy media waters, like them. I nodded acquiescently, resisting a nasty urge to ask how their superior media savvy was working out for their careers.

I was slightly disturbed by the way Bone kept calling Pursglove 'Minister', as if to indicate he believes the strange young man is destined for great things, but for once I kept my mouth zipped.

The basic message from Tweedledum and Tweedledee was that I'm not to do any more media without first running it by a man called Nick Wood, who was head honcho in the Conservative Party press office half a century ago. Apparently he has great contacts in the lobby and is very in with IDS.

I gently informed them that I'm doing Radio 4's *Any Questions?* programme on Friday and have been invited onto *Marr* this weekend.

'You're on *Marr*?' Bone spluttered.

Guess he's never had the pleasure. I smiled sweetly and said I'd let them know how I get on.

11 NOVEMBER

Eric Pickles has written to the Electoral Commission saying Vote Leave should be disqualified from getting official designation following the CBI student stunt. Old Five Bellies accused them of running 'an open campaign of nasty tactics' that falls foul of official guidelines on playing fair.

Pickles may be a Remainer, but I love him today.

I dropped Andrew Neil a line to put it on his radar. 'This goes against the grain totally and it pains me to say this but on this occasion Sir Eric Pickles is right,' I said.

> If we are to gain the trust of the British people in this campaign then provocative stunts and schoolboy politics is not the answer. This is a serious debate about a very serious matter and we now have to conduct ourselves accordingly. Stating that this is going to 'get nasty' (as Cummings has said) helps no one.

'Very tactical,' he replied.

12 NOVEMBER

The *Mail*'s running a poll tomorrow putting Leave ahead! According to their survey, it's Brexit 53 per cent; Remain 47 per cent. Fantastic news at this stage. Emailed Gerry, who replied, 'Awesome!'

He thinks the final vote will be 55 per cent Leave. I feel we're on track with our messaging.

The lobby thinks next week's press conference is our official launch, so we're making a big effort. I'm arranging some high-quality branded freebies – mugs, pens, bags etc. – and we'll make sure we have a decent line-up of speakers. Cambridge Analytica will be there to explain what they do. When the lobby see the calibre of people we've hired, perhaps they'll take us more seriously.

13 NOVEMBER

Gunster's recipe for victory

Gerry has devised a brilliant battle plan which hammers home the points the whole team needs to understand. He stresses that referendums are very different to elections. There's no personality to promote – it's about an abstract message.

He says:

> Messengers must come from variety of backgrounds. Define terms that appeal to the self-interest of voter e.g. family, your budget, your future. [Be] Emotionally charged but maintain discipline – confused voters vote to maintain the status quo. Top three messages: 1) Border control 2) Keep money at home 3) Make our own laws / Control our own destiny. Separate each of these issues for male and female audiences. Action plan: 1) Secure the base 2) Persuade the persuadeables 3) Win the tossup vote 4) Dent the hard remain.

Our three top messages are polling well: controlling borders, keeping money at home and controlling our own destiny by making our own laws. In each case, more than 70 per cent of people find the argument convincing. None of the top three Remain arguments

– on the economy, security and the risks of leaving – score that high, which is surprising and encouraging.

Gerry is quite clear: 'In the real campaign environment, the Leave messages will win against the Remain messages.'

I am feeling energised and positive about our prospects. I am convinced we can pull this off against the full might of the establishment, because it's what people want.

Any Questions?

Just back from *Any Questions?* in Basingstoke and glued to the TV watching the terrible news in Paris.

Hundreds of innocent people are dead or critically injured following a series of co-ordinated shootings and suicide bombings all over the French capital. Absolutely unbelievable events.

This raises many very serious political points – including questions about how the EU's open borders policy has affected security – but tonight's not the night for that.

I spoke to the team to ensure everyone knows we won't be using this tragedy for political gain. Gerry agreed we should stay off Twitter and told us not to post anything, even if it's not immigration- or terror-related. We'll continue this policy over the weekend and return to business on Monday.

Any Questions? went well. I was up against Energy Secretary Amber Rudd, Scottish Nationalist John Nicolson and Tony Blair's old chum Charlie Falconer. As always, Jonathan Dimbleby was in the chair. He kicked off by introducing me as UKIP's biggest donor, diamond mine owner etc. etc., which attracted predictable boos. We discussed the ethics of the drone strike which killed 'Jihadi John', the ISIS executioner with the London accent.

I said I thought our boys did the right thing in this case, but the government needs to be careful about edging towards anything like judicial murder, which got a clap. The final question was about Cameron writing to his local council to complain about library closures. Cue widespread ridicule about him sounding off about his own budget cuts. I declared that I had nothing good to say about Dave but acknowledged his right as a local MP to write the letter. I was pausing to think about what to say next when the audience clapped, so I quit while I was ahead.

Left the studio feeling I'd struck the right note. Toby Blackwell sent a nice message tonight describing me as 'the quiet, credible voice of common sense'. Two fingers to Bone and Pursglove!

Am exhausted and depressed by what's happened in Paris and have decided to cancel my appearance on *Marr*. It's disappointing but it's a high-stakes gig. I need to be on top of my game.

Drearybones and the foetus will probably assume I was bumped for a bigger name, but I've shown I can hold my own on the airwaves.

14 NOVEMBER

Lisa from *Any Questions?* has been in touch with one of our press officers to say I was great – 'thoughtful and not shouty' was her feedback. They want me on again. Result.

18 NOVEMBER

Gerry and the bear hunters

Very buoyed up by our Westminster launch. As always, Nigel was a grumpy git ahead of the event, moaning that nobody would turn up, it would all be a shambles, we were hopeless at organising anything etc. etc.

He was annoyed because we decided not to put him on the platform, and he was forced to sit in the audience for once while we took centre stage.

The Happy Hippy was also full of doom and gloom, complaining there was nothing behind the main lectern, the backdrop was reflective, table-top microphones went out with the ark, there was no lighting and the room was too big.

We'd hired a hall within walking distance of the House of Commons, with Gerry, Tice and a woman from Cambridge Analytica as key speakers. As I'd hoped, Gerry was very much the star turn. He was on comfortable ground talking about his record in the States, where he's been involved in all sorts of strange referendums, not all as epoch-making as our own. In Maine, they even had a referendum on bear trapping methods. The question was whether the use of jam doughnuts and pizzas to lure the animals to their deaths should be banned.

'What happened?' asked one of the hacks.

'The bears lost,' replied Gerry, deadpan, which got a laugh.

Afterwards, Nigel and the Happy Hippy had to eat their words, grudgingly acknowledging that it had been a success.

Lucy Thomas, Will Straw's deputy at Britain Stronger in Europe, cranked out a press release this afternoon trying to spin it as a 'relaunch' and describing it as 'lame'.

'Leave.EU wouldn't even allow UKIP's Nigel Farage on the panel today because they were afraid he'd overshadow their event,' she said.

Texted her to say nobody's ever accused me of being limp before and invited her to lunch.

David Wall, who organised that business cruise during which Farage met Elliott, has been in touch. He's a big Tory donor who runs an umbrella group for wealthy Midlands industrialists who vote Conservative but flirt with UKIP. He wants me to renew efforts to join forces with Elliott. He batted off my concerns about Vote Leave briefing against us, saying Cameron's henchmen are the bigger threat. He wants me to crack on with a formal letter proposing a merger.

I am keen to keep all the politicians in the loop. David agreed, but told me to hurry up. 'A bunch of MPs are waiting to hear, carpe diem, my friend,' he said.

Have told Andy to get something drafted.

19 NOVEMBER

I have not changed my opinion of Elliott, but I do understand real-politik. So in a slight (!) change of strategy, we're love-bombing him. Have sent him a letter saying we should join to create 'one united and irresistible force'. I've proposed merger talks with no pre-conditions. Two rival campaigns slugging it out is a waste of time, money and effort; the competition has kept us sharp but in the long term it will only help the Remain side.

Teeth gritted, I paid tribute to VL's 'great technical analysis' and its links with 'big businesses' and politicians. Kept my language diplomatic and measured. They have the SW1 skills; we're the ones with the people power. We complement each other. We've piled on 300,000 supporters in three months and have a huge social media presence. Every day we receive small donations from ordinary people wanting us to succeed, and hundreds of local councillors and small businesses have signed up.

David Wall was pleased: he says it paints me as the good guy. Maybe we can combine the campaigns under the Leave.EU banner and let Matthew focus on working with the politicians? Ideally Cummings will have to go. Tice thinks we should hold fire now until they respond. We haven't given the letter to the media, but I'm pretty sure it will leak, as we ended up cc-ing it to thirty-five MPs.

Going off grid for a while for the East African Safari Classic Rally in Kenya. It's one of the highlights of my year. There's nothing quite like hurtling along dirt tracks at breakneck speed in a battered old banger. We'll cover 2,500 miles or so of Kenya and Tanzania in nine days, dodging floods, craters and wild animals. My kind of fun!

When I stagger out of that rust bucket after a day careering over potholes, my bottom feels like a bruised nectarine, I'm covered in dirt and my muscles are so seized up I look like a turtle with a dislocated neck. Elliott and Cummings will be the last thing on my mind. It's a massive adrenalin rush and, best of all, it raises thousands of pounds for Love Saves the Day. Can't wait.

20 NOVEMBER

Our ex-SAS security guy says he'd rather shoot Taliban than do this rally. Day 1's been a ballbreaker. Spent the day rattling through the bush in a 1968 Ford Escort Mexico with my old friend and partner in crime Tim Chesser, who's a trauma surgeon in Bristol and one of my neighbours. We play squash together and this is our third car rally. We share the driving and navigation and try not to kill each other.

Today we did a jump that nearly went horribly wrong. We hit the launch at full speed, achieved take-off, then there was a deathly silence as we hurtled through the air before thudding back to earth with a deafening crash, the windscreen caked in a layer of billowing dust. Somehow we emerged in one piece.

'Don't break your bloody neck, we need you here,' was David Wall's response when I regaled him with the day's adventures.

The compensation for all the hardship on the road is the accommodation: luxury lodges where you can kick back, have a hearty dinner and catch up with what's going on back home. I checked my emails tonight and found a sniffy holding response from Elliott. Says they need to have a board meeting before they can give us an answer. Meetings about meetings about meetings – sums them up.

The truth is, they're all over the place. Wall says they were shocked by my letter and don't know how to respond. The word in the Vote Leave office was that it can't have been written by me as it was far too diplomatic and professional. I can play that part when it suits me! Apparently they're worried about it going public. The board is split, and there are big ructions. Piss-up and brewery come to mind.

23 NOVEMBER

Elliott's twigged that he's under surveillance. Wiggy thinks he'll try to use David Wall to find out if it's us, and sent me an urgent email telling me to keep my mouth shut.

Banksy,

Call me when you can.

Two things. If you are asked by DW if you have put ME under surveillance deny it point blank – do not admit anything.

ME is convinced that he is under watch and says he has evidence so plead the 5th amendment that you know nothing…

Decided to try to head it off at the pass by emailing Wall to tell him I'd heard that Elliott is making allegations. Incidentally, I think David would be a good chairman of the merged campaign. There's no doubting his sincerity or commitment to the cause: he's well tapped in with lots of donors, and seems to get on well with everyone.

Thought I'd switch off from the campaign while I'm out here, but I'm too immersed to detach.

Got a message from UKIP peer Malcolm Pearson praising my letter to Elliott.

'Bravo! Well Done! Upon such a tide are we now afloat,' he wrote grandly, misquoting *Julius Caesar*. All we can do is wait.

24 NOVEMBER

We're mid-way through the rally and have a day off. Couldn't come soon enough! We've skirted Kilimanjaro and we're now in Tanzania by Lake Manyara, which Ernest Hemingway called the loveliest lake in Africa. We're supposed to be sightseeing (we're near the famous Ngorongoro crater, which is amazing for wildlife watching) while the mechanics service the rally cars, but I can hardly move from the hotel.

26 NOVEMBER

Been back in the rust bucket all day having my bones rattled. We're heading for the Tanzanian city of Arusha, after which we plunge into the Pare Mountains, before crossing back into Kenya. It's been hair-raising. At one point I told Tim to 'go left, slow' and what does he do? Goes right and fast and lands us in a ditch. I hope he knows left from right when he's operating on patients.

Wiggy emailed, helpfully reminding me that if it all goes tits up, I could take advantage of some of the insurance services we offer.

'If you've had an accident in the last 3 days call our expert no-win no-fee lawyers; you could be entitled to £3,000 compensation,' was his idea of a joke.

Checked back with base and apparently Elliott's been briefing that there's no deal on the cards. Publicly, they're still considering our olive branch. It's frustrating, but I'm not giving up. Have suggested Tice and I fix a cosy lunch with John Mills, the Labour Leave businessman who chairs Elliott's board. I reckon it's a better option than the official channels. Tried to do the same with Wheeler, but he says he doesn't want to complicate things. Grrrr.

27 NOVEMBER

Flashdance at Old Down Manor

So happy to have missed the latest embarrassment with Liz's 'Christmas No. 1'. Let's just say it's not Band Aid.

Some bright spark came up with the idea of shooting a video to go with the song, using the call centre team as backing dancers. The 'choreography' – if we could call it that – was a cover of Taylor Swift's 'Shake It Off'.

Very much against my better judgement, Liz decided to run with it in case it generated a bit of extra publicity and pushed the tune up the charts. She was told that if we could get all our subscribers to download it, it would be a genuine contender for No. 1.

To give him his due, for once even Wiggy was sceptical. 'This is entirely a Liz Bilney one, this. I'm not taking ANY blame for it,' he said tersely.

Liz conscripted all the call centre employees and I suggested they could use Old Down as a set. Having seen the video tonight, I have my regrets.

I can conclude that my team are great at working the phones but are about as good at dancing as Ann Widdecombe on *Strictly*. One of the guys claimed he was a professionally trained dancer but, judging from the footage, that's definitely a lie. Another of the boys had just turned twenty, never danced in his life, and kept getting confused between left and right. Apparently they sounded like a choir of cats but, wisely, this was dubbed over in the final cut.

According to Pamela, who was in charge of logistics, the whole event was a cock-up from the start. They all descended on Old Down to find Antonia hadn't shown up. Apparently she was flying in from abroad and would be there 'in a bit'.

They'd hired some fancy choreographer who'd claimed to have worked with celebrities like Danny Dyer and was supposed to be amazing. Her brief was to teach the team the moves to 'Shake It Off', but she only gave them sixty seconds' worth, after which they were left standing around.

After a total of fourteen shoots for one minute of footage, they waited three hours for Antonia to pitch up. She's not the type of diva for whom I'd have hung around, so I've got to pity my staff on that score.

Then apparently there was some bitchy showbiz drama between Antonia and the choreographer because someone had given someone a dirty look or snubbed the other at some point. Cue the choreographer having a tantrum and refusing to teach the team any more moves.

They spent the rest of the shoot sitting on their backsides on the stone-cold stairs, mouthing the chorus. For some inexplicable reason, they were all holding candles. Unfortunately, they didn't even know the lyrics, so all you can see is their mouths moving up and down without any synchronisation. They kept swivelling their eyes to the right, where Kim was standing with a flip chart pointing at the words.

The overall effect was a bunch of stoned students at a séance.

28 NOVEMBER

Last day of the rally. Back to base at Whitesands on the Indian Ocean, avoiding the traffic on the main Nairobi–Mombasa route. Beat-up vehicles are par for the course in Kenya, but our old bangers take it to a new level and are best kept off main roads.

The whole thing has been an amazing adrenalin rush. We rolled three times, killed several unfortunate goats and a dog, hit a donkey and had a tyre come off at 140km/h. One morning the gearbox went after just 75 km and we were stuck in third gear for the rest of the day until the thing conked out. We had to be towed out. Another day, we ended up upside down in a ditch. I was lucky not to need Tim's trauma services.

I reckon I've lost at least a stone.

We finished thirty-fifth out of fifty, not bad considering how many knocks we had. One of the other cars finished with a bad mash-up at 120mph, so we consider ourselves proud.

29 NOVEMBER

Heading home. More grief over the Antonia Suñer thing.

Liz is mortified by the 10,000 CDs which are destined for landfill, though the song did get an airing on Radio 1. Wiggy almost crashed his car when it suddenly came on, after an announcement from the DJ that he was going to play something so bad it was good.

Antonia's people have been desperately trying to put a brave face on it, insisting it could work. Her team have been bombarding Liz with emails, asking how she intends to push it on Facebook etc. 'Do you have any plans to email members to download?' one of her team asked. 'I was thinking of POP WEEK. POWER OF PEOPLE WEEK. Dec 13th to Dec 20th. I feel that we could achieve 50,000 downloads thus making lucrative sum of money for campaign, BBC news and sky news plus even more interest for our people's movement!'

We replied saying sorry, but the videos are shit and this is not going to go anywhere.

Antonia herself keeps emailing, telling us to repost the video, but Liz has finally acknowledged that she's flogging a dead horse and has been avoiding her pleas. She's even blocked her on Facebook.

Meanwhile, some smart alec has discovered that one of dancers in the video is Slovakian. Cue predictable crap about 'hypocrisy', because we want to reduce migration from the EU. We've never said we want to ban EU citizens from coming here. We just want to be able to control the numbers. Hardly unreasonable.

Nigel's been tied up with the Oldham by-election in Manchester following the death of Labour's Michael Meacher. It's a very safe seat – Meacher had been representing the area since 1970. That said, UKIP came second in the constituency at the general election, and Labour's tanking under Corbyn, so it's not impossible. Wiggy and I are planning to go to the count on 3 December. UKIP's intelligence is that postal votes are very low, and Labour rely on those. Best guess is Labour to win by 1,000, but with four days to go we could still pull it off. According to reports from the doorstep, lots of voters are saying they'll stick it to Corbyn. Should be an interesting night.

30 NOVEMBER

Back from Kenya. Nigel has been bringing me up to speed with the latest developments. The Turkish government is trying to exploit its ability to control the tide of refugees from Europe to extract new concessions from the EU. They want free movement for Turkish citizens in the EU and fresh accession talks.

Nigel reckons this is a game-changer and I agree. Don't those dimwits in Brussels realise Turkey borders Iraq and Syria, and therefore the Islamic State? The EU must be nuts if it's seriously considering caving in to this blackmail.

Met up with Lucy Thomas and Will Straw at Stronger In about

a potential City of London debate. I like them both, strangely enough. Lucy thinks Vote Leave is a bigger threat to Remain than us. Wiggy and I laughed. We'd rather be underestimated and over-deliver. They still don't get what they are up against.

We broached the concert idea (we're calling it BPop Live) and they love it. We've pencilled it in for 8 May at the NEC in Birmingham. The arena holds 17,000 people. It's going to be spectacular and will really break new ground, not just for us but for British politics in general. So pleased they're up for it!

DECEMBER 2015

2 DECEMBER

Met John Mills at Tice's office in the hope of thrashing something out. Sadly, we didn't get anywhere. I think we've reached the stage where it's wishful thinking to believe our two groups can work together. As I told them, leopards can't change their spots. That goes for both sides. John admitted they have a far bigger problem than us when it comes to hostile leaks and briefings because they have such a big board and lots of politicians involved. We can't work together, but we have at least agreed a ceasefire. I'm determined to honour it. Fired off an email to everyone on the team warning them to ignore Vote Leave and concentrate on our own campaign.

3 DECEMBER

In Oldham for the by-election count. Been getting regular updates from Nigel and he's unusually optimistic. Apparently he's getting a great reception on the doorstep.

Wiggy and I booked rooms at the Lowry in Manchester, where we arranged to meet Nigel for a quick bite to eat before heading to the count.

On the way up in the car, we were listening to Iain Dale's LBC show and who should come on but Wiggy's old chum Derek Hatton, a former member of the Trotskyist Militant group. He and Andy have known each other for years. He was tearing into UKIP on LBC, barely giving Dale a chance to get a word in edgeways. However, he let slip his admiration for Nigel. After Dale wrapped up the interview, I persuaded Wiggy to give Hatton a call to ask if he would help support the Brexit campaign. Wiggy put him on speakerphone.

'Fuck me, Wigmore, you Tory c***. How are you?' Hatton said, sounding surprised at this call out of the blue.

Wiggy informed 'Degsy' (as he likes to call him) that he was in a car with me. There was an awkward pause.

'That Banksy bastard? The guy that gave a million to UKIP? Seriously? What are you doing with him?' he replied.

Wiggy told him that we were on our way to the by-election, to which Degsy responded that we were wasting our time, as it would be a 'fucking stitch-up'.

'Tell Farage he's a c*** but is welcome to come for a beer with me,' he concluded.

It seemed a perfect opportunity to ask if he would support our campaign.

'If Bob Crow were alive, he'd be tearing into Cameron and the Remain campaign,' Wiggy coaxed. 'The EU is bad for workers' rights.'

'Damn right I will!' replied Degsy enthusiastically. 'But only if the Tories aren't involved.'

We've agreed to catch up next week.

When we arrived at the Lowry, Farage seemed a bit down. He was convinced the postal votes would be a stitch-up.

'What's the point?' he moaned. 'Our system is corrupt and we cannot do a damn thing about it. Let's have a drink.'

Ten G&T's later, we were all at the bar when Nigel turned to his press officer and said we'd better put out a comment before the count starts. As if on cue, we got a call from his campaign manager, who said a group of imams had just walked in with boxes full of postal votes. He claimed 98 per cent of those in the first box had gone to Labour.

It certainly sounded a bit fishy. In no mood for a sober assessment of the evidence, Nigel delivered a characteristically uncompromising verdict.

'Fucking hell, it's bent,' he declared, and told his aide to tweet accordingly.

Realising that the boss was a bit squiffy, the aide looked at Wiggy for clarification.

'Just do it,' Wiggy confirmed.

Seconds later, Wiggy got a text from Sebastian Payne.

'Farage says bent. Any comment?'

'Not you, Seb, just the election,' Wiggy replied rudely.

Within about five seconds, the Westminster village was in full cry about us being homophobic, which was not unreasonable.

In truth, we've developed a soft spot for Seb. He may be a Vote Leave groupie, and we like to complain about him, but he's rather sweet, and we use him to leak stories.

We apologised on Twitter for pressing send.

Nigel decided there was no point going to the count so we stayed up until 4 a.m. drinking the bar dry and complaining that everything was rigged. In the end, Labour held on to the seat with a majority of more than 10,000.

4 DECEMBER

Feeling flat. The Corbynistas are crowing about Oldham. I can't help thinking UKIP should have done better, but I don't believe it means anything for the referendum. Oldham has had a Labour MP for forty-five years. Let's not over-interpret the result.

7 DECEMBER

Bone and Pursglove have accepted an invitation to Lysander House the day after tomorrow.

I'm looking forward to showing them what we do. We have stacks of letters and cheques coming in; people hammering the phones to drum up supporters and donations; social media whizz-kids creating graphics; marketing teams working on branding. This is what the beginning of a mass movement looks like!

8 DECEMBER

The great fudge-off

The Great British Fudge-Off is taking shape. The samples have arrived and they taste surprisingly good.

People aren't as easily fooled as the PM thinks. It doesn't take a genius to work out that his diplomatic mission will generate nothing but spin.

We've produced a leaflet and a website dissecting his re-negotiation. There's even a recipe for Dave's euro-fudge – sickly, full of artificial sweeteners and no money back.

This is an eye-catching way to make a serious point. Donald Tusk, the President of the EU Council, has given his first official response to Cameron's gentle requests and it's painfully obvious that the PM won't get a fig. There won't be any treaty change – meaning nothing they agree will have the full force of law.

Of course there will be the usual bullshit 'tough talks' in Brussels, no doubt culminating in a symbolic all-nighter, at the end of which an 'exhausted' Cameron will stick out his chin and triumphantly declare that he's beaten the EU hands down and secured a great victory for Britain. Examine the small print, and you'll find diddly squat. The EU isn't interested in reform and doesn't care what Britain says. Which is why we have to get out.

12 DECEMBER

Bone and Pursglove enjoyed their visit. Got a joint email from them saying they were 'very impressed by the whole operation'.

'It was very pleasing to see such a hive of activity. Grassroots campaigning was actually happening, something we've never seen in SW1 ... You are absolutely right that the campaign needs to focus across the UK ...'

They're planning to set up an organisation called GO, standing for 'Get Out' or 'Grassroots Out', to bring together Leave activists all over the country. They reckon they can attract lots of MPs. I've told them it's something we will back.

13 DECEMBER

In the Alps with Katya and the kids. It's a school trip. We've done this for the past five years and we all love it. It's a no-frills holiday – the parents and kids all set off together by coach and take an EasyJet flight from Stansted. I find it quite relaxing, because the children all pair up and ski together, leaving the adults to have a good time.

Had another email from Jamie Huntman from UKIP. He thinks it's 'time for a new UKIP'. He's been reading an article in *The Economist* which says the party's limping along after the failure to break through in Oldham and is full of 'unrisen fruitcakes'. I couldn't agree more. If it wasn't for Farage, I doubt the party would get anyone's vote.

16 DECEMBER

Cameron goes to Brussels

Cameron's off to strut his stuff at the European Council, and I'm having no trouble containing my excitement. I honestly don't know why he's bothering. All the polls show people want to end open borders; for us to be able to make our own trade deals; and for our own Parliament to have the final say on our laws. It's basic stuff. Yet all he's doing is grandstanding about ending migrant benefits, which won't do a thing to reduce the number of people wanting to come here and which he won't get anyway. No doubt he'll come home with some kind of guarantee about stopping our path to 'ever closer union' but no actual change in our circumstances.

Ashcroft's published one of his big polls and it's encouraging. He surveyed 20,000 people, asking them where they stood on the referendum on a scale of 0 to 100. Zero meant they'd definitely vote to stay in, and 100 meant they'd definitely vote Out. Less than 40 per cent are leaning towards Remain. The majority put themselves somewhere between 51 and 100 – meaning they're inclined to vote Out. And 14 per cent don't have a clue. All to play for! Incidentally, three quarters think immigration is out of control. Three quarters? God knows what planet the other quarter lives on.

18 DECEMBER

As expected, Cameron came home empty-handed. Nigel got it right: 'He came, he saw, and he got hammered' – though presumably not on the house claret.

Carswell's been making a tit of himself on Radio Essex. Claims UKIP's performance in Oldham means it's time for a 'fresh face'. If he's looked in the mirror lately, he'll know he doesn't fit that description, but he's never been one to let reality get in the way of his towering ambition. Three people from Vote Leave have subsequently been on TV trying to undermine Nigel. So much for the ceasefire I agreed with Mills!

19 DECEMBER

The *Daily Express* has been doing Nigel no favours by giving Carswell's nonsense the oxygen of publicity. Wiggy got onto their political columnist Macer Hall to ask if that means they now prefer Vote Leave to us. They know we back Nigel to the hilt.

Hugh Whittow wrote back to say they're giving us all an equal shout and that their aim is to win the referendum. He says he's more than willing to carry any Out message. Quite right.

20 DECEMBER

Still annoyed about Vote Leave jumping on the bandwagon over Nigel's leadership. We should have been uniting to highlight the PM's woeful efforts in Brussels, not talking about UKIP. Have written to Mills saying how disappointed I am.

I told him I hope the Vote Leave board will reflect and ensure there's no repeat performance but signed off on a pleasant note, wishing him and his family a merry Christmas.

21 DECEMBER

BPop Lives!

Have updated Jim Mellon about plans for BPop Live. We're looking at Duran Duran, the Rudimentals from South Africa and Shirley Bassey. I can see Nigel coming out to the sound of 'Hey, big spender … good-looking, so refined'. I'm sorry to say the London office isn't any more enthusiastic than they were when we first floated it. Jack Montgomery thinks that it will be a total embarrassment, painting a nightmare image of the acts saying they're going to vote Remain and the millennials in the audience jeering Nigel and chucking plastic beer cups at him. Let's prove the doubters wrong.

Grassroots Out takes off

Bone and Pursglove have updated me on their plans to launch Grassroots Out. They've given it a lot of thought and I'm extremely impressed. They suggest twenty or so launches around the country at the end of January and want to get the campaign up and running in the New Year. Kate is on board. This could be the way to end the deadlock between the rival campaigns.

Various Tory MPs including Liam Fox and Bill Cash have been saying they're willing to share a platform with UKIP during the campaign. I should hope so too.

22 DECEMBER

That fat Tory foghorn Nicholas Soames has come out and said his grandfather Winston Churchill would have been appalled by the campaign to leave the EU. He's been telling people his ancestor was 'a profound believer in the values of European co-operation'.

What tosh. Soames is a pompous old bore whose blind Europhilia would make Juncker blush. The only thing he and his fine ancestor have in common is their waistline.

23 DECEMBER

My latest missive to John Mills riled him. He's usually very mild-mannered. He's sent me a long email moaning about this and that. He thinks a merger will be 'very difficult in the current circumstances'. Tell me something I don't know!

Whatever. As Frank Sinatra said: 'The best form of revenge is massive success.'

Have asked a couple of economists including Ruth Lea if they can do an analysis of Cameron's plans to restrict migrants' benefits for four years. At the same time, it's government policy to hike up the minimum wage. So will the two added together push immigration up or reduce it? They say it's complicated and needs a welfare expert to look at it. No quick and easy answers, sadly.

24 DECEMBER

Apparently I've sent all the staff luxury hampers for Christmas. People kept coming up to me in the office to thank me. I smiled munificently and made a note to thank Liz.

I did know we'd sent Fortnum's hampers to our favourite journos, including Heffer, Pierce, Christopher Hope from the *Telegraph*, Caroline Wheeler on the *Sunday Express* and Sam Coates at *The Times*. Wiggy had obviously been at the cherry brandy early, as he suggested we should send one to Sebastian Payne. I vetoed that one.

Heffer's thank-you note said he'd found his hamper when he got in from 'an arduous day killing pheasants'.

'We shall now get even fatter at Christmas than we were going to already,' he said, promising to drink to the cause tomorrow – as will we all.

Am on the sherry, watching *To the Manor Born*.

25 DECEMBER

Christmas at Old Down. I always like to do the cooking, and made a fantastic lunch for the whole family, after which we opened presents by the tree. I gave all the kids hoverboards. I lasted three seconds before I hit the Labrador and went flying into the air, twisting my ankle. Alcohol may have been involved.

27 DECEMBER

Some Christmas cheer from Vote Leave. Elliott's briefed the *Mail on Sunday* that we have put 'operatives' on his tail. He leaked that email I sent him months ago in which I told him we have a surveillance company.

The *Daily Mail* rang wanting to follow it up tomorrow so I cranked things up a bit by telling them I'd only written to Elliott after discovering my own communications were being tampered with. 'At the time, I assumed the In camp were responsible. I never considered that the source of surveillance was from our own side.'

The *MoS* also had some daft tale about Bernard Jenkin being a nudist. Apparently George Osborne's crony Daniel Finkelstein (a journo on *The Times*) has been putting the story about. Jenkin gave the story legs by being suitably outraged. A 'friend' was quoted describing it as 'an attempt to sway voters undecided about Europe that one of the leading anti-EU gang is a bit odd and loves walking around without any clothes on'. He'd better not get his tackle out round here.

30 DECEMBER

Angela Merkel's New Year message is being released with Arabic subtitles at the behest of her 'integration czar', who also suggests it be translated into Pashtun, Farsi and Tigrinya (a new one on me).

No mention of failing security or the uncontrolled numbers of immigrants now flooding into Germany thanks to her giant 'welcome' sign.

If she wants to turn these migrants into good Germans, as opposed to a million foreigners who've just rocked up, pitched their tents and are now waiting for handouts, she should be hammering home the message that they need to learn the language. What's more, the subtitling is being done by ZDF, the German state broadcaster. How long before the BBC give the Queen's Christmas message the same treatment? Honestly, words fail. Wiggy needs to bash out a suitably punchy, Trump-like statement.

Our own social media campaign is knocking the others out of the park. We have 322,890 supporters. Vote Leave is on 28,000! We are not far behind Labour's 417,680 and at this rate should overtake them in mid-February. No thanks to the *Express*. Despite Whittow's sweet words, Wiggy says they've ignored our last five press releases. I detect the hand of their former political editor Patrick O'Flynn, who left the paper to become a UKIP MEP. He's in Carswell's gang, and is probably telling Whittow to big up Vote Leave. I'll deal with this via advertising. Hopefully money will talk.

31 DECEMBER

New Year message

Gerry Gunster sent New Year's greetings and said he was toasting 2016.

I told him I'm all fired up and ready to go. In fact, I have punted out my own New Year message. If I get any grander, I'll be running for Pope. I think 2016 is going to be momentous for our country. Britain will vote Out – and the repercussions will be as big as the fall of the Berlin Wall. It will take a lot less to knock down the crumbling edifice in Brussels. A stiff breeze should do the trick. We're preparing something a lot more powerful than that.

PART 3:
JANUARY—MARCH 2016

JANUARY 2016

2 JANUARY

Tice on the skids

Wiggy and I are still nursing hangovers, but Tice is full of New Year vim and vigour and is off to Switzerland for what he called 'some winter sport'.

I like a spot of skiing myself, but a couple of gentle runs down some blues before a slap-up lunch at a nice mountain restaurant is quite enough for me. Tice prefers gruelling days of high altitude thrills, jumping out of helicopters on remote peaks and skiing back to civilisation off-piste. I doubt he even allows himself a glühwein at the bottom.

Being clubbish and proper, he's also a member of the Cresta Run Club in St Moritz, a sort of sponsored head-first suicidal toboggan race down three quarters of a mile of frozen ditch. In theory anyone can do it, but in reality it's the preserve of a very smart London set.

Apparently you lie on your stomach on a steel sledge and plunge head-first down a ribbon of polished ice with your nose three inches from the surface, trying to avoid getting what aficionados call 'the Cresta kiss' – in other words, shredding off your face. Every year, the least skilled participants end up in a coma, breaking limbs, or worse.

There's no way I'd be hurtling down a mountain on my front at 60mph, even if my belly does provide a bit of cushioning, but Wiggy, who's always fancied himself as a bit of an action man, got very excited.

'Go on, Richard, you handsome devil. Fuck all the referendum crap. You deserve a break. Remember to send us some pics.'

I hope he makes it to the bottom in one piece. It'd be a crying shame if those chiselled features were disfigured.

$$\approx$$

John Nott, Maggie's old Defence Secretary, has been in touch to wish me luck and say how impressed he is with our campaign. He's a vice-president of Conservatives for Britain and very tied in with Vote Leave. Nott said how important it is that we all work together. Told him I'd tried.

3 JANUARY

A vision in Lycra

Maybe we shouldn't have asked Tice to send us pics. This morning he emailed a very gay-looking selfie. He's grinning inanely in a skin-tight blue Lycra onesie, standing to attention with his tea tray in the background. I don't know if it was taken before or after the death-defying feat, but he appears remarkably unscathed and very pleased with himself.

It's captioned 'Your co-chair doing the Cresta Run'. I told Andy to tweet it out to distract attention from anything more serious. Wiggy and I have only ever seen him in a suit and almost died laughing.

('Jesus!!!!!! Put me right off my cornflakes,' was Wiggy's response.)

He duly posted it for the world to see. Tice was straight on the phone.

'How many people have seen it? I'm mortified!' he protested.

What did he expect us to do – keep it to ourselves?

≈

Richard Murphy, our ground campaign guy, who used to work for Vote Leave, has asked me to suggest a lawyer to sue them over unpaid fees.

That would give me such pleasure, but I suppose I'd better give John Mills the chance to sort it out first – I'm trying to be nice to him after all!

Who'd want to kill Nigel Farage?

The *Mail on Sunday*'s splashed on an assassination attempt on Farage.

Wiggy and I have known about it for ages but he wanted to keep it quiet. It was all very fishy. He'd been driving his Volvo back from Brussels back in October 2014 when all of a sudden one of the wheels fell off the car on the motorway near Dunkirk. It turned out all four wheels had loose nuts. The French police told him they'd never seen anything like it and suspected they'd been unscrewed deliberately. If he'd been going any faster, he might have been a goner. As it was, he had to jump a crash barrier to avoid an oncoming lorry.

We knew he'd be accused of paranoia if word got out, so it was kept very tight. Only a handful of Kippers knew, including Carswell and Suzanne Evans. Wonder how it leaked?

Of course the *MoS* put the rocket boosters under it, even though Nigel himself is quite cautious about jumping to conclusions. Either way, I still can't believe he isn't given taxpayer-funded security.

By this afternoon, the story was trending online and everyone was speculating about who'd tried to kill him. 'Douglas Carswell???? Isn't he fairly cross at the moment #justsayin' was Wiggy's mischievous tweet. Carswell went ballistic. We are blissfully ignorant of the full extent of his rage because he's just blocked us on Twitter, but the gist of it was that it was disgusting, despicable, and should be reported to the police. For once, the Twittersphere was on our side, and told him to pipe down.

Wiggy annoyed him even more by saying sorry in a tone that clearly indicated he wasn't sorry at all. 'Just a quip Dougie, sorry…'

Talk about not being able to take a joke.

4 JANUARY

Carswell's mugshot is all over the front of *The Sun* and they've made him look a complete pillock. The headline reads 'Carswell forced to deny he plotted to kill Nigel Farage' and they've used a picture of him looking like a rabid dog. All the papers have followed up the story, with varying degrees of scepticism over whether it was a real assassination attempt.

Pierce rang Wiggy last night looking for a quote, and Wiggy helpfully suggested he write something about 'Nigel Garage and the Carswheels saga'. Apparently Carswell was practically foaming at the mouth when he saw it in the paper. We thought it was all very funny, but Nigel was less impressed. Six missed calls, so we took cover. He wouldn't stop ringing, so eventually we tossed a coin to decide whose turn it was to take the bollocking and call him back.

Wiggy lost.

'There's no upside. He's made himself out to look like a victim. We're not in a good place with this,' Nigel fumed.

Oh well, he'll soon calm down. We've got a nice surprise for him when he comes to visit in a couple of days.

Scandinavia shuts the doors

This is what happens when head-in-the-clouds liberalism finally smacks up against reality.

For the first time since the 1950s, Sweden has told anyone coming in from Denmark that they will have to show ID at the border. The Swedish government says it can't cope and believes there's a 'serious threat to public order and national security'. That's what happens when you lose all reason and open your doors to everyone. They've had 80,000 asylum seekers since September in a country of less than 10 million.

I think this is a turning point. Euro elites can no longer shut their eyes to the crisis of mass migration.

A few hours after the announcement, Denmark said it would do the same on its border with Germany. Of course, none of this does anything to address the underlying problem – the Brussels dogma of free movement of people. As soon as migrants have an EU passport, they're free to live in any member country they want. We need to get out of this racket.

6 JANUARY

Nothing like a good swear-fest

Nigel came to see us in Bristol today. We knew he was still in a grump about the Carswell thing, so we thought 'fuck it', and blew up an A1-size poster of *The Sun*'s front cover. As he walked into the office, there was Carswell's scrunched-up mug boggling out at him.

He tried desperately not to laugh but he just couldn't keep a straight face.

'You're a bunch of c***s,' he told us. 'The pair of you, bunch of c***s, it's not funny. This is serious.'

'Of course it's serious, but come on – that Carswell thing was a joke.'

'Yeah, I know, I know.'

We swore ourselves stupid and got it out of our system, which we do far too much, I admit.

≈

I'm sick of all the doom-mongering from the Remain camp. Stuart Rose has spent the weekend spouting nonsense about threats to British jobs and trade, relying on the Brussels-funded CBI as his main source of information. That is, the same sorry shower who predicted Apocalypse Now if we didn't join the euro. Wrong then, wrong now. The truth is, that lot think we're too small, too poor and too stupid to make our own way in the world. The only thing that makes me feel better about all the negativity is the conviction that it won't work.

7 JANUARY

A new hire – through gritted teeth

We're giving Pete North's old man Richard a job. Could be a big mistake. The pair of them hate UKIP, and are always slagging us off. However, I'm still keen on North Sr's concept of 'Flexcit'.

Tice thinks I'm mad. He sent me an uncharacteristically fruity message.

'Jesus, toxic, he can be very dangerous – beware.'

Admittedly, it was a slight moment of weakness on my part. The guy has a reputation for being difficult. He and his son have been emailing me abuse for weeks. At one point they claimed the campaign was being run by a 'chimpanzee on drugs' (they meant me, not Wiggy/Tice.) They also accused Nigel of making a 'total prat' of himself and talking 'total, unmitigated bollocks'.

North Sr actually shared an office with Nigel for five years, working as a researcher, but they fell out, partly because North thought freedom of movement and immigration were non-issues. Oh well, I've got a thick skin.

It's a shame our competition for the best essay on what shape Brexit should take never really took off. We didn't get the quality of entries we'd hoped for. I suppose it goes to show the scale of the challenge for the government if Britain does vote Out. Nobody's pretending it's going to be a walk in the park.

Hold tight.

8 JANUARY

A funny turn

Important Brexit debate today at the Foreign Press Association, with me as a key speaker. I was up against BSE director Will Straw, who I quite like, but who is not the most daunting opponent, so I had a few sound bites pre-cooked and wasn't too bothered.

Or rather, I wasn't too bothered until I woke up this morning feeling as if I'd been flattened by a truck. I was hoping breakfast at Claridge's with Wiggy would clear my head, but I just wasn't feeling myself. The truth is I was a bit nervous. TV's one thing, with a couple of cameras and a pretty make-up girl, but having a horde of hacks eyeballing me like I'm addressing school assembly makes me twitchy.

Wiggy could see I was out of sorts. One of our security guys handed me some hokum-pokum herbal medicine he'd picked up on his travels. 'Try this!' he suggested. 'Works a treat!' I'm not usually one for weird stimulants, especially not in granular form, but given the challenge ahead, I thought it was worth a try.

'What am I supposed to do with it?' I asked.

Wiggy shrugged and suggested I just eat it, so I ambled off to the gents to wash it down with a glass of water. I was a bit unsure whether this was wise, but after seeing my tired reflection in the mirror, I decided I didn't have much to lose. I gulped it down, not much enjoying the taste, and headed back to the reassuringly serene surroundings of the dining room.

'I don't feel anything,' I told Andy. 'What was that stuff?'

He assured me it was nothing untoward but seemed a bit concerned.

'How much did you take?' he asked.

'All of it,' I replied matter-of-factly. 'Is there a problem?'

'Christ, Arron! I don't think you were meant to take the whole lot!' He quickly (and unconvincingly, I must say) composed himself. 'Well, hopefully it will work. You should be full of beans.'

I was a bit concerned by his reaction and beginning to feel queasy, but the clock was ticking so we paid the bill for breakfast and set off for the debate. As we were heading out of the hotel, suddenly, to my horror, I realised I was going to be sick. There was no time to get back to the gents so I rushed towards the nearest hedge, where I promptly threw up. I don't think anyone noticed, but embarrassed doesn't cover it.

By now Andy was looking really worried.

'What the hell was that stuff?' I hissed, quite angry now and not a little alarmed. He didn't say anything, but I could see he was uneasy. What was done was done, however, so we continued on our way.

By the time we arrived at the venue I was feeling truly terrible. The environment could not have been worse for someone feeling sick. The room was nauseatingly stuffy and the bright lights were making me sweat. As I surveyed the expectant-looking press pack, my head was spinning.

With a metaphorical drum roll, the organisers announced the key-note speakers and I wobbled up to the stage. Steeling myself, I began the opening statement I had prepared. I was only a few sentences in when I began feeling so weak at the knees I thought I might collapse.

Wrapping things up rather quicker than the hacks expected, I mumbled my apologies – 'Sorry, ladies and gentlemen, I'm not feeling well' – and staggered away from the lectern to a seat at the back of the stage.

'Can someone get him a cup of tea?' asked Wiggy brightly. 'He's recovering from a stomach bug.'

A few minutes later, warm tea inside me, I began feeling better. Top of the dial, in fact. Suddenly I was overwhelmed by a sense of supreme confidence and wellbeing. It's all going to be all right, I thought. I look good. I sound good. Everyone wants to hear what I have to say.

Straw's performance was polished, slick even – but very far from the 'positive and patriotic vision' we've long been promised by those who wish to sell off our sovereignty for another generation. It was just a rehash of the old fear-mongering, half-truths and scare stories pro-EU types have been pitching for years – three million jobs lost, half our jobs disappearing, and all the rest.

Beaming, I bounded back up to the lectern just in time for the Q&A and gave what I thought was one of the best performances of my life.

Poor Will wasn't up to much when he wasn't giving a pre-prepared speech, with a fine old gentleman from the Norwegian press taking him to task over the way he was misrepresenting life beyond the gilded cage of EU membership. Will mumbled lamely about (literally) the price of cheese in Norway, receiving a pitying smile from the veteran journo.

'Yes, Mr Straw, but, being outside the EU, we Norwegians can afford it.'

I held up under pressure rather better. Under fire from the German contingent, I pointed out how much damage the German-dominated euro was doing to countries along the Mediterranean.

'But surely you are not a good European with this Brexit vote, Mr Banks?'

'No, I'm not a good European, I'm British,' I came back with a wink. Applause.

Gazing benevolently at my interrogators, I wondered if I might not be smiling a little too radiantly. (What on Earth was the active ingredient in Wiggy's dubious elixir?!)

They all applauded. I gazed at them benevolently. I loved them.

Will Straw looked defeated; I reigned supreme. Baron Banks of Brexit.

But that's the last time I trust Wiggy's mystery medicine chest.

My general malaise was not improved by the reaction to our belated press release about recruiting Richard North. I've had a barrage of emails, including one from someone called Jeremy Wraith from the Sutton branch of UKIP, who says North is bombastic and always disparaging about the party. Richard put out something saying he'd be working with us as a consultant for the duration of the campaign 'unless, of course, we fall out and slaughter each other'. Given our many run-ins so far, it's entirely possible.

Anyway, North is not exactly a key figure. It is great for the campaign that the top three jobs in the office are now all-female – Liz Bilney, the CEO, plus Alison Marshall, finance director, and Caroline Drewett, who is in charge of getting businesses on board.

11 JANUARY

Brex and the City

We put out a heavyweight briefing today on how Brexit will benefit the City. About time we redressed the balance a bit – every day the *FT* runs some nonsense about how our financial services industry will evaporate if we vote Out. The City has everything to gain from Brexit and nothing to fear. We're the number one global financial capital, ahead of New York and Hong Kong. The top-ranked Eurozone location, Frankfurt, is just fourteenth in the table, while the top three European centres are all outside the Eurozone: London, Zurich and Geneva. Paris is thirty-seventh.

We account for less than 1 per cent of the global population, but we have the world's fourth largest banking industry, third largest insurance sector and second biggest fund management and legal services sectors. Are the Remainers seriously saying we can't manage without Brussels?

What with the never-ending regulation needed to prop up the Eurozone, the financial transaction tax they want and the constant changes to rules, the EU actually poses a huge risk to the City. Far from trashing everything, Brexit would breathe new life into the UK's financial services. Onward!

Raheem Kassam has written a piece for the right-wing website Breitbart about a poll showing that Nigel would be more popular as the leader of the Leave campaign and is even more popular with the ladies than Boris. He'll be delighted.

12 JANUARY

Toyota has said it will stay in the UK whether or not we're in the EU. Akio Toyoda, the founder's grandson, said he hopes that in 2090, when they dig up the time capsule they buried at their Derbyshire plant, they'll be able to say they are a truly British company. Good on him. Finally, a multinational telling the truth. The constant scare stories from BSE just don't stack up. VW has already said it thinks the UK is a 'good place for investment' and when the CEO of Rolls-Royce was asked if they'd pull out of the UK if we vote Leave, his response was, 'Are you kidding me?' Executives from General Motors and Nissan have also committed to staying, and Jaguar Land Rover is investing £120 million in a new factory. Time to knock this nonsense on the head.

13 JANUARY

I've had a delegation of Kippers staying at Old Down. It almost ended in tragedy when the MEP Margot Parker fell into the swimming pool. She can't swim and we had quite a business holding her out.

Margot's a splendid creature in her seventies who had a very successful career in the fashion industry before she became a Kipper. She used to be chief buyer for a South American lingerie company, and still loves to dress for the occasion.

We had all gathered for a pre-dinner drink near the pool and, as she sailed towards us in full regalia, luxurious fabrics billowing in her wake, she tripped. To make matters worse, the pool had a plastic cover over it. There was a tremendous crash, and we all turned round to a thrashing lump under the PVC.

Several people rushed to the rescue and, after much flailing around, managed to fish her out. It was quite a drama, and we were all shaken, particularly Nigel, who is very fond of her.

Other than the near-drowning, the evening went according to plan. We gave the MEPs a presentation on what we're doing at Leave.EU, and tomorrow they're coming to see round Lysander House. They're having a similar tour of Vote Leave's premises before deciding who they want to back. I'm quietly confident that when they see what we're doing, they won't be in any doubt.

≈

Have had another go at John Mills as all the duplication and competition between the two campaigns is undermining the cause. Told John about a call I got from a high-profile donor last night who said that if Dominic Cummings were removed, that would open the way. I said that Matthew does have talents, particularly political (which I don't regard as a compliment, by the way).

14 JANUARY

The MEP visit seems to have been a great success.

Paul Nuttall's just emailed thanking me for dinner and saying they were super-impressed with our operation. They have their doubts about Richard North, though, who seems to have fallen out with anyone who's anyone in the Eurosceptic movement.

I'm exhausted by the effort of hosting them all and am slumped in an airport lounge – dry January starts now. Paul said he couldn't get his head off the couch and is 'back on' dry January. That is the kind of self-discipline I can identify with.

Ashcroft's old friend William Hague has been on telly claiming Brexit could lead to the break-up of the UK. To think he used to masquerade as a Eurosceptic! The economic case for Scotland breaking away is even weaker than when it lost the

SNP their last independence referendum. More rubbish from Project Fear.

16 JANUARY

I am up on the High Veld in South Africa, but not letting that distract me from my push to unite the two campaigns. Another donor told me that Dominic is the big obstacle ('pure acid'), though he thinks Matthew could stay.

Our social media accounts should have more detail of the local activities that our people on the ground are organising. Have told Andy to sort this ASAP. VL are doing this better than us at the moment, but Wiggy says a lot of it is what he calls 'astroturfing': look carefully at the pictures and you'll see they're all the same people.

17 JANUARY

Two referendums

Some idiots are still going on about having two referendums. I can't understand why this is still getting traction. Proponents think it would reassure worried voters that they will get the chance to approve our exit deal, but I think it's mad. The choice here is simple: Remain or Leave. It's not an opportunity to extract better terms. It's a once-in-a-lifetime chance to get out. If people think voting Out may not actually mean we leave, it could be fatal to the cause. Let's dispense with these silly wheezes.

Am writing to Elliott to appeal to him to help shut this down. It's inconceivable the Electoral Commission could give designation to a campaign group that looks like it's not serious about leaving. Will tell him I still think we should merge – as long as he gets rid of Cummings.

≈

Grassroots Out is taking shape and was making progress with VL until a story in today's *Times* suggesting the whole thing might be a ruse to leak Tory data to UKIP. I can't believe these people. Here we have a genuine attempt to bring everyone together via a neutral third party (run by two Tories!) and they turn it into some kind of conspiracy. Needless to say the story quotes 'Vote Leave sources'. I've also been shown an email from Matthew suggesting our campaign is racist and homophobic. He went on to say that when Westminster understood this, it would preclude us from going for designation.

I take massive exception to this, particularly the racist jibe. I fund multiple charities in South Africa, focusing on women and child poverty, and numerous educational bursaries. I am actually hurt by these slurs.

I may need to get lawyers on to it, but I'll wait to see how it plays out. Some MPs are very angry about the allegation. I'm sure John Mills would not condone these smears. Apparently he's having a very rough time with Elliott and co.

18 JANUARY

Am enjoying my break but still seething at the lies about GO. These politicos are awful people. My understanding was that GO approached VL in the same way as they approached me, suggesting they could form an umbrella group.

Surprise surprise, they were rebuffed, while I offered to help with no pre-conditions. I guess Elliott and co. needed to come up with an excuse for rejecting a perfectly constructive solution to the deadlock, so they concocted some cobblers about it posing a risk to Tory data. I reckon they're feeling the heat. The last thing they want is MPs joining GO rather than their outfit.

We released my letter to Elliott about the double referendum thing. I called Cummings a 'liability and a danger' and the only thing standing in the way of a merger. I can't understand his refusal to cut his ties with the man. He's actually a nutcase, though I didn't put this in the letter.

I am far from convinced that all the key players at Vote Leave genuinely want to leave the EU. Everything they do suggests what they really want is reform. I don't know about Cummings, but I strongly suspect Elliott's primary objective is to run an 'impressive' campaign that establishes him as a bigger figure at Westminster.

Nonetheless, almost all the donors still think a merger makes sense, and I'm not giving up yet. Had a useful discussion with Malcolm Pearson about next steps. He's written to Mills sympathising with the terrible time he is having at VL.

'You don't deserve it,' he told John, which is true.

He put our offer on the table – Mills as chairman and Cummings chucked overboard, with me stepping down in return. I know my late-night missives to Elliott wind him up and that he feels he can't work with me, so I'm willing to remove myself. If John left, the Labour window-dressing would be removed and there is no way Elliott's crew would get designation as it would be clear they are just a load of Tories.

Had a great lunch with Liam Fox, even though we spent the whole time talking economics. We got so absorbed in talking about the markets that I somehow forgot to ask him if he'd speak at a big event we're planning at Westminster on 19 February. We've got a number of gigs planned in the next few weeks and I can't believe the scale of demand. It's only taken three days to sell all the tickets for a rally we're planning to hold in Kettering with Nigel, Kate Hoey and Tory MPs. Not to mention BPop! I reckon it will be the biggest political rally since the war.

There's a lot of speculation that the referendum could be as soon as June, and the tension among Eurosceptic MPs and donors has escalated dramatically in the past week. Relations between the various warring factions have never been more strained. To borrow one of Gerry's favourite phrases, it's getting hot in the kitchen.

'I can see the flames from DC!' he says.

20 JANUARY

Preaching from the Pope

The latest big-shot foreigner debasing his office to lecture the British on how to govern their country is none other than the Pope. His Foreign Minister has said the Catholic Church would see our departure from the EU as 'not something that would make a stronger Europe. Better in than out.' I thought Henry VIII had seen off meddling Popes 500 years ago, but there you are.

The background music for this papal preaching is all the talk during the migrant crisis about how nobody has been doing enough and how the Holy See is 'not in favour of walls'. We lampooned this ludicrous rhetoric by posting pictures of the gargantuan stone ramparts that surround the pontiff's own palace with the caption 'Meanwhile, at the Vatican'.

Guardianistas love the papal intervention and are trying to use it to besmirch people with legitimate concerns about uncontrolled immigration. Time to point out just how immoral it is to recklessly encourage sea crossings that kill people in their thousands and pour dollars into smugglers' pockets.

Anyway, if the EU is so great, why isn't the Pope filling in his application form? Could it be because the Vatican's finances are so dodgy they aren't too keen on anyone having a look?

I instructed the social media team to get stuck in and make it really punchy.

I was working myself into a state of righteous indignation about all this when it suddenly occurred to me that Wiggy had gone curiously quiet.

'I don't think we should be going after the Pope,' he said falteringly.

'Why on earth not?' I replied.

I was taken aback by his reticence. This is the guy who was kicked out of school for flogging communion wine when he was an altar boy, after all. Indeed, he's so profane that I've heard it suggested the title of his memoirs should be *Fuck a Priest*, his favourite phrase when things are going awry.

'Because I'm a Papal Knight,' he admitted sheepishly.

Along with a string of other obscure titles that he has inexplicably picked up along the way ('Queen's Messenger', 'Senior Justice of the Peace' and 'Trade Representative of the Government of Belize'), it turns out that he's a member of something called the Archconfraternity Guild of St Stephen. Apparently it's especially for altar servers, though you'd have thought selling the wine might have proved a disqualification.

I gave him the ribbing he deserved, to which he looked quite wounded.

'Have a look on my desk, mate, there's a book on my Order there. It's actually quite serious.'

When it comes to Wiggy, wonders never cease.

Anyway, Pope Francis is in good company. Goldman Sachs, the bank whose boss has said it's doing God's work on earth, is throwing money at BSE. A 'substantial six-figure sum', according to the reports. Golden Sacks quite likes the status quo? Quelle surprise.

If they'd offered us money, I'd have told them where to shove it.

Tory dirty tricks against Nigel Farage

Finally, the media's waking up to the scandal over Thanet South in last year's general election.

We've always known it was a stitch-up and that the Tories were willing to go to any lengths to prevent Nigel winning the seat. Every man, woman and dog they could muster piled in to swing the vote against him. Now it's all beginning to come out.

We'll never know how much Operation Stop Farage cost, because most of those who helped will never have to declare what they spent, but Channel 4 reporter Michael Crick has made a start. He's revealed they spent twice as much as allowed under election law. He's found hotel bills that prove they parked senior campaigners there for the whole election period. They tried to pass it off as a national expense on the grounds that these people were doing work in other marginal constituencies too.

It's a paper-thin excuse and won't hold up – Thanet is stuck right out in a corner of the country and nobody would stay there unless it was where they planned to work.

This is the tip of the iceberg. There are many more skeletons rattling in that cupboard.

21 JANUARY

Am in Kimberley, South Africa, checking on progress at the mines. Had some fun sifting through diamonds and found a lovely eight-carat stone, which made my day. Most stones are two or three carats and all sorts of odd shapes, but a stone this size usually means there's a vein of other good ones nearby. I've got a bad case of what the South Africans call diamond fever – it's like hunting for treasure and really finding it!

I'm getting slightly better vibes from John Mills. He's become a pivotal figure in the rift between us and Vote Leave. They desperately need him to burnish their 'cross-party credentials', but he seems to feel very conflicted. He says he wants a meeting to try to put relations 'on to a more even keel' following the successful launch of Labour Leave. It's a referendum grouplet designed to bring together what's left of the Old Labour Eurosceptics once led by Tony Benn and encourage Labour-minded voters to give Brexit a fair hearing.

It's worth a shot.

I've been having an entertaining email exchange with a bloke from France who contacted me saying how much he's looking forward to Britain leaving the EU because we're such crap European partners. He believes with us moaning Brits out of the way, they can hit the gas on their plans for a federal European superstate.

I reassured him that we'll still be buying their cheese, champagne, truffles and handbags. He added Airbus planes, cars etc. to the mix and said the Scots will use this as a great opportunity to have another referendum to leave the UK. I pointed out that the Scots aren't going anywhere, as all the nationalists' grand plans hinged on oil at $100 a barrel. It's currently down below $30.

Besides, a Leave vote would transfer all sorts of new powers to Edinburgh from Brussels, particularly over fishing, which the EU has hit particularly hard in Scotland. The SNP asking voters to leave Britain in order to give powers away to Brussels would be a ridiculous spectacle – 'an anti-independence referendum', as Nigel puts it.

Meanwhile, the French can enjoy the migrant crisis, Eurozone implosion and Brussels central planning. And we'll keep the Airbus wings, which we make here.

22 JANUARY

Piss-up with the FT

I invited Jim Pickard from the *FT* and his colleague Kiran Stacey (a notorious Kipper baiter) for a spot of lunch at Old Down Manor or, as Crick likes to calls it, Downton Abbey. (Unlike the Earl of Grantham, I earned my money.)

Pickard's editor, Lionel Barber, is a shameless Europhile, so our relations with the paper have always been a bit tricky. Whenever Pickard's name comes up in conversation, Wiggy produces some snarky one-liner. 'So good he was named after two *Star Trek* captains,' he sniffed, when I told him they were coming for lunch.

Needless to say, Pickard and Stacey weren't going to let any of that get in the way of a jolly day out of the office, and accepted my invitation without hesitation.

I'd have been quite happy to send my driver to pick them up from the station, but the pair of them (and their photographer) pitched up in a taxi, which they'd taken all the way from London. Obviously newspaper industry cutbacks haven't affected expense accounts on the *FT*.

The snapper obviously wanted shots of me looking like a rich knob, so I posed obligingly with the manor in the background, next to a huge bronze stag I picked up a few years ago at the Chelsea Flower Show.

I showed them around a bit and then took them into the dining room.

'Do you mind if we record this?' Jim asked as we all sat down.

'Not if you don't mind if we do,' Andy replied cheerfully.

So we all sat round with the two tape recorders blinking ostentatiously on the table.

I knew perfectly well Jim and Kiran had come with a view to stitching us up, but I didn't mind playing along with their game.

It was all rather formal over the starters, but the conversation became more lively the more they drank. We began with a couple of bottles of red, after which I produced the Jack Daniels, as well as a spot of champagne. Before too long, they were pissed, which was precisely the plan.

Of course Andy couldn't resist regaling them with his party piece about once being mistaken for a £1,000-a-night gigolo, a story he's been dining out on for at least two decades. I smiled indulgently and just gave them more drink.

After a while they were so squiffy they became very indiscreet.

Around 6 p.m., we poured them into their taxi and they headed back for London – and very sore heads the next day.

With the ammunition I've got on my little tape recorder, I doubt they'll be printing anything bad about me any time soon.

23 JANUARY

Grassroots Out – the big launch in Kettering

Wiggy and I headed up to Kettering for the big launch of Grassroots Out.

Our troops had donned lurid green T-shirts emblazoned with the GO logo, and Wiggy wanted me to wear a tie in the same horrible colours. I told him we might be mistaken for a pair of gameshow hosts from Butlin's and that there's only so far I'm prepared to go.

The launch was deliberately grassroots not glitz, but it was a sell-out and it was a pin to pop the Westminster bubble. We chose Kettering in Northamptonshire. It's on the railway line that goes from gleaming St Pancras, where EU groupies board trains to Brussels, to Sheffield, where the locals are on a permanent diet of Nick Clegg and wages crunched by immigration.

The venue was a bleak sports hall built of yellow 1990s bricks. The main nearby attraction was a Lidl supermarket. The hall's polished wooden floorboards, marked out for a volleyball court, reminded me of panting around at school during PE.

Somehow we pulled off the complicated choreography required to get an array of political parties on the platform together. The speakers were Nigel and Kate Hoey, plus the inevitable Bone and Pursglove. (From now on I'm calling them Boneglove, because I don't want to waste precious seconds of my life writing out their names.)

We also unveiled Liam Fox, the former Defence Secretary, who is proving surprisingly willing to extract himself from his usual stamping ground (five-star hotels near the Palace of Westminster) and get down with the people in less salubrious parts. He was obviously quite nervous before the show as the crowd grew and he kept pacing up and down. Sammy Wilson from the Democratic Unionist Party in Northern Ireland completed a real cross-party line-up.

The size of the crowd was the first surprise for our politician friends. Clearly taking their cue from Nigel, Boneglove had been moaning continuously at us, saying the event would never come together because we were amateurs and had no idea how to organise anything. They had done precisely fuck all to contribute except whinge, and obviously their plan was to claim the credit for it all if it was a success and blame us if it wasn't.

The BBC reckoned we pulled in 2,500 people. I wasn't counting, but Wiggy thought there were a thousand in the hall itself and another thousand or so snaking back to the train station.

It had been our call centre operation at its best, and all rustled together in three or four days. We rang round 30,000 homes in Kettering and the two neighbouring constituencies to drum up interest. In fact, there were so many people that Wiggy got a bollocking from the police for failing to give them any notice. They complained that they were having to deal with three-mile tailbacks on the roads.

The second surprise for the politicians was how well they got on. Kate had been particularly nervous at sharing a platform with Nigel, but when she and Brendan Chilton (general secretary of Labour Leave) met him for the first time tonight, they quickly realised he's not the monstrous racist they'd been led to expect. Nigel worked his charm and soon they were all chatting like old friends.

In any case, there was a far easier target for hostilities, in the shape of Pursglove, a character so irritating that Wiggy recently felt compelled to issue a no-thumping-Pursglove edict to staff.

The boy's tantrums over his hair and make-up before the rally were priceless and his diva behaviour would shame the Kardashians. He demanded that any cosmetic applied to his face be a precise colour match for his chubby pink cheeks and stipulated that it should have a specific moisture content.

Our 25-year-old events organiser Victoria Hughes became increasingly exasperated as she was forced to make a succession of journeys to Boots to find products that met his exacting requirements.

'What the fuck does that even mean?' she hissed to Wiggy, as she was dispatched for the umpteenth time to find creams with more impressive hydrating properties. Her unkind conclusion was that he was a 'total t*** who was obviously born old'.

As always, Nigel was the stand-out performer and went down brilliantly with the predominantly Tory crowd. Backstage, there was some consternation at the rousing applause, especially when he got a standing ovation.

Kate seemed to find his grandstanding a little distasteful and asked me to get him to tone it down. 'Oh, he's such a show-off,' she said. 'Can't you stop him, Arron? He mustn't just wander round the stage like that.'

In the end, though, she had to give him his due.

As the event drew to a close, Nigel became quite emotional. He has been through so much in the last year and occasionally the mask slips.

Elated by the warmth of the reception he was getting, he mingled with the crowd, shaking hands and posing for pictures, surrounded by supporters of all political hues.

Finally, all the MPs signed a document we grandly christened the Kettering Declaration, promising to work together to win this campaign.

It was such a success that Sammy has suggested we do something similar in Belfast, and I'm wondering about Scotland and Wales too.

Kate texted me late tonight to thank me for everything I am doing for the cause. I replied that she'd been very brave.

25 JANUARY

Am seriously considering suing Vote Leave for putting it about that I'm a racist and that GO could be a mechanism for leaking data to UKIP. This nonsense is still circulating and I can't let it stand.

I told John Mills, who asked me to put things on hold until we've had a chance to talk it all over at lunch on Thursday.

I agreed to do that – and I also repeated the offer. He becomes chairman of Leave.EU, with an equal number from left and right on the board. A full merger would then follow, with Elliott running the donor side of things and other posts to be negotiated. Cummings out is a red line, though.

Also told John we will continue to support GO after that superb launch.

～

Stuart Rose gave an embarrassingly bad interview about BSE today. He didn't know his own job: 'Stuart Rose and I'm the chairman of Ocado, I'm chairman of – sorry – Stay In Britain, Better In Britain campaign'. Later on he tried again and managed: 'I'm chairman of the Better In Britain campaign, Better Stay In Britain'.

Yes, he'd better stay in Britain – he's helping us no end. I'd pay good money for him to keep cocking things up.

26 JANUARY

Tice and his tax return

Richard is becoming crosser and less corporate by the day. He rang me this morning in a state of great indignation to inform me that HMRC is sniffing around his affairs.

I could barely get a word in edgeways as he bellowed about an 'establishment stitch-up'.

After a lifetime of faultless tax returns and audits, he's had a menacing letter accusing him of living beyond his means. They're threatening a full inquiry and demanding three years' worth of bank statements, credit card bills and so on.

'I can't believe the lengths they're going to,' he said angrily. 'They're trying to discredit me in the City. They want to put people off becoming big donors.'

I tried to calm him down, telling him anyone who's anyone gets grief from HMRC. It's why a lot of super-wealthy people try to avoid appearing on the *Sunday Times* Rich List. Told him that if he's done nothing wrong, he should see it as a kind of badge of honour.

But he was still furious, muttering about the establishment 'working in mysterious ways' and people needing to appreciate 'the lengths to which it will go, even in one of the greatest, most stable democracies in the world'. He's convinced he detects the hand of No. 10. 'You and I were the first business people to stick our heads above the parapet on the referendum last year. Bet someone in Downing Street's encouraged HMRC to have a little look,' he said darkly.

There may be something in it. I would put nothing past those bastards.

≈

We have had a very touching donation of £10,000 from a retired accountant in the Midlands who says this is a huge sum for him but he's doing it out of profound conviction. He may give us the same again. He sends us 'best wishes for what will undoubtedly be the most stressful, intense and bloody political campaign which has ever been fought in the UK'. It feels like it already is.

27 JANUARY

I had a long discussion with Peter Bone about Vote Leave. Their show is just that: a show. It's all about egos. We're about people power. We now have half a million supporters in the country, with numbers growing at 5,000 a day. Peter told me he and Pursglove had both come to the conclusion that Leave.EU has to play a prominent role. He said they'd spoken to the Electoral Commission, who indicated pretty clearly that if Leave.EU and Labour Leave all folded into GO, it would be hard for them to ignore. Bone clearly thinks his outfit should be in charge.

Kate is going to join me for lunch with Mills at 5 Hertford Street tomorrow. I'm glad she's coming along. I don't like to waste her time but I'm feeling exposed, as Mills is coming mob-handed, with Elliott and a few others.

She was over the moon when I told her that the Kettering videos have been watched by a quarter of a million people, including 40,000 for her speech on the Facebook page. It is amazing the way this is reaching people now.

Lucy Fisher's been in touch, asking for an interview for this Saturday's *Times*. I said yes right away. We're meeting at Bentley's in Mayfair, one of my favourite restaurants. Am well up for it, especially as I've had to cancel her a few times recently. Am also on the BBC tomorrow and ITV wants to do a profile. Five hours of filming for twenty minutes!

28 JANUARY

Vote Leave is imploding. Apparently there's been an attempted coup against Cummings. According to today's *Times*, Bernard Jenkin is behind it and demanded Cummings be kicked off the board.

Sadly, it failed, but Bernard has immediately gone up in my estimation. He's far from the only MP pissed off at VL. Reports of infighting have reached fever pitch. It's all very entertaining, but ultimately it does no good for the cause.

Lunch with Elliott and co. today was a very depressing experience. It was dominated by endless dreary discussions over whether to have an overarching committee or a steering committee and all that boardroom crap.

I'm convinced our efforts must go into Labour Leave to turn Labour voters our way. They are a key target. That's why I've already funded a TUAEU leaflet attacking the TTIP trade deal between the EU and the US. My sense is that John Mills feels stuck because of the huge amount of time and effort he has invested in trying to make VL work. I understand his position. John and Richard Tice are meeting again on Sunday but I don't hold out any hope.

Kate has just emailed saying she thinks I was very patient and restrained at all the negativity. Says she just gets furious. She still thinks my efforts to get John in as chairman of the merged group may pay off, particularly as he is fundamentally a nice guy. I agree.

Lucy Fisher had to cancel, which was a shame. Glad it's not me standing her up for a change.

30 JANUARY

Managed to stifle my temper and have a civilised conversation with Elliott about the need to merge and on what terms. He continues to defend Cummings to the hilt and blindly insist that no Cabinet minister will join a group with UKIP participation.

If Labour Leave agree to support GO, it would bring things to a head. We could merge our talents and resources and would have a great chance of winning. Kate pointed out to me later in the day that UKIP's only MP sits on the VL board, though clearly Carswell is not remotely interested in talking about immigration.

31 JANUARY

Tice loses it

The change in Tice's personality is getting quite alarming. He's now a very different man to the buttoned up corporate automaton Wiggy and I first met a year ago.

We have reached peak People's Front of Judea/Judean People's Front with Vote Leave and, what with the HMRC thing, he's extremely stressed. In recent days his characteristically neutral facial expression has been slowly morphing into something resembling The Scream. It all came to a head this morning, when he rang Wiggy, apparently simply to let off steam.

'Where are you?' he demanded aggressively, when Wiggy picked up the phone.

'At home,' replied Wiggy amiably. 'Just knocking up some bacon and eggs for Mrs Wiggy and the kids.'

'Can't talk to you if they're in earshot,' Tice replied menacingly. 'Can you move out of earshot?'

'OK, I'll go into the garden,' Wiggy replied, beginning to feel nervous. 'Right, I'm on my own now. What's up?'

'C***, C***, C***, C***!' yelled Tice.

For once, Wiggy was shocked into silence.

'JUST C*** C*** C***!' ranted Tice again.

'Have you finished?' Wiggy responded pleasantly.

'Uh, yes,' replied Tice, now sounding a bit sheepish.

'What was that all about?'

'Those fucking c***s at Vote Leave; all the fucking MP c***s; all the c***s in the media; the c***s at HMRC who think I'm tax-dodging; they're all fucking, fucking c***s. That's all. Sorry. Not your fault.'

Apologising again, he wished Wiggy a happy Sunday and hung up.

Disturbingly, I think he's turning into us.

≈

I've left Tice to talk to Mills today. I'm 100 per cent convinced nothing will come of it. My suggested structure is that Leave.EU and GO jointly apply for designation from the Electoral Commission as the official campaign. The only thing that can make it happen is for Labour Leave to come over to GO. Richard and Andy will make an offer to LL tomorrow – in essence an office and a decent budget, say £30k a month. Plus a marketing budget. I just spent an hour on the phone with Brian Denny from the RMT signing off anti-TTIP leaflets for the trade unionists. This is the kind of thing we should be doing much more of.

I'm not going to waste any more time in London arguing with Tories. It's all about prestige and peerages, as opposed to winning the referendum campaign.

FEBRUARY 2016

1 FEBRUARY

Mills is a very successful businessman, and I'm surprised he hasn't learned the same lesson as I have over the years: sometimes it's best to cut your losses. Most of the regrets I have in life revolve around not doing the right thing earlier. Whether it's business or personal, failure to grip a problem inevitably leads to a worse outcome.

I had a final stab at persuading him to cut his ties with Elliott and Cummings. I think he knows he should. I told him:

> Business has taught me that whatever the history or degree of investment made, that you need to approach the decision based on the facts as they stand today.
>
> This is about the future of the country not the egos of two paid executives who clearly can't see the wood for the trees.
>
> I spent an hour on the phone to Matthew ... but I fear he would rather destroy all he has worked for than compromise in any way.

I suppose I was naïve to think that everyone involved in this referendum would put the need for a co-ordinated campaign first.

Kate tried to cheer me up, saying I'm just a 'decent' outsider in contrast to the 'calculating careerists' in the other camp. 'I don't think you are naïve,' she said. 'I just think you are dealing with calculating careerists who in some cases (not John) care more about their careers and future prospects than the so-important once-in-a-lifetime chance of uniting to get us out of the EU.'

We agreed that arrogance and entitlement are what being a Tory is all about these days.

Peter Bone's also given me a bit of thanks and encouragement, which is very welcome right now. I told him that when I played rugby, no sod got past me. It's time to dig in for the designation battle. It's looking like Labour Leave will come over very soon now.

Tice, who has rediscovered his inner Buddha, reckons we need to dial down the hostility. He said he thinks me and Andy should take the moral high ground and stop tweeting against VL as it's damaging our cause and putting off MPs who may otherwise be tempted to jump ship.

2 FEBRUARY

Am off to Kimberley to see how things are going with the mines. Was about to leave when Lucy Fisher rang wanting to revive the interview, so we ended up having to meet at Heathrow. We sat in a noisy branch of Carluccio's in Terminal 5.

I adopted my usual policy of saying exactly what I think. I informed her about our plan to sue VL for defamation ('Mishcon de Reya. Bosh,' I told her, smacking my hands together) and revealed that Wiggy enlivens the mornings at Lysander House by giving daily impressions of one or other of the characters from the campaign. He does a great Matthew piss-take, saying, 'Arron, I want to suck your earlobes' and 'Oh, Arron, this is such a distasteful situation.' I said I call him 'Lord Elliott of Loserville' because he's so desperate for a peerage.

Some choice words about Will Straw followed: 'not quite there in the IQ stakes'. She trotted off happily to write it up. Told her not to stitch me up.

～

I have now registered the Leave Group as a limited company all ready and waiting as the umbrella organisation to help us go for designation with the broadest possible support. Leave.EU, GO, Labour Leave, UKIP and others will all be able to come into the company when they're ready. Each group gets one share and the right to nominate a board member – as long as they are not a politician. I want this to be the vehicle for the full merger.

The Brussels billet-doux

Donald Tusk, the dour former Polish Prime Minister who heads the European Council, has responded to Cameron's meek list of 'demands'. It's extremely thin gruel.

Dave promised an 'emergency brake' on paying benefits to migrants. Tusk says he won't get it unless it is so watered down there's nothing worth having left.

He wanted EU treaties changed to make it clear we have nothing to do with 'ever closer union'. Instead, there will be no treaty change, only a pinkie promise that won't be worth the paper it's printed on.

The other 'concessions' are so mind-numbingly trivial and boring they're not worth reporting. If Cameron thinks this will win it for Remain, I want to know what he's been smoking.

3 FEBRUARY

Nigel Lawson chairs Vote Leave

That octogenarian Ghost of Thatcherism Past, Nigel Lawson, has been made chairman of Vote Leave. Greetings to the man who pegged the pound to the Deutschmark, wiped out what was left of British industry and, late in life, finally saw the error of his ways.

This is a complete kick in the teeth for John Mills. Lawson taking over finally rips off the disguise and exposes the group for what it is: a Tory operation. The 'stars' of the Vote Leave show have been dining out on Euroscepticism for years, preaching to a congregation of pinstriped bores who will lap up any glib Shakespeare quote thrown their way with a chorus of smug guffaws.

Now that Brexit is a real possibility I think they're losing their nerve. Instead of painting a strong, confident vision of Britain outside the EU, they are trying to woo undecideds with a muddled and gutless double-referendum strategy cooked up by Cummings. He's a man long on glowing references in sympathetic outlets like *The Spectator*, where his wife is a commissioning editor, but remarkably short on actual accomplishments. His CV includes a stint as director of strategy during Iain Duncan Smith's disastrous tenure as Tory leader; founding an airline flying from Russia to Vienna which failed on its first day; and getting sacked as Michael Gove's adviser at the Department for Education because no one could stand him. He seems to relish his notoriety as 'the most self-aggrandising and destructive agitator the modern Tory Party has produced', as a colleague describes him in *The Guardian*, and shows absolute contempt for anyone who does not agree with his views.

This self-appointed Eurosceptic aristocracy are still clinging to the rigging of the sinking Vote Leave ship. They see the EU debate as their personal property and will not work with anyone else, dividing the campaign and presenting a confusing picture to undecided voters.

I guess they're banking on the token presence of Tory turncoat Carswell and Labour's Gisela Stuart to fool their chums in the Electoral Commission into giving them the designation. Mills, a decent, honest, hard-working guy who believes in the cause, has been humiliated and bumped down to deputy.

Anyway, we need to take advantage of the disarray as this could all help our arguments for a merger. The press release is ready to go.

Kate has confirmed she wants nothing more to do with Vote Leave and is 'absolutely committed to GO'. She's told me that getting 4 million Labour votes is key to winning the referendum. Dead right.

≈

Steve Baker may just be the most pompous Tory MP I've dealt with so far and there's fierce competition for that accolade. We've been trying to use him as a go-between with Vote Leave, but Wiggy is losing the will to live. He keeps getting texts from Baker saying things like 'United against a common foe'. Where do they find these people?

A blockbuster is born

The music industry is proving hard to crack but we're not going to be put off showbiz by a few minor setbacks. Next up: the big screen.

We've been talking to some people about the possibility of a Brexit movie.

According to a breathless email I've received from a potential producer, our grassroots network is 'phenomenal' and 'could we utilise it to find examples of everyday businesses and entrepreneurs who are hamstrung by EU regulation?'

I'm not exactly rushing to buy popcorn on the basis of that marketing pitch, but there may be something in it. They've been chasing us for a meeting and clearly want our contacts and cash.

Liz's Christmas 'No. 1' farce taught us a lesson and we're wary, especially as the trailer they've produced to whet our appetites is very lame. Wiggy was particularly peeved when he found out they'd been hawking their plan round Elliott's lot as well. He wrote to them saying that we weren't going to give them a donation until we saw it and we certainly won't back it if they're in bed with Vote Leave.

He got a very indignant response from the director, Martin Durkin:

> I cannot say loudly or emphatically enough that we are most certainly not, repeat not connected to effing Vote Leave or any other outfit. I put together that short taster together at high speed from a position of complete ignorance about the various factions that I now see are at war.
>
> Believe me when I say that this film will be very red-bloodedly calling for Brexit. 100% no compromise. I will not be doing half measures on this. As far as the EU goes, I am going for the jugular. The film will feature Nigel F

prominently (who I love dearly) as well as the likes of Kate Hoey and others.

This was all a bit drama queeny, but helped put discussions back on track. We've agreed this can't be like some kind of short film by *Newsnight* and that, in Durkin's words, it will 'entertain and shock and inform'.

They want fifty grand, which is small beer considering the effect it could have if done right, so I'm giving them the benefit of the doubt and forking out.

We still haven't got to the bottom of their links with VL, but as long as they do a good job and give our perspective, we'll live with it. We'll go heavy with the promotion as well. Exciting!

4 FEBRUARY

Betrayal by Steve Baker

That little greaseball Steve Baker double-crossed us last night. Told Wiggy he was trying to work 'behind the scenes' for a peace deal after the attempted coup against Elliott and Cummings, then went parading on *Newsnight* an hour later saying there won't be any deal because of a 'genuine disagreement about strategy and tactics' and that Farage is toxic. Wiggy texted him asking what the hell he was up to and Baker replied dismissively, 'I'm going to bed.'

It didn't exactly augur well for today's lobby lunch, which they were both attending. Wiggy had been invited by Nick Watt at *The Guardian*. These lunches are a long-standing tradition among parliamentary journalists and always feature a guest speaker who's supposed to give a witty speech after a meal in Moncrieff's, the hacks' dingy canteen. Today it was Stuart Rose, so we were keen to be there.

Wiggy arrived to find the place packed with VL types, including Cummings, Baker and Oxley. He had been ruminating on Baker's treachery and was itching to give him a piece of his mind. As soon as he found him, he delivered a verbal wazzocking and demanded to know what the hell he was playing at, pretending a deal was in the offing and demoting poor old John Mills in favour of Nigel Lawson.

'We just have to be patient,' Baker stammered. 'Now that Lord Lawson is in charge—'

'Who the fuck is he?' Wiggy snapped, exasperated by the strange obsession among VL Tory boys with relics from their supposed glory days. 'With all due respect, who the fuck is he?'

Baker was at a loss for words. Apparently it was like watching Raffles the Gentleman Thug tearing through a particularly pathetic victim.

'He is, ah, a respected figure in the group...' Baker replied falteringly.

'We're supposed to be trying to win over the whole country, not a handful of pensioner activists at the Conservative Party conference!' Wiggy snapped.

At that point Baker's phone started ringing.

'I've got to go, it's Lord Lawson,' he declared, looking relieved.

'This is a pointless, pointless exercise,' replied Wiggy, eyes rolling. 'I'm off.'

The end of a beautiful friendship. Not.

≈

John Mills has finally blown a gasket.

The Guardian has got hold of an excoriating email he sent Elliott and Cummings, telling them Labour Leave is 'fed up with the way they have been treated by VL' and begging Cummings to stop being rude to Nigel Griffiths.

> Dominic – what on earth are you doing generating more and more ill feeling like this entirely unnecessarily? I thought you had promised to stop doing this sort of thing. Don't you realise that this kind of behaviour puts more and more

damaging and unnecessary strain on everyone? It certainly makes my life more difficult, entails me spending more and more inordinate amounts of time pacifying people and defending policies in some of which I don't really believe and wearing down such credibility as I still have because of the need to undo damage to the relationships which your insensitivity causes.

I think we have reached peak poison in this campaign.

Richard Tice sees the light

Tice's slow descent into madness continues apace.

He turned up for coffee with Wiggy at a Millbank café called Crussh in a state of agitation.

'There's been a leak. We're being bugged! I thought we were running a tight ship,' he cried.

'Oh, that will be Kate Hoey,' Wiggy replied airily. 'What's it about?'

'Never,' declared Tice. 'I've known Kate almost twenty years. She's a woman of principle. She's just not like that.'

He was in a flap because someone had told someone that his latest pet scheme for bringing all the warring factions together had hit the buffers.

'Was it Arron?' he demanded belligerently.

By this stage Wiggy was almost crying with laughter. Kate is indeed a woman of principle. She backs fox-hunting; has been a long-standing supporter of leaving the EU; and her proud refusal to toe the party line has been annoying Labour leaders for decades.

'Look, Richard, I'll call her. Let's get to the bottom of this,' Wiggy offered.

'Oh no, that would be embarrassing. We mustn't suggest she'd leak something, or do anything underhand.'

Wiggy called her anyway. After brief pleasantries, he came right out with it.

'Did you leak that story? It was brilliant!'

'Yes, I know, I'm so glad I did that,' replied Kate in her finest steely Ulster tones. Wiggy told her it was a great tactic and that we weren't going to respond, to which Kate merrily responded: 'Oh good, oh good.'

'I don't fucking believe it,' exclaimed Richard, as it finally dawned on him that even the very nicest politicians simply cannot help being politicians.

5 FEBRUARY

Farage hits Manchester

My big interview with Lucy Fisher is in tomorrow's *Times*. Lucy's just sent me a link and I'm pleased with it.

She was heading out to Copenhagen for a press conference with Cameron this afternoon and called en route with some quick-fire questions to go alongside the main interview. 'Champagne or cider?' that kind of thing. (Answer: 'Blimey. Both.')

I told her not to blow me up too badly as this is a four-month campaign and she will need access.

The interview went up on the website tonight and I texted to thank her.

She's put in a line comparing my 'rabid' rhetoric to Trump, and described how we've elbowed our way into the debate using punchy social media and provocative press releases. I quite like the way she depicts us as the Brexit bruisers and acknowledges that 'behind the rhetoric is a shrewd calculation that lambasting his opponents in colourful terms will garner media attention and could destabilise them'. Spot on.

For good measure, I managed to piss on UKIP's electoral wicket too, commenting on last year's election: 'UKIP delivered a victory for the Tory Party, which is reason enough for it to be disbanded.' I didn't remember saying it, but I suppose it was on tape.

Nigel has been up in Manchester at a GO rally. Apparently the local MP, a popular senior Tory backbencher called Graham Brady, didn't like the thought of a Kipper getting a standing ovation and attempted to choreograph things such that it didn't happen. His efforts failed and Brady was none too happy about being upstaged.

What the Tories don't realise is that Nigel is the reason people come to these events. When we took him off the billing in Glasgow, the place was nearly empty. This one was packed, and he was cheered to the rafters. Afterwards, Kate was starving, so Jordan and Victoria from the press office ended up having to hustle her, Boneglove and the immaculate Mr Tice into a McDonald's for an impromptu supper. In a show of true Labour authenticity, Kate smuggled in a bottle of wine, forcing a rather sheepish security guard to tap her on the shoulder.

'You can't have glass bottles in here, miss.'

Thinking fast, Kate simply tipped what was left of the bottle into an empty McFlurry carton before handing it over, seeming happy enough to sup from that. I can only imagine the look on Tice's face!

≈

Am supposed to be on *Marr* on Sunday, but have decided to take the weekend off. Wiggy says I'm being a wimp, but has told the Beeb I'm in Lesotho.

7 FEBRUARY

Kate has talked to the *Telegraph* to explain why she got out of VL. She pulled no punches, accusing them of wrecking attempts to form a united campaign, calling Cummings 'strange' and saying they've been spreading 'lies' that we are a UKIP front, which she says is rubbish. She's done us proud.

8 FEBRUARY

Following Nick 'Tubby Two Belts' Soames's attempt to invoke the ghost of Churchill, desperate Remainers are now trying to claim Thatcher would be on their side.

Her biographer Jonathan Aitken has joined the chorus of ridicule against her former foreign policy adviser Charles Powell, who has been making absurd claims that she would have voted to stay in the EU. Aitken emailed Pearson today describing it as 'utter codswallop'.

> As you and I and many others know, she was virulent in her opposition to the EU. I have some chapter and verse not only in my biography from the lips of MT but Charles Powell himself said some interesting things about his and the Foreign Office's failure over the Single European Act ...
>
> Keep up the good work! I am sure we are winning the country at large despite the views of the London metropolitan establishment.

Still in South Africa and it all seems very far away. I'm not very interested in fat political biographies.

Kate has sounded a warning note that it's important Nigel is not seen as the head of GO as this could create problems and not just with the left. This is no criticism of Nigel, who, as Kate said to me, has been subjected to an irrational amount of venom. I will sort it with him carefully – he does get it. But he is in need of some love right now. It's been a long, hard road.

Largely thanks to Kate, several of the Labour Leave people have now vacated the VL office and moved into a new office next to ours. I have issued them with passes and am sorting out their finances. The IT people have come up from Bristol to sort out the computers.

This evening, Nigel and I got talking about Eurosceptics from the Thatcher era, which reminded me that Wiggy is to blame for a legendary anecdote about Cameron's old boss, Norman Lamont. Following Black Wednesday, the young editor of the *Times* diary column – one

Andrew Pierce – called Wiggy looking for a story. Wiggy playfully suggested that Cameron, who was working as Lamont's special adviser, had overheard the Chancellor singing Edith Piaf's 'Je ne regrette rien' in the bath.

It was complete bollocks and, when he saw it in the paper, Cameron was livid. Pierce grassed Wiggy up, but it was too late and the story has become part of the folklore of the John Major years. Andy has been on the Tory naughty step ever since.

≈

Very hush-hush, but Tice claims that Ruth Lea, the veteran Eurosceptic who chairs Economists for Britain (which is linked to VL) has resigned with the usual complaints. She isn't convinced they actually want to leave the EU. Seems to be a recurring theme in the defections from that place.

I feel totally knackered. Probably because after four months on the go, I have suddenly stopped.

9 FEBRUARY

Beautifully peaceful out here in South Africa, if you don't count the dramatic electric storms every day at 6 p.m. After the lightning, it gets fresh and cold. That's when I light a fire and sit outside, listening to the noises in the bush.

It turns out Farage's car was not the last of his security problems. He was at a gig in Newcastle this evening and a maniac tried to bring a machete into the tent. As we told the plod, our security guys took 'appropriate action for the situation'. Let's just say the nutter won't be trying that again any time soon. He even had the chutzpah to accuse us of 'grievous bodily harm' and say he was going to sue. Just shows how contemptible it is that the police continue to refuse to give Farage protection.

Apparently Elliott's trying to sign up David Owen, the former

SDP leader and Labour Foreign Secretary back in the 1970s. Vote Leave seems to think he's some kind of grand eminence who will impress the Electoral Commission. For fuck's sake. First Lawson, now this. Where did they dig him up? What next? Grave-robbing? Jeremy Thorpe? We are pushing for the big unions, who can actually bring in some votes.

I've been hearing about some fancy display lorry you can hire with drop-down sides and platforms that extend out, a bit like a mobile library. Subway sandwiches have bought it up for weekends, but the beauty of it is that their panels are only velcroed on the sides. We could replace them with Leave.EU or Labour Leave displays in less than an hour and drive it round during the week. Sounds fun.

Tice's intel on Ruth Lea was right. She's confirmed with Liz that she's resigned as head of Economists for Britain, saying she wants to be free to work with whoever. 'The powers that be in Vote Leave seemed to have no interest in what I was doing at all (I think they were more interested in my contacts),' she said. 'I've decided to be a non-aligned, free spirit and help those who genuinely wish to leave the EU (which may, or may not, include the powers that be in Vote Leave!).'

Very telling.

10 FEBRUARY

Delayed guilt trip about telling Lucy Fisher that Will Straw's a dimwit.

Texted him to say it was out of order and I'd overstepped the mark. Asked him out for a beer. No reply.

The think tank Migration Watch has brought out a new report that shows the sheer scale of the crisis created by free movement of people across Europe. It quotes official EU figures showing 1.8 million illegal border crossings into the EU in 2015 alone and 3 million more expected by the end of 2017. It's a scandal and demonstrates how the EU cannot control its borders and why it is heading for further catastrophe.

11 FEBRUARY

Back from South Africa but not in the UK for long. It's half term and Katya and I are going skiing with Wiggy, Mrs Wiggy and all the kids.

Was due to give an interview to Sky's political editor, Faisal Islam, but am rushed off my feet and had to pull out. Islam got a bit stroppy, claiming he'd cancelled a trip to Hamburg with the PM to fit it into his diary. I told him I'd be happy to try next week after I'm back from a short ski trip in Switzerland. He asked if it was possible Leave.EU might choose not to go for the designation so the path is clear for GO. I told him that it's very possible.

12 FEBRUARY

Extortion by the DUP

The DUP is demanding cold, hard cash in exchange for its support! Thirty grand a month, to be precise. I know Northern Irish politics is dirty, but this is crazy.

It all came about because Farage is mates with Ian Paisley Jr, who's a DUP MP. (I can see how they became friends: Ian Sr was the only man to have caused more of a fracas in the European Parliament than Farage. It's not everyone who has the balls to shout 'Antichrist' at the Pope, as he did when John Paul II was giving an address at the Parliament.)

We already know the DUP are Outers. The question is whether they endorse us or Vote Leave. Nigel suggested I talk to a guy called Chris Montgomery, the party's chief of staff at Westminster, and see if we could sign them up.

I was a bit wary of getting at all sectarian about the campaign and we're keen to make sure everyone who supports Leave, whether they're Unionist or Sinn Féin, comes on board. Sinn Féin are officially backing Remain, but we'd already had one DUP MP, Sammy

Wilson, speaking at Kettering in January (he was the one who suggested we do an event in Belfast), so I thought it was worth pushing for wider support.

Unfortunately, Montgomery and I did not hit it off.

He was in the throes of house-hunting while we were trying to fix a meeting, and texted me saying that 'the two most important men in my life today are the slimy turd from Foxtons [the estate agents] and the man who might save Britain', by which he meant me. 'I already prefer one of you greatly.' Cringe.

We arranged to meet at 5 Hertford Street, but he got in a muddle and thought we were meeting at Strangers' Bar in the House of Commons. I sat waiting at 5HS getting increasingly irritated while he rushed over from Westminster.

When he finally turned up, he shamelessly announced that if the DUP were to come on board, they were going to need thirty grand a month for four months.

I told him he must be bloody well joking if he thought we were going to hand over that amount of money (allegedly 'to spend on the campaign'). Made it clear that's not the way we operate and that we want the support of parties who believe in what we're doing, not people who can be bought.

Swiss bliss

We're in Wengen, where Wiggy has a ski chalet. I love Switzerland. No sign of the EU anywhere and the Swiss seem to be coping just fine.

Kate Hoey told us to watch out for Matthew and Dominic trying to crash into us on snowboards.

We're in the Hotel Victoria spa, which has great views of the mountains and lakes. The place feels like a throwback to a simpler time when the European project didn't exist.

I'd like to detach from the campaign, but my phone won't stop ringing and I can't ignore all the calls.

The Tories seem to have forgotten their leader doesn't want to leave the EU. They've set up their own 'steering committee' for the referendum. It goes from stupid to crazy. They must be following orders from ze VL bunker – 'Shoot all resisters'...

Gerry's been in touch inviting Wiggy, Farage and me to the annual White House Correspondents' Dinner in April. He reckons American journos will be keen to meet Nigel and talk to us about Brexit.

Thatcher's former private secretary Sir Mark Worthington's also been in touch asking me to call. I thought I was going to get a ticking off, but we had a very pleasant email exchange. I told him Tice and I have been asked to give evidence to the Treasury Select Committee, who are doing an inquiry on the EU. I said it was a chance for me to be my reasonable self.

'Reasonable?' he fired back.

Unfair. I'm very reasonable. I've lost my temper no more than five times in twenty years.

I'm glad to be in the mountains, leaving the magic wand in the hands of Mr Tice. Click your shoes together three times, wave the wand and everything will happen, as Dorothy would say in *The Wizard of Oz*.

13 FEBRUARY

Bone and Pursglove have been bending Nigel's ear about getting some more 'serious' media operators to run GO. He wants to draft in Nick Wood, who runs a PR company called MIP and helped him out during the 2010 European elections.

I asked Nigel what exactly these PR geniuses do in return for their fee (£50,000 a month!).

'Well, they got me in the *Express* all the time,' came the reply.

I told Nigel that every time he rings the *Express* they're happy to run his stories. I'm not happy forking out £50k a month for that, but, against my better judgement, I have agreed. I suspect it won't end well. We now have ten press officers and three comms directors across Leave.EU and GO. Absurd.

14 FEBRUARY

Valentine's drinks in Wengen

Even at the top of a mountain there's no peace. It's Valentine's Day and I had hoped to spend it relaxing with Katya and the kids, maybe with a bottle of bubbly.

Instead I find myself discussing Liam Fox at the summit of Männlichen, where we had got the cable car with Wiggy. It has some incredible views, it's a really romantic spot and it's the perfect place for Wiggy to woo me. And what does he want to talk about?

'Liam Fox has just been on the BBC news as a GO spokesperson,' he exclaimed. Complete mood killer.

I woke up to news that the Beeb is planning to run a smear story about our Facebook pages. Through no fault of our own, some advert to the BNP appeared on a link. It's absolutely nothing to do with us. Robbie Gibb is being quite helpful and says he's trying to hose it down.

16 FEBRUARY

Apparently the DUP has been up to the same money-grubbing tricks with Vote Leave. It seems they've tried to play us off against each other. Apparently they demanded more from Elliott than they did from us (£50,000 a month, I'm told).

I tried to call Chris Montgomery a couple of days after our meeting to smooth things over, and got a message saying he couldn't talk because he was 'at lunch in Norfolk'.

'My wife will neuter me if I answer the phone,' was his lame excuse.

I texted him this morning to say I've heard they're about to throw in their lot with VL. I told him we're planning a massive public meeting in Belfast with Farage, who's popular in Northern Ireland. Nigel is going to appear alongside Kate Hoey, who's also a big draw as she's from those parts. I added that I didn't care what the DUP was doing: we'll just sign punters up at the event.

For some reason he took umbrage at this and started randomly accusing me of making threats.

'Good luck with that in Ulster,' he added darkly.

'No threats,' I told him cheerily. 'See you in Belfast.'

He seems to think a Belfast gig will 'bring needless bad publicity'.

'Not at all,' I told him. 'We plan to go to every part of the UK and Northern Ireland.'

He sent a snotty reply pointing out that Northern Ireland is in the UK and that I should make sure I realise that if I am going to try going over there.

I suspect that's the last I'll hear from him. What a slimy turd, to coin a phrase.

≈

Tice was right. I was an idiot to hire Richard North.

The idea of being anywhere near Nigel again brings him out in a rash and he's blown his top over our plan to let GO take the lead in applying for the designation. He described it as 'little more than an extended suicide note for the Leave campaign', puffing that there was no longer any 'room' for him at Leave.EU. Andy tried to play for time with the stroppy old prima donna, but he went full Tonto, claiming there was 'absolutely no way' he could work with or be associated with GO. 'I really don't have any option but to resign and disassociate myself and Flexcit from Leave.EU,' he declared.

I think we might just survive without him.

17 FEBRUARY

Elliott and co. seem to have declared cyberwar on Labour Leave, taking control of their website (apparently with the agreement of John Mills).

I got an email from Nigel Griffiths, the former Labour minister, who's one of the people co-ordinating. He said he hates the new version and is furious that the Labour contingent is now being 'controlled by former Conservative ministers' special advisers and others who have acted against the Labour Party'.

This is coming to a head.

18 FEBRUARY

Bitchfest

Private Eye has run a very funny number about all the infighting, which they've branded a 'septic Eurosceptic bitchfest'.

They've laid into all of us, saying our Twitter operation is run by 'pea-brained Kippers'. I'm 'multi-millionaire Arunonthe Banks' and Wiggy is described as 'Farage's evil spin doctor'. Which he loves.

'SHIT is a badge of honour', he texts me when I tell him.

Vote Leave hasn't escaped either. It's described as a 'well-funded, cross-party front runner to be the official "Leave Lead" campaign, now in such disarray that it is no longer well-funded, or cross-party or front runner'.

We couldn't have said it better ourselves.

Thanet election scandal deepens

Fantastic news: the Electoral Commission is investigating Tory spending in South Thanet. This is a vindication for Michael Crick's investigative skills at Channel 4, and the Tories should be very worried. This is just the beginning.

The word is that as many as thirty MPs may have fiddled their election expenses, with help from Tory HQ.

Meanwhile, the Norths have been giving us more grief. Pete North, who calls Wiggy and I 'two bozos', has been emailing us accusing us of 'stringing people along with false promises and bogus intent'.

'Every email exchange you have made sits in my inbox waiting for release on the day of our inevitable defeat, where it will be made public just how duplicitous and deceitful you have been,' he tells us.

Lovely bloke; real chip off the old block.

Big deal

Cameron is in Brussels for the final stage of his renegotiation. No surprise, there was no real progress today. All nicely choreographed for a triumphant last-minute fake 'deal' tomorrow that he will promote as a great concession that secures our future in Europe.

Much bigger deal

We're planning to herald the grand finale of his diplomatic marathon with a big rally at the QEII Centre near Parliament. We're expecting 2,000 people and will have various speakers. The wild card will be 'Gorgeous George' Galloway, probably the only politician in Britain who winds people up more than Nigel. It's bound to provoke a reaction (good and bad).

He may be a bellend, but he's about the only one still carrying the torch for the left-wing democratic Euroscepticism Tony Benn once represented.

I've been busy on the designation document, which we'll submit under the aegis of GO. We're in a good position and need to hold our nerve.

19 FEBRUARY

Galloway day

Cameron's back from Brussels. What an anti-climax. He didn't even produce a hat, never mind a rabbit.

He's trying to claim we now have some kind of special status, but he's got nothing, and he knows it.

We'd promised a 'surprise keynote speaker' at the QEII conference event, and revved up the press to expect a big name.

We'd set the capacity low at 1,300, even though we expected more like 2,000, because Wiggy thought it would look better with the audience huddled cheek-by-jowl.

The result was carnage and the venue went into lock-down, as officious health and safety types wouldn't allow anyone extra in. ITV's Robert Peston got shut out and had a massive 'don't you know who I am' strop. David Davis suffered the same fate but, like the good ex-SAS reservist that he is, left the rest of them standing while he arranged to have himself smuggled in through an underground car park. We ended up with a hefty bill for damage to doors by an over-eager crowd fighting to get into the hall, but it was a price worth paying for the terrific atmosphere.

About half an hour before kick-off, Wiggy disappeared backstage with Nigel to usher in our mystery guest. Wiggy hadn't been entirely convinced that Galloway was the star turn we needed ('holy crap' were his exact words when he heard) and was still in an anxious state, needling Nigel about whether it was a good idea.

'Isn't this going to backfire?' he asked nervously, knowing that the assembled press were anticipating some A-list knockout and were about to be confronted by the most irritatingly sanctimonious left-wing political has-been known to man.

'It's going to be wonderful,' Nigel boomed. 'Suck it up. This is going to work.'

To tell the truth, I was a bit unsure myself, and still in a bad mood because of the exasperating Nick Wood and his team. Wood's been parking his tanks all over our lawn and kept telling everyone what to do and what to say, as if he'd organised the whole event himself.

Eventually I lost my rag and texted Bone making it clear I'm not putting up with it any more. I told him they were causing havoc.

'Things have in many ways got out of hand,' Bone agreed, and tried to calm me down with a little flattery. 'I for one very much appreciate what you have done. It has been superb. In fact, Vote Leave are on the ropes … With regard to MIP there has been a terrible misunderstanding but that can only be sorted face to face.'

Anyway, there was no point dwelling on it, so I made my way into the throng and waited to listen to Nigel, whose speech prompted thunderous applause. Then the doors at the back of the stage were thrown open and out bounded George in his trademark black fedora.

A brief moment of shocked silence ensued.

'Fuck,' exclaimed *Times* reporter Sam Coates, who was at my elbow. I laughed nervously, and then all hell broke loose. Half the conference hall was disappointed it wasn't a Hollywood star; the other half was outraged that they were being forced to listen to Hamas's chief British propagandist.

UKIP MEP Tim Aker stormed out and an Israel supporter at the back started yelling abuse and had to be removed by security. When everyone finally calmed down, our man started to speak, and before too long, he'd won over what remained of the crowd.

Say what you want like about him, but he's a fantastic orator, and his call to arms about 'winning the country back' was pitched just right. The press can sniff – and they did – but Nigel's right: Galloway's probably the only Brexit supporter who can engage much of the Muslim community who traditionally vote Labour and would never listen to UKIP.

Afterwards, Wiggy and I were elated and headed to the Westminster Arms for a few pints. The place was mobbed, and I was just getting stuck in to a beer when Nigel's press man tapped me on the shoulder, saying I was wanted for an interview on Radio 4's *World Tonight* about Cameron's not very triumphant return from Brussels.

That will be easy, I thought – there's nothing to say. So I hot-footed it to their radio car, bunged on the headphones and waited to be patched through to the presenter.

'What's your reaction, Mr Banks?'

'He's got absolutely nothing,' I replied.

There was a long pause, which I didn't fill.

'Would you like to say anything else?' the presenter enquired.

'No, not really. That's it. It's a non-deal,' I replied. It was blowing a gale outside, and there was a really annoying echo on the line. I could hear my voice bouncing back at me and just wanted to get back to the pub.

'Oh, OK then, thank you,' said the presenter.

And that was that.

20 FEBRUARY

All systems go

The papers have shredded Cameron's deal. I would love to have been a fly on the wall inside Downing Street when the first editions dropped.

The *Mail* did a wholesale demolition job, splashing with the headline 'Call That a Deal, Dave?' and running a full-page editorial on how crap it was. *The Times* said that 'from the land of chocolate', Cameron was 'always destined to bring back fudge'. *The Sun* splashed on a silly story about 'two randy EU officials caught romping in the loo' but also looks likely to come out for Leave. Even *The Guardian* and *Mirror* struggled to sound enthusiastic.

Cameron must be horrified by the reaction but he's still trying to claim success.

What little he's got is already unravelling. Justice Secretary Michael Gove, who's going to campaign for Brexit, thinks his feeble concessions will be chucked out by the European Court of Justice. A handful of other big hitters are also backing Out, including Iain Duncan Smith, Chris Grayling, Theresa Villiers and Priti Patel. It's a good start, although they're aligning with VL (no surprise). What a shame Theresa May isn't backing Brexit. Boris is still making up his mind, claiming he needs to examine the small print over the weekend.

Anyway, finally we have a date. The referendum will be on 23 June, much to Richard North's spluttering indignation. He's been telling anyone who'll listen (which is not many) that there was no way the date could be anything other than late 2017.

Perhaps this will put a dent in his unshakeable sense of infallibility, but somehow I doubt it.

Gerry says Washington is buzzing about the news and wants us to go to DC for a couple of days to hold a forum in the Capitol with Congressmen and the press. He reckons VL are up to something similar and we should beat them to it.

21 FEBRUARY

Boris Johnson comes out for Out – sort of

After leading the press on a merry dance all weekend, Boris has finally declared for Leave. Great news! He'll be a massive asset, though I wish he'd stop pissing around. He's written a very strange column for tomorrow's *Telegraph*, reviving the double referendum idea. Claims the EU 'only really listen to a population when it says no'.

Faisal Islam, Sky's political editor, texted me to say he thinks Nigel and I may be 'onto something' when we say we're not sure some of these politicians really want to leave.

He interviewed Boris today and was surprised by his attitude to the objective of voting Out. 'When he said "to get a better deal" to me on live TV I could not quite believe it,' he said.

I told Faisal this is going to come back and bite Boris big time. This is an In or Out situation; Shake It All About isn't on the ballot paper.

23 FEBRUARY

Maggie's man

There is no greater expert on how the establishment works than smoothie-chops Sir Mark Worthington, who was Maggie Thatcher's private secretary for more than twenty years.

Andy's known him for donkey's years and he's being very helpful behind the scenes. We've met up a few times at Caffè Nero opposite the Home Office and he always tells us we have no hope of getting the designation. 'You do know that VL are going to get the designation, don't you? And that's because of the impression they give, they just feel like the establishment bid. I don't agree with it, but you have to recognise that,' is how he put it.

I told Malcolm Pearson what Worthington thinks and he entirely agreed. 'I'm afraid you're going to lose before you've even started because the establishment will make sure Matthew Elliott gets it,' he told me.

The way I see it, we have two choices. We can pretend we are establishment greasers just to get that designation, or we can stay true to ourselves – the naughty outsiders shaking up the way things work – and see how it plays.

If we tried to change it wouldn't work anyway, so I've always thought we should just keep doing things the way we know best. We're fighting the establishment, not gagging to be part of it – and that's what our supporters love about us.

Malcolm's circulated a mass plea to 100 or so Brexiteers appealing to us all to hold hands. 'How can we fight a cohesive ten-week campaign after a six-week slanging match?' He had a bit of a go at me for starting a 'pillow fight in the nursery', but I didn't much mind.

Elliott has told us we can expect a response from Lawson to our latest peace feelers. I can hardly bloody wait.

The BBC's booked Wembley Arena for a massive referendum debate two days before polling day. They're also planning a *Question Time* special and something up in Glasgow. Wish Cameron had the balls to agree to a head-to-head debate with Farage. Now that would be worth watching.

25 FEBRUARY

Thinking about it, I see it as a badge of honour that Tory ministers who back Brexit don't want anything to do with us.

If they think a moth-eaten Lord Lawson – who did more to destroy British manufacturing than the Luftwaffe – is a better look for the campaign than Nigel Farage, they are plain wrong. We are having this referendum because of Farage's bravery against the poison of the establishment. He is a great man, who always puts me in mind of that speech by Teddy Roosevelt with the quote: 'The credit belongs to the man who is actually in the arena.' Gove, Grayling and the rest of Elliott's pet Tories haven't been in the arena a week, yet suddenly we're expected to airbrush Nigel out of the campaign and defer to them? I don't think so. At school I used to love reading about Roosevelt and his Rough Riders, the volunteer cavalry in the Spanish–American War.

I was out last night canvassing in our neighbourhood with my dad. Everyone we spoke to vehemently for Out. Dad, who is not quite as fire and brimstone on Brexit as me, was taken aback by the strength of feeling.

Pearson has put me in touch with his godson, who's in the advertising world. He can get us the best billboard sites in London for our poster about the referendum being Independence Day. Ashley is half-Jamaican and half-Lebanese, a true diamond in the rough and Malcolm thinks I will love him. He sounds just the ticket.

27 FEBRUARY

Project Fear alert: Osborne is now saying Brexit would be a shock to the whole world economy. Well, if we are really that important to the whole globe, you'd think we were strong enough to decide our own future.

28 FEBRUARY

Our election analyst Ian Warren has been doing some work with Brendan Chilton and Labour Leave. This is great, as we're focusing on Labour voters this week. He says the Labour Party is putting

Me on *Marr*. I can't remember what made me pull this silly expression, but no doubt it was some nonsense from the Remain camp's Project Fear.

A youthful Wiggy with Ronald Reagan. He managed to blag staying at the President's ranch for six months in the early 1990s when Thatcher was writing her memoirs.

A deliberately provocative social media 'tile'. We used these to spark debate and engage people in the campaign.

Peter Bone and Tom Pursglove, two of a very small number of Tory MPs who liked us. Our relationship with them didn't end well.

ABOVE Dinner in McDonald's after a Grassroots Out gig. We got into trouble for the wine, so Kate Hoey decanted it into some McFlurry cups.

LEFT Our post bag after Peter Hargreaves's mailshot. I loved all the letters from ordinary people desperate to leave the EU.

Wiggy poses with Alan Greenspan, former chairman of the US Federal Reserve. He mistook the economist for Watergate reporter Carl Bernstein, and tried to talk to him about Deep Throat.

BREXIT LIVE PRESENTS

b**POP**
LIVE

LIVE ACTS INCLUDE

MR BLOBBY | SID OWEN | SONIA | THE WURZELS
THE REYNOLDS GIRLS | MIKE READ | THE RACIST ONE FROM S CLUB
VANILLA | VERA LYNN | 28.7% of SO SOLID CREW

SUNDAY 19TH JUNE, NEC, BIRMINGHAM, ENGLAND, MY ENGLAND

TICKETS START FROM £23 NO JOHNNY FOREIGNERS ADMITTED

ABOVE This spoof advert sums up the disaster that was BPop. Our plans for a Brexit concert descended into farce. We only gave up when the Electoral Commission warned us that Liz Bilney might go to prison.

LEFT Nigel and the PM bumped into each other in a corridor before ITV's referendum debate. Downing Street had told TV bosses not to let this happen. A super-awkward moment.

Bob Geldof and his luvvies at the Battle of the Thames. An amazing day highlighting how the EU's Common Fisheries Policy is destroying livelihoods.

Lunch on polling day: Posh George, Nigel, Wiggy, me and Chris Bruni-Lowe. Nigel would not snap out of his gloomy conviction that we'd lost.

Nigel mobbed by the media at our party on referendum night. Here he is gloomily conceding defeat before the votes had been counted. I was very annoyed.

Wiggy swigging champers on the morning of 24 June. We'd been up all night and were about to have a celebratory breakfast at the Ritz.

Behind the scenes in UKIP's office on the morning of 24 June. We were waiting to watch Cameron resign.

Nigel on College Green on the morning of 24 June. After twenty-five years of campaigning for Brexit, he still couldn't believe it had happened.

ABOVE Nigel was touched by this full-page advert we'd booked to appear in the *Telegraph* on 24 June. Win or lose, we wanted to thank him for spending twenty-five years of his life fighting for UK independence.

ABOVE Hanging out with Trump in Mississippi. We were all thrilled to be invited to join him at a fundraising dinner and a rally in the States. Nigel spoke at both events.

BELOW Trump introducing Nigel at a Republican rally. We only told him about the invitation at the last minute, because we feared that if he had too much time to think about it, he would freak out and refuse.

A quick recharge on the campaign trail.

TOP Farage doing more media in Las Vegas after the final Trump *v.* Clinton debate.

ABOVE Farage and Judge Jeanine sharing a joke.

The great Lord Ashcroft with fellow Belizean Wiggy waiting to see Trump.

Farage with
Kellyanne Conway
in Trump Tower.

The picture
of 2016: Trump
and Farage – two
happy men.

Governor Phil Bryant with the Bad Boys
overlooking the White House.

Farage, Wiggy and I at the Ritz Party hosted by
Freddie Barclay.

Wiggy meeting the Queen… again.

Nigel telling Californians how they can win their own referendum.

LEFT Tice, Wiggy and Farage in the London office ahead of Article 50 being triggered.

BELOW Nigel celebrating Article 50 Day, true to form, with a pint and a cig.

a hundred 'mobilisers' into target areas as they are privately very worried about what they're hearing on the doorstep.

MARCH 2016

1 MARCH

Big-shot mailshot

Have spent the day at Old Down with Peter Hargreaves and am quite excited about our conversation. He founded the only FTSE 100 company to be started at a kitchen table. He's worth around £3 billion and has 750,000 customers who trust his advice.

He came for lunch and we sat in big armchairs with glasses of wine and talked about what he could do. Peter, who's just had a heart bypass, told me he's had Elliott on the phone every other day trying to persuade him to join Vote Leave, bending his ear about how we can't be trusted, we're just a Farage front organisation etc. etc. He told me that if I knew what they were saying about me privately, I'd throw a chair through the window.

I know Peter is a quiet Kipper. He's been discreetly donating money to the party for a while, but he gives small amounts that don't exceed the £7,500 threshold above which it has to be publicly declared. I can understand why. It's not because Peter would be embarrassed but because he doesn't want to put the company in an awkward position.

I've been quietly courting him for three months and now it looks like it's going to pay off. He has come up with the idea of writing to millions of people when the time is right about why we should leave the EU. If it all works out as planned, it will be worth around £5 million, the biggest donation ever made to a campaign in this country. Seriously exciting stuff. Have emailed Gerry, who will be thrilled.

2 MARCH

Rock and a hard place

I'm afraid Tice reverted to type today. He and I are the yin and yang of this operation. When we want to put our case in sensible, statesmanlike tones, that's a job for Captain Collegiate (or, rather, it used to be, before he began morphing into us).

When we want to blow things up, it's time to roll out the howitzer: me.

If we're not sure which way to play it, we scrap among ourselves.

That's what happened today when the world's biggest asset manager, BlackRock, joined Project Fear, issuing a ludicrous warning about the potential consequences of Brexit. Parroting the Osborne script, they claimed it would trash the City, knacker growth, kill jobs, mean 'big risk' and 'little reward' and generally result in economic meltdown.

Going for the jugular is our standard approach. If we try to match the establishment's technique of lining up well-paid 'experts', we'll just get buried under a heap of suits. So we issued a statement that went straight for the kill, highlighting the company's murky record over insider dealing and pocketing millions of pounds helping the EU and the IMF screw up the Eurozone crisis.

Tice reacted as if he had been zapped with a cattle prod when he saw it. He was straight on the phone warning that they could sue.

'Has this gone out?' he asked anxiously. 'Are you sure of your facts?'

Of course I wasn't. The press office just Googled for some dirt, cut and pasted the worst stuff they could find and hammered out a release – quick, decisive and calculated to undermine. It had all been said before anyway.

At this, Tice became even more alarmed.

'Right, right,' he said. 'It's just that these guys sue absolutely everyone who comes after them. We just need to tone down the rhetoric.'

I decided to let him handle this one, and the next thing I know, our punchy social media graphics have been replaced with some totally vanilla effort which began with the words 'Irish MPs describe BlackRock as ...' and meandered on for ever. I told them it was 'crap' and instructed them to 'get edgy'. What I had in mind was something Tice would call defamatory. There ensued a barrage of emails from the Bristol office, cc-d to Wiggy, protesting that they did not want to be sued.

To which my response was quite simple: 'Fuck it.'

The result was a social media post to the effect that 'BlackRock have a habit of providing dodgy risk assessment to profit from insider knowledge. Are we really trusting their word on Brexit?' Nice.

I don't know what Tice's reaction was, but I imagine it was despairing. So far we have not heard from BlackRock.

Fall-out with Frank

I had dinner with Frank Field, a famously independent-minded Labour MP and Eurosceptic. It was all very pleasant, but he's still shilly-shallying about whether he's going to support Leave. I followed up with an email telling him to get motoring, to which he took great umbrage. He's a gent and I didn't want to upset him, so I grovelled and admitted I'm not one of life's natural diplomats. Mentioned the episode to Kate, who told me not to worry as Frank is 'a bit odd' and sometimes takes a contrary view just for the sake of it.

Have told Wiggy to work on getting Norman Lamont on board, which may be a bit tricky, given their bath-time history. There is cause for optimism, however. Lamont sat next to Jim Mellon at dinner the other day and told him to ignore his 'snootier colleagues in the Tory Party' and let Farage know that he's right behind him and that he should keep going on immigration. He also mentioned that he is now the PM's trade envoy for Iran and can help on anything Iran-related. I know we like to lampoon crusty old Tories but we'll make an exception for him.

We're planning a big telephone bank exercise on 11 March with Nigel and David Davis, targeting 400,000 Labour supporters. I remain convinced that they're key to winning this referendum.

4 MARCH

The Belfast rally

Our Belfast rally today was a triumph, with 1,500 people turning up for an event we cobbled together in four days. It nearly didn't happen at all. Tensions were running high after a bomb went off this morning. The atmosphere was strained and we had representatives from six political parties, including Sinn Féin and the DUP, who weren't speaking to each other.

Things were so bad that, a few hours before kick-off, we considered cancelling the event. However, local councillors insisted it go ahead.

In the end, Nigel gave the Sinn Féin people an ultimatum: 'If you don't get on this stage, we're going to tell everyone that your party is only backing Remain because you get EU funding.' They fell into line.

We'd booked the Titanic, a great big shiny conference centre on the old dock where they built the doomed liner and lots of other great ships. It has the advantage of being fairly secure as it sits all by itself, making it relatively straightforward to control who enters and leaves. Lucky we were thorough: our security team discovered a man carrying a knife.

Somehow we managed to herd our cats onto the podium, including Sammy Wilson and dozens of other DUP people as well as eight Sinn Féin councillors who had signed up against the policy of their party leadership. Wiggy artfully organised the seating so the worst enemies didn't have to sit next to each other.

To me, it was a symbolic two fingers to Chris Montgomery and the DUP bosses who had led us on a wild goose chase and clearly never had any intention of backing us for the designation. They were just using us to screw more money out of Vote Leave, whose nomination they duly signed.

But most people had turned up to see Nigel, and the thing was a triumph. We'd taken the same approach as we did in Kettering: just throwing it together as a genuine grassroots event, with people of every political persuasion and none. We used the call centre to drum up interest. There was no careful preparation of agendas or agonising over who spoke after who. We just rolled with it.

Towards the end, the simmering tension between the politicians descended into farce. The various parties had agreed to sign a declaration to put aside their differences during referendum campaigning, but nothing is simple in this part of the world. The words had somehow been printed in green ink, which, being an 'Irish' colour, the Unionists disliked. They refused to sign the document. Only when someone pointed out that the green looked sort of gold under the light did they agree. Some idiot managed to leave a sticky patch on the document and made a cack-handed effort to remove it with white wine and boiling water. So we ended up with a stinking, filthy sign emblazoned in green/gold ink, but at least all the Ulstermen departed friends.

French farce

In his desperation to frighten voters, Cameron has press-ganged François Hollande into hinting that if we leave the EU, the French will abandon border controls at Calais.

Between them, they tried to paint a picture of shrugging French immigration officers languidly puffing on Gauloises and waving through streams of migrants clinging to the axles of Dover-bound lorries.

We watched Dave grin away while his socialist chum claimed he didn't want to 'scare' the British, 'just say the truth'.

'There will be consequences,' he claimed darkly.

What a shame he failed to agree a line with the man actually responsible for borders, French Interior Minister Bernard Cazeneuve.

Poor Hollande, who always has the expression of a man who's been presented with a cassoulet when he ordered duck à l'orange, was left looking a bit of a twit when Cazeneuve took to the airwaves to contradict it all.

He says France will 'go on building with Britain a good immigration policy, especially at Calais' – and no wonder: scrapping the Le Touquet agreement, which sees our money and our border guards lending support in France, would make his job ten times harder too.

Touché!

Highland charge

To listen to 'Gnasher Sturgeon'* you'd think no one north of the border would dream of voting Out.

But, whatever the SNP leader says, Scottish Euroscepticism is a thing, especially in fishing communities, and it would be daft just to write off the Scots in this campaign.

Cameron's been up at the Scottish Conservative Party's conference, claiming that the EU is good for jobs in Scotland. He seems to have forgotten what Brussels has done to key industries up there. Perhaps he doesn't realise that the EU has wrecked the livelihoods of fishermen in Scotland's coastal and island communities, and that the EU squeezes wages, guzzles our resources and exploits Scotland in every way possible. Brussels is no friend of our Scottish partners.

Of course Dave doesn't care about the disastrous effect of the Common Agricultural Policy on Scottish farmers or anyone else up there. Why should he? The Conservatives have precisely one Scottish MP. I think that if we can persuade enough Scottish voters to switch sides, it could make all the difference.

We overtake the Tories on social media

Today is a red-letter day for this campaign. The Leave.EU Facebook

---

* Don't ask

page has overtaken the Tories' page with upwards of 550,000 likes in under six months. It's an incredible achievement. It's whetted the appetites of a kind of 'people's army' who now want to get our numbers up to a million. I like their attitude. It shows the depth of public feeling over this campaign. We are cutting through.

6 MARCH

Bailing out the Commonwealth

Wiggy and I have been asked by the Royal Commonwealth Society to support Commonwealth Day on 14 March. Wiggy deals with the society because of his Belize connections. It's the oldest Commonwealth entity in the world, supported by the Queen, but it's had a few historical financial problems. About five or six years ago it nearly folded because the Foreign Office no longer seems to give a toss about it. Wiggy and I have agreed with the big boss Mike Lake that closure's not an option and will continue to do what we can to get it financially stable.

Along with a few others, including Ashcroft, we've been pitching in to keep it going. To us, it seems the government is blithely cutting ties with our Commonwealth friends, many of whom are subjects of the Queen and look up to her. They are bound to us by centuries of history, common law, language and culture.

Last year, the annual Commonwealth Day celebrations came within a whisker of being cancelled altogether. The royal family, various heads of government, ambassadors and a string of other dignitaries were due to attend, but the FCO seemed reluctant to extend the funding, which didn't become apparent until just three days before the event. How embarrassing is that? They needed help or it was off. Wiggy offered to stump up a third of the funds if I'd cover the rest, so together we managed to keep the show on the road and thankfully the FCO made an additional financial commitment.

It would have been fun to leak the story in the run-up to the election – 'UKIP donor bails out Commonwealth, while Cameron can't even be arsed to turn up to the reception' might have caught the public imagination.

However, we were specifically asked by the director of the Royal Commonwealth Society and George Osborne's father-in-law Lord Howell, who's its president, to keep it quiet, so for once we exercised some self-restraint.

After the commemorative service at Westminster Abbey on the 14th, we've also been invited to attend an evening reception to celebrate the Queen's 90th birthday at the Guildhall. Exciting!

Slave Labour

Horror stories about the way Labour MPs and activists are being treated inside Vote Leave. They're being subjected to petty mind games that have no place in a serious campaign. According to Brendan Chilton, they're being made to complete reams of paperwork to get financial authorisation for leaflets and campaign expenditure that's handed to the Tories without question. They find themselves logged out of their email accounts and are told it's a 'technical error' while everyone else's computers are working fine. They were allowed to go ahead and prepare a Labour for Britain launch party only for Cummings to scrap it at the eleventh hour. Their researcher, who's very young, is apparently being treated like crap, working fifteen-hour days in return for the living wage.

7 MARCH

Ousted

A furore today over the sudden resignation of John Longworth, boss of the British Chambers of Commerce. He's an Outer and has been summarily suspended from the BCC for having the temerity to suggest that Britain could have a bright future outside the EU. It looks suspiciously as if No. 10 may have been involved.

This seems grotesquely anti-democratic and heavy-handed and will backfire. They've made him look like a martyr and his profile has soared. He's going to be a huge asset.

Altitude sickness

Am in Méribel skiing with a mate. Glorious sunshine and snow, but Boneglove are giving me a headache. It's all to do with Peter Hargreaves's plan for a mass mailshot to millions of households. Given how much money he's spending, I don't think it's unreasonable to let him decide what's on the leaflet.

However, Boneglove are kicking up a fuss because he wants the text to include a line taking a swipe at politicians and, being creatures of Westminster themselves, are whining that their kind are subjected to a 'relentless stream of abuse'.

I gave them short shrift. Hargreaves doesn't want anything to do with MPs or civil servants, which is the whole reason he's drawn to Leave.EU. If he knew about Boneglove's moaning, his antipathy to the political classes would simply be reinforced.

The truth is that Boneglove have another agenda. They want me to stick £1.2 million into their bank account for their own mailshot. They think the Hargreaves project might undermine their chances because I've not yet agreed to theirs. And quite honestly, who would the average member of the public rather hear from? A genuine entrepreneur who's built a massively successful company giving people solid financial advice, or two nonentity MPs? Very reluctantly, I've agreed a compromise which will involve the Hargreaves mailshot featuring both Leave. EU and GO branding. 'Leave.EU, part of the GO movement' or something like that. But I suspect this isn't the last we'll hear of it.

Tice said Boneglove are still acting hurt that I don't hold politicians in the highest esteem, and I suppose I'd better rein it in. Got to keep my eye on the prize. Will remind the team we have to treat them with respect, however tempting it is to tweak their tails.

8 MARCH

Wiggy's in a strop because Boneglove have been dissing his skills as a spin doctor and trying to cut him out of the loop. They seem to think he doesn't understand the media, when he is largely responsible for creating just about the most successful, left-field viral campaign this country has ever seen. He's annoyed that Nigel seems to concur. He emailed me rather plaintively, saying: 'They don't want me involved – don't think I'm good enough to make decisions and Nigel's not really helped by telling them he agreed with them … very, very fucked off.'

I told him Nigel's just trying to manage some awful Tories in the most efficient way he can. Plus, he's very tired, and may not be thinking straight. Wiggy wasn't pacified. 'Thought Nigel was on my side. Clearly not,' he replied grumpily.

Evidently the pressure's getting to him.

9 MARCH

Hargreaves coughs up

Still in Méribel. Had a call from Hargreaves to say he was just about to transfer the £3.2 million to our account for the leaflet. Quite a moment.

We have scaled down the cost as we don't think we will need to print as many copies as we initially planned.

I told Nigel about the donation and he was over the moon. I asked if he reckons it's the biggest-ever single donation, and he reminded me that Stuart Wheeler once gave the Tories £5 million. I told him that doesn't count as the money was donated during Michael Howard's leadership so it was a waste.

Her Majesty comes out for Brexit

The Sun has a great scoop that the 'Queen backs Brexit'. They claim Her Majesty gave Nick Clegg a dressing-down for his Europhilia when he was Deputy Prime Minister in 2011, and made no secret of her disdain for Brussels.

The Palace is in a tizzy about the breach of protocol and say she would never air her private views, but I think most people suspect she's a closet Outer. With most of the establishment lining up for Remain, we've got the one who matters.

Wembley arena

Someone's leaked the BBC's provisional line-up for the Wembley debate.

George Osborne, Alan Johnson, Tim Farron and Caroline Lucas versus BoJo, Nigel, Iain Duncan Smith and George Galloway.

If this is true, I am not at all happy. Politicians across the board, and our lot will look like a bunch of old farts on a day out from a Bournemouth bowling club. They're hardly going to resonate with the public, beyond Galloway making their toes curl.

What about Kate Hoey? Hell, what about Priti Patel?

The Beeb's denying the report is accurate but I don't trust them an inch.

Have written to the Trust saying they're trying to make Brexiteers look like a bunch of grumpy old men.

10 MARCH

Wiggy v. Woody

Back from the Alps to find Wiggy on the warpath.

Nick Wood and his insufferably pretentious PR company are driving him mad. They have something they call a 'news grid'. It's several times the size of Ed Miliband's 'Ed Stone', which they use to schedule daily media activities. Every second is accounted for in minute detail, as if they're lawyers charging clients by the quarter-hour.

Wiggy and I like winging it. Every day, we hold what we call 'morning prayers', during which we try to cobble together some sort of plan and appeal to a higher authority for it not to hit the skids within the first half-hour. When Wood's lot smugly present their meticulous schedule and we don't produce something similar, they tut disapprovingly at our 'disorganisation' and give Wiggy dreary lectures about the importance of the 'news cycle'.

Wood reckons we're not in the papers enough and should release a story at four o'clock every afternoon to maximise our opportunity of getting on the front pages. Don't get me wrong: we love being in the papers. But we'd rather generate controversy on social media, and go to places like Manchester and Kettering, where we can convert people.

Besides, our own little press team in Wiggy's London office clocks more media mentions than Wood's lot every day! Instead of wasting time on elaborate grids and interminable meetings, they pounce on likely stories straight away. I've given them a broad remit to use their initiative and keep it punchy – and we're getting results.

I emailed Wood and Boneglove, making it clear I stood firmly behind Andy.

> People who have long meetings and use grids may want to call us disorganised, but results are what matter and that's what we're achieving. If this is badly organised, then I'm a Dutchman. I've been in business long enough to realise most people would rather fail than be unconventional. Our team have been working their socks off. Finally, we may be a bit anti-politician but believe it or not, it's pretty popular.

Frankly, I am sick of Wood and I will not be paying his £50,000 a month bills much longer.

Kate is on *Question Time* tomorrow with that patronising harpy Anna Soubry.

I am very anti-Tory right now.

11 MARCH

A voice of reason from Norway

Remain keep suggesting the City of London will wind up looking like Homs if we leave the EU. Today, the chief exec of Norway's $830 billion sovereign wealth fund exposed what a nonsense that is. He says they'll continue to invest in the UK at the same level – perhaps even increasing the amount – 'no matter what happens'.

With uncharacteristic relish, Tice bashed out some quotes taking aim at those EU apologists Goldman Sachs and BlackRock, calling them 'predatory' and attacking their judgement.

The *Daily Mail* gave it great welly and ran a few of Tice's choicer lines. Unfortunately, Wiggy didn't notice the mention and rang political editor James Slack to complain that they've been ignoring us.

Slack very politely pointed out that we were in their main EU story of the day. The giveaway was the long quote from Tice together with the big picture of him looking at his most boring, sitting at the desk with a lunchtime bottle of tomato juice beside his keyboard.

Wiggy immediately put his hands up and admitted he'd been an arse. I told Pierce, who emailed me with a kiss: 'Bless him. Do keep up the pressure boys. X'

12 MARCH

A culture shock for Gerry Gunster

Gerry is in the UK for two weeks, and I suggested he and his colleague Rob Leggat stay at Old Down tonight.

Unfortunately, I'd forgotten Katya's mum was having a birthday party and I was expected to put in an appearance. It was the last thing I felt like doing, especially with Gerry, but in the interests of marital harmony I reluctantly agreed.

When I broke the news to Gerry, he didn't exactly sound

enthusiastic and I can't say I blame him. It's bad enough going to your own mother-in-law's party, never mind someone else's. I told him not to worry about what to wear and assured him he wouldn't stay long.

By the time I got home from work, the party was already in full swing. I waited for Gerry to arrive, and we made our way to the function room at Old Down. It was at this point that we began to notice that everyone was wearing strange clothes.

Already slightly bewildered, we headed to the bar, where the first person Gerry encountered was a tall man wearing a black suit and a large white hat.

'Hello, I'm Gerry, from the States,' he announced politely.

'I'm a White Russian,' the fellow replied confusingly.

Neither of us had any idea what was going on.

I assumed the man was referring to the cocktail in his hand, until it belatedly dawned on me that we were at a murder mystery party. The guests had all been primed to play a part. Except us.

I'd rocked up in my gym kit, Gerry was in his slacks, and everyone else was some kind of Cluedo character.

Before I'd had time to make any introductions, someone thrust a piece of paper in Gerry's hand and I was dragged off to talk to one of my Russian relatives. Through the mêlée, I could see him studying the piece of paper, trying to get his head round the instructions for the part he was supposed to play.

After ten minutes, I decided to do a runner. Much as I love my in-laws, after a long week at the office, it was all too much. By now Gerry was on the other side of the room, looking alone and confused. I didn't dare make my way through the throng to tell him I was leaving, for fear of being waylaid by some cousin or aunt and getting stuck for another half-hour. So I abandoned him to his fate.

As I slunk out of the house, hoping nobody would notice, I bumped into my son Peter.

'Go and rescue Gerry,' I instructed. 'He's the American. The one not dressed up.'

I sat outside in the car waiting. A few minutes later, Gerry bolted out of the house looking ashen.

'What was that all that about?' he demanded.

All I could say is that the Russians are a law unto themselves. I've never seen anyone look so relieved to get away from a party.

13 MARCH

100 days and counting

We have 100 days left to win this campaign, and I'm increasingly optimistic.

Remain has tried to create what pollsters call a 'settled view' on the economy, in the hope of convincing people that Brexit will come at an unbearable price, but I think they're overplaying their hand.

I am determined that Leave.EU won't copy these tactics. People are sick of being told to accept the status quo and made to feel there's no hope of anything better. Negative campaigning is not engaging the public at all. We are going to be the keen, bright-eyed optimists, showing how this great country can benefit from controlling its own destiny. As we get closer, the pendulum seems to be swinging in our favour. This is ours to lose.

BPop Bust-up

BPop seems to be hitting the buffers.

Wiggy got a bit carried away and decided to leak the names of the hoped-for headliners. Cue front-page images of Ella Henderson and Pixie Lott under the headline 'The Brexit babes backing Britain'.

One small problem: neither of the artistes concerned had actually signed on the dotted line. Their agents hit the roof and have been frantically ringing round journalists trying to kill the story. At this rate, Antonia Suñer may be the best we can muster.

Lord Ashcroft's 70th birthday bash

Went to Ashcroft's 70th birthday party at the Grosvenor House Hotel on Park Lane last night. It was absolutely spectacular and must have cost a fortune, but then again, he very nearly didn't make it to seventy after falling seriously ill last year.

He played up his Bond villain image by hiring an actor to play Blofeld stroking a white cat in the corner, with a couple of appropriately sexy girls in attendance. I had my picture taken next to Ernst Stavro, of course.

As guests filed in to the lavishly decorated venue, actors dressed as paper boys handed out mocked-up newspapers with headlines threatening to sue anyone who suggests he's reached such a grand old age, a play on his reputation for pursuing his foes through the courts. Then everyone was ushered into a low-lit reception room for pre-dinner cocktails, champagne and caviar.

David Cameron had issued a fatwa forbidding any Tories from attending, following his fall-out with Ashy over that business with a pig's head. Naturally, any Tory worth their salt was there anyway, including Theresa May, William Hague and Iain Duncan Smith.

The seating plan was deliberately designed to cause trouble. In a classic Ashcroft ruse, Boris Johnson was mischievously positioned between two stunning models, while May was put on the same table as David Davis, with whom she does not exactly see eye to eye. The compère was Rory Bremner, who took the piss out of Boris for his dithering over Brexit. Adopting Johnson's plummy Old Etonian tones, he mocked, 'It's a cause I've believed in for – what day is it now? Saturday? Almost two weeks.' Wiggy and I were on some sort of naughty table with Richard Desmond and Nigel Farage as well as a Miss World and, to stir the pot, some of Elliott's biggest donors. We were ringed by Cabinet ministers on surrounding tables. Poor Elliott was too far away to hear what we were saying, and had to sweat it out while I made small talk with Peter Cruddas and Bob Edmiston, two of the wealthy businessmen bankrolling Vote Leave. We were pleased to see that Mark Wallace, who writes endless glowing pieces about Vote Leave on Ashcroft's website, ConservativeHome, was seated somewhere near the exit.

I also had a nice chat with Peter Lilley and his wife Gail, who is an artist. Back in the 1990s, when Wiggy was working for Peter, he claims to have offered himself up as a model for her to practise her life drawing technique. To his chagrin, she seemed to have no recollection of this episode or if any painting resulted. She can't have been that desperate.

The fun and games went on into the small hours, with entertainment from soprano Katherine Jenkins, Denise van Outen, a magician off *Britain's Got Talent* and Michael Bublé.

My 50th's in ten days. I will not try to compete.

14 MARCH

Turkey can get stuffed

It's a slow burn, but people are beginning to wake up to the prospect of Turkey joining the EU. This is toxic for Remain and Nigel's very keen to push it.

I think most voters are very uncomfortable with the thought of a Muslim country becoming part of an organisation that enforces free movement between all member states.

Yet Cameron officially supports Turkey joining the EU. We need to hammer home the message that this could really happen.

We commissioned a poll, which the *Express* ran today, that confirmed the scale of unease among voters about the prospect of a country with a population of 77 million people being able to take advantage of our NHS and benefits system. A third of people we surveyed said they'd be more likely to vote to Leave if it looks like Turkey is joining the EU, including more than a quarter of those who currently want us to Remain. This is strong stuff.

I wrote a piece for the *Express* pointing out that Turkey's aggressive and paranoid dictatorship is being paid billions to speed up its entry to the EU, with Cameron one of its chief cheerleaders. President Erdoğan isn't just demanding suitcases of cash in return for doing something to stem the tide of migrants coming through Turkey to Europe, but also visa-free travel to the Schengen area and fast-track negotiations for EU membership. This is tantamount to a protection racket – and Brussels is forcing British taxpayers to cough up!

The Foreign Office told the *Express* it still supports Turkish membership despite having no idea how many immigrants would come here as a result. Privately, they like to brief journalists that it's all a clever ruse to keep the Turks on side in the Middle East. Too clever by half and far from convincing – it's not hard to dig up awkward video footage of Cameron lavishing praise on the Turks and saying how much he is looking forward to helping them join. Feeble protests that it's all a diplomatic game won't wash.

A royal encounter

Katya, Mrs Wiggy, Wiggy and I finally got to meet the Queen.

It was the Commonwealth Day reception at the Guildhall. I was genuinely over the moon to have been invited as a thank-you for all the support Wiggy and I had given to the Royal Commonwealth Society. A major part of our involvement in Brexit was because we value our historic global connections and believe the Commonwealth has a great future to play post the referendum.

Wiggy knows the Queen's assistant private secretary and she is entirely aware of our propensity for high jinks. We were under strict orders to behave, which we understood meant no talking about Brexit, and certainly no mention of the *Sun* splash the other day.

Various overseas dignitaries attended, including former Prime Ministers of Australia and New Zealand and Baroness Scotland, the Commonwealth Secretary General. I was first introduced to the Duke of Edinburgh, a man with a great sense of humour, who smiled as he shook my hand. Then the Queen arrived and began greeting guests. I was thrilled to meet Her Majesty, who thanked me for our work with the Commonwealth and charities, and we had a brief chat.

Her Majesty then turned to Wiggy, and they had quite a detailed discussion about Belize and why the Commonwealth still matters.

Lord Howell, who is president of the Royal Commonwealth Society, looked nervous, clearly fearing we were going to throw caution to the wind and attempt to engage her in a full-blooded Brexit debate. I didn't want to lose eye contact with HM, but I could see him bobbing up and down on his toes, braced for a diplomatic incident. I could also see Wiggy's friend from the royal household giving him daggers. I would never dream of embarrassing Her Majesty or the Duke; meeting them was genuinely one of the highlights of my life – a very proud moment that I will treasure.

Despite our schoolboy excitement, I'm proud to say we managed to behave.

We came away more convinced than ever that Commonwealth countries have a major role to play in Britain's future outside the EU.

16 MARCH

Butt out, Barack

Obama is paying us a visit next month. Not content with lining up the entire British establishment, Cameron is attempting to turn the referendum into a global stitch-up by getting all his G7 accomplices to wade in.

No doubt the British electorate can expected to be treated to some banal nonsense like 'when Britain succeeds, America succeeds', and 'Britain is stronger when we have a unified Europe' and a convenient glossing-over of the hypocrisy that no US President would ever be willing to cede power to a supranational Pan-American Union with its HQ somewhere like Guatemala City.

Six politicians (Kate Hoey, Nigel Farage, Bone and Pursglove, plus Kelvin Hopkins from Labour and Sammy Wilson from the DUP) have written the President an open letter telling him to butt out.

If he can't resist interfering, I suspect it will do the campaign for

Brexit nothing but good. If there's one thing the British are sick of, it's being dictated to by condescending US Presidents.

We told Obama: 'This is a chance for the British people to choose the path of their country. Interfering in our debate over national sovereignty would be an unfortunate milestone at the end of your term as President.'

How mediocre and disappointing he has been.

≈

On the sly, Kate has forwarded me a letter from Brendan Chilton to John Mills describing Vote Leave as 'the most disgusting people' he has ever encountered.

He told Mills:

> I cannot stay involved any more under these conditions.
>
> I'm no longer working I am simply spending my time managing argument after argument, dispute after dispute and lie after lie most of it as a direct consequence of the actions of those in Vote Leave. Our campaign has done no real work for weeks because of the crap they keep throwing at us.
>
> They are the most disgusting people and the foulest campaign I have ever encountered.
>
> I do not know how good Labour people can remain in Vote Leave. I really think you and all those remaining should resign from that group. They are treating all of us with utter contempt.

My own disdain for VL plumbed new depths after an unexpected visit from an 86-year-old concentration camp survivor who found refuge in Britain and made his fortune teaching children with special needs and producing books and toys that were successful worldwide. He wanted to help. He went down to the Leave.EU office and, by the by, told us he had also donated to VL. He says Elliott told him I am only interested in immigration and basically a racist.

17 MARCH

General alert

We've been pumping out social media tiles based on an article General Sir Mike Jackson did for the *Mail on Sunday* last weekend, in which he said the EU makes him 'bristle with indignation'.

Lovely quotes and just what you'd expect from a former para and head of the army. Unfortunately, despite the lively Eurosceptic language about his dismay at being 'hidebound by petty rules and regulations devised by unaccountable bureaucrats in Brussels', the General ultimately bottled it, saying he used to be a Leaver but is now going to vote Remain with a 'heavy heart' as he thinks the EU is good for our security.

Just another establishment figure playing it safe.

Still, his reluctant endorsement came with a clear admission about the loss of sovereignty, and an acknowledgement that people must vote for Brexit if restoring that sovereignty is their main concern. We pumped out selective quotes on social media tonight, and hope it gets a reaction.

~

Peter Bone has had a hilarious wind-up phone call from someone claiming to be Donald Trump, offering to fly us all to Florida for a meeting in his private jet. Kate did not quite see the funny side and told us to ignore it even if it really was The Donald. 'We have enough enemies,' she said. Lighten up!

18 MARCH

I loved the Mike Jackson social media quotes we've been posting and was very annoyed to discover they'd been taken down last night.

'Why is this?' I demanded.

A rather sheepish Pierre, our head of research, told me the General had called him yesterday and given him both barrels. He was furious that we made him look like an arch-Eurosceptic and browbeat Pierre into apologising and promising not to include him in any future social media posts.

'Why did you do that?' I demanded. We're not one of his soldiers and we don't take his orders! I told Pierre to ring the General and say we were putting it back up. 'Tell the General there's a chain of command and admit that you broke it,' I instructed.

It was a tetchy conversation which Pierre didn't enjoy, but I'm happy. The Remain campaign love quoting us out of context, saying, 'Leave campaigner admits X, Y, Z', so it's nice to be able to turn the tables for once.

Gerry emailed this evening to tell me that our warning to Obama has been picked up by ABC News. Good.

IDS gives Cameron two fingers

All hell has broken loose at Westminster. Iain Duncan Smith has finally had it with Cameron and Osborne and has stormed out of the Cabinet. They were about to make him the fall guy for a humiliating reversal on benefit cuts to the disabled and he finally blew.

By Westminster standards his resignation letter is devastating. He says:

> The latest changes to benefits to the disabled and the context in which they've been made are a compromise too far … they are not defensible in the way they were placed within a Budget that benefits higher earning taxpayers … I am unable to watch passively whilst certain policies are enacted in order to meet the fiscal self-imposed restraints that I believe are more and more perceived as distinctly political rather than in the national economic interest.

Kapow! Coming from a former party leader, this is weapons-grade. Now he's liberated, he can really hit the campaign trail.

19 MARCH

I was due to appear on *Marr* tomorrow but have been bumped in favour of IDS. Bloody hard for us non-politicians to get a look in sometimes.

I have been giving a lot of thought in recent weeks to the future of UKIP. Going to talk to Nigel about carrying on our Bristol operation after the referendum and switching it over to a relaunch of UKIP. I can put money in.

21 MARCH

Joining the Trots

We'll talk to just about anyone if it helps win this referendum, which is how Wiggy found himself nipping to north London – that great bastion of the proletariat – to hobnob with the Commies. Somehow, he'd fallen in with a bloke called John Sweeney, an old comrade of Jeremy Corbyn, who remembers campaigning with the future Labour leader against membership of the EEC back in 1975.

Sweeney has a reputation as something of a Godfather figure among old trade unionists, and is well tapped in to the leftie scene, not least in the People's Republic of Islington, where he's one of Jezza's constituents.

Of late, he's been telling people how surprised he is at the Labour leader's unconvincing 'conversion' to the Remain cause, and offered to introduce Wiggy to some kindred spirits who might back our designation bid.

It did not prove straightforward.

It transpired that, in addition to Corbyn's wing of the Labour Party, there are no fewer than three Red outfits devoted to class war and the struggle to end private property: the Trots, known as the Revolutionary Communist Party of Great Britain (getting a bit past it now); the original Communist Party of Great Britain (seen as rather right-wing for the real Islington vanguard); and Sweeney's allies, known as the New Communist Party.

'People's Front of Judea' springs to mind again, but that's the left for you.

Wiggy's (admittedly cursory) due diligence suggested that the New Communist Party were comically unashamed Stalinists. Nonetheless, he gamely scootered over to an Islington bar, where he was introduced to some comrades from the organisation.

I don't know if he was intimidated by the four Red Guards who pretty much had him surrounded in the back room of this place, but the evening did not go exactly to plan. In hindsight, Wiggy may not have been the most suitable choice of ambassador. Part of his misspent youth had been occupied traipsing behind the Iron Curtain with a backpack stuffed full of Western propaganda leaflets, and, while his natural charm is undeniable, he's not exactly a son of toil. I could just picture him breezing through and greeting these unreconstructed old revolutionaries with a cheery 'All right, chaps?', looking as out of place as if he had just sauntered in wearing a pith helmet at a jaunty angle.

Nonetheless, he deployed the diplomatic charm that enables him to sail through functions from the hallowed halls of the Foreign Office to the palaces of African despots, and soon had them eating out the palm of his hand. He told me proudly that he didn't even have to sing 'The Internationale'.

The bad news is that the night culminated with Wiggy coughing up a large amount of cash.

He told me that when he arrived at the venue, Sweeney's cronies thrust him a copy of their manifesto, while Sweeney himself sought to reassure them that their dapper visitor was not a member of the Conservative Party.

'He's got a bit of a posh voice, but I promise he's not a Tory,' John insisted.

The men looked sceptical, as well they might.

Once Wiggy had warmed them up, he waved our designation document beneath their faces, assuming they'd happily sign on the dotted line. We wanted the broadest possible church, after all, and you don't get more leftie than a Marxist-Leninist lot who think their main market rivals are wet-blanket revisionists.

At this point the evening became even more surreal. The New Communist Party was happy to be part of the struggle and sign up as brothers and sisters to our cause, but – much like Chris Montgomery from the DUP – they wanted cold, hard cash for their trouble.

Not collective payment, but £250 each. They also insisted that Wiggy join the party.

Sweeney helpfully explained that it would be a grand for the four members present, plus another grand for the wider party. Perhaps this included a small fee for his 'introduction'?

Having devoted an evening to the mission, Wiggy was loath to allow this relatively modest sum to derail him, and dutifully trotted off to the cashpoint, returning with the requested funds.

Having handed over the readies, he was duly signed up and, in return, they signed our designation document.

Now he's a fully paid-up, card-carrying Commie, so he won't be first against the wall when the revolution comes after all. Not till I grass him up, anyway.

~

We still have a huffing, puffing General giving us grief.

He's complained to the *Express*, who'd picked up on our tiles, and chewed their ears off until they printed a long whinge about how 'anyone seeing these posts would think that I supported the argument to leave the EU'.

Which is precisely our point.

I was not feeling the slightest repentant and told the team to stick to their guns.

'Retreat? Never!' I exclaimed, and got Wiggy to issue a punchy statement making our position crystal clear: 'We never actually say Sir Mike supports Brexit, we just cite things he has said on the issue, and which are on the public record. Far from apologise, we have issued a second post.'

Tice knows the General, so we made a vain attempt to use him to make peace. Jackson sniffily declined an invitation to lunch, whining about feeling 'badly misrepresented'.

Back in 1999 in the Kosovo War, when a gung-ho American General told him to clear out some Russian troops who were in the way at Pristina Airport, he had balls. 'I'm not going to start the Third World War for you,' he told the Yank. Now he claims to be hurt by a bit of gentle political knockabout. Pah!

22 MARCH

Elliott gets served

Wiggy and I are hardly wilting violets. We give it both barrels and expect a bit of blow-back. Sparring with politicians and the press is half the fun.

When it comes to our businesses, however, we have to be serious. We've spent decades building successful companies and when someone jeopardises our work, we have to act.

When you have shareholders, stakeholders, compliance laws, good practice reports and all that stuff, some accusations are more than just Westminster knockabout. Which is why I finally decided today to serve Elliott with a writ.

I already suspected him of bad-mouthing Tice in the City, so when I heard that he and Jenkin were still putting it about that I'm a racist homophobe and misuse personal data to boot, Bernard still wasn't having it.

I decided to sue the bugger – or at least scare him a bit – to teach him a lesson about responsibility.

With civil cases, you physically have to serve the writ to the person you're suing. It's practically a daily occurrence in Mayfair and I'm told it's partly why oligarchs have so much security, so that they can physically prevent plaintiffs from getting close enough to serve papers. Apparently Roman Abramovich doesn't do handshakes with Chelsea fans any more because he once got served by someone posing as a true blue supporter.

Near 5 Hertford Street is the Cartier boutique where Abramovich once denied being served a writ by the now-dead oligarch Boris Berezovsky. I'm told they had to show the CCTV footage in court to prove he'd been given the papers. (Roman was there with his detail, Boris turned up with his mob and the security guards had some sort of rugby scrum down in the middle of this luxury boutique until Boris got through to Roman, who promptly put his hands in his pockets. Anyway, you get the picture.)

I fancied reproducing a bit of this drama for Elliott's benefit, so I asked Mishcon's to serve him a writ for defamation.

Conscious we would need proof that he'd got the paperwork, I sent an undercover cameraman down to Elliott's office to record the episode.

The resulting footage is quite entertaining. Out comes Elliott for a cigarette, perching on a bench outside the office. As he puffs away, no doubt dreaming of the day he will ascend to greatness as Lord Elliott of Loserville, he is approached by a seemingly innocuous gentleman brandishing a document and asking if he's Matthew Elliott. He immediately looks suspicious and tries to demur. Then it all gets a bit Monty Python as the question is repeated, and Matthew actually denies being himself. Finally, our man says: 'I have information that you are indeed Matthew Elliott,' explaining that he has instructions to deliver the envelope. Elliott can't really refuse and the last image is of him with palm outstretched, looking apprehensive and bewildered.

That should shake him up a bit.

~

We have been getting our supporters to lobby the Electoral Commission endorsing our bid. Within two and a half hours 7,500 of them did so, successfully crashing the EC's servers. It's probably more emails than they've had in their whole history.

≈

It's my 50th today. No party for me. Wiggy and I have been hatching a plan for a joint bash at a beach hut in Cuba at some point after the referendum, but we've not had a minute to organise anything. At this rate we'll have to do it for our 60th.

23 MARCH

The people love Peter

The Hargreaves mailshot has started dropping through 8.1 million letterboxes, with a tear-off slip at the bottom to donate. Peter reminded people this was the biggest vote of their lives and set out his ten top reasons for leaving (his full list stretches to 115!). It's powerful stuff: 'I urge you to listen to real people and entrepreneurs who create wealth, not heads of big institutions whose cushy lives will be disrupted by change.'

Bang on message for our campaign of the people versus the elite.

Already, the public response has been fantastic: it has clearly struck a chord (mostly a good one). We are reaching an audience politicians ignore and dismiss. We've had thousands of responses and the website and call centre are in overdrive.

We emptied out the sacks of mail on the floor and had great fun sifting through them all. It was like being a child opening thousands of birthday cards. One cheque was for £3,000.

I reckon we will hit a million supporters within a few weeks.

The responses are not uniformly positive, however. A few people took the opportunity to inform us that they weren't convinced. One bloke even took time out of his (probably not very busy) day to send us a letter that read: 'I have attached a crude drawing of a cock with which you can go fuck yourself. Regards. A Remain voter.' Attached was a fairly impressive drawing of a handsome cockerel, alongside an image of the other kind of cock.

Keeping it classy.

Sticking it to the Electoral Commission

We are the real people's campaign. Our supporters have now sent 45,000 letters and emails to the Electoral Commission saying we deserve the official designation. Ordinary people trying to make their voice heard.

The Commission clearly found the whole exercise very distasteful and called the office begging us to stop the mailings. They made it clear that, as far as they're concerned, this mass support counts for nothing. So much for their prattle about the official designation going to whoever can command the 'widest range of support across the political spectrum'! I guess they'll just choose whichever campaign manages to sign up the greater number of Cabinet ministers, run by the people who can best navigate the Westminster cocktail party circuit. Which means we're fucked.

I fired back a letter telling them exactly what I thought of their disdain for ordinary voters. Tice did a Tice and told me to stop winding them up.

25 MARCH

Fisting for GO

Poor Peter Bone. Politics likes colourful characters but everything about him is grey, right down to his early career as a chartered accountant. In the Commons, he likes to reassure everyone that he's not as sad and lonely as he looks by making constant references to 'Mrs Bone'. (The one he keeps at home, not Pursglove.)

However, he looks so much like a lost extra from *The Addams Family* (somewhere between Lurch and Uncle Fester) that an audible groan can be heard whenever he gets up to speak. Even Cameron has taken the piss out of 'Bone groan's' domestic life, once complaining that he felt 'trying to give pleasure to Mrs Bone' had become 'a very big part' of his life.

Who knows whether Peter's tireless efforts to get us out of the EU are fully appreciated by his wife Jennie. What I can say is that they're widely appreciated elsewhere. Alongside support from the more predictable quarters, Grassroots Out is becoming a very broad church indeed, spawning all sorts of interesting offshoots, including Students 4 GO, LGBT 4 GO, Fishing 4 GO and even, apparently, an outfit called Fisting 4 GO! There was much hilarity in the office when this new 'affiliate' popped up online, prompting Wiggy to email Liz praising her for 'reaching the parts other campaigns dare not go'.

For once I had a sense of humour failure, and told our social media team to get on to Facebook and ask them to take it down. Wasn't entirely optimistic, but by the end of the day I'm relieved to say the offending 'affiliate' had vanished.

Presumably it's a piss-take from the other side. If so, it's a good one. If it's genuine, well, let's just say I'll leave them to themselves.

28 MARCH

Neil Kinnock is a bellend

The Guardian has had a go at us for employing Eastern Europeans in the Bristol call centre. It quotes a spokesman for Remain saying we're 'beyond parody', though it does graciously concede that my beef is with uncontrolled immigration, not with all immigration in general.

That didn't stop Neil Kinnock weighing in, accusing me of 'hypocrisy' for running a 'campaign based on division and demonisation' while employing EU workers. Showing that old age hasn't diminished his propensity to be a total twit, he claimed I should hang my head in shame.

I regard it as a badge of honour to be slagged off by the bellend of all bellends, a man who enriched himself for years by scoffing at the Brussels trough, along with most of his family.

Happily, *The Guardian* also talked to one of our EU workers, an excellent fellow from Slovakia called Rudolph Svat. No doubt to the disappointment of the journalist, he said he thought we should leave the EU and bring in proper border controls.

Good lad.

29 MARCH

I have sent Andrew Pierce some Ipsos MORI polling showing that Farage is the most popular of all the party leaders, with a higher satisfaction rating than Cameron, Corbyn or the unheralded and unknown Tim Farron. Good news for Nigel, though I admit it's not too hard to be more popular than that grisly trio.

We've booked the Leave.EU campaign truck to deliver our designation application to the Electoral Commission the day after tomorrow. Should be fun.

30 MARCH

Liz has done a superb job on our designation document for the Electoral Commission. Even Boneglove contributed positively in the end.

Meanwhile, donations and letters prompted by Peter's leaflet are still pouring in. It's so encouraging and great for identifying potential helpers.

A pensioner called Ruth wrote saying she couldn't afford to donate, but wished us all the best: 'Have my vote to leave by all means – if I could I would definitely make a donation. Good luck and blessings for people with common sense!'

Another lady called Val said she was 'disabled, blind in one eye, limited sight in the other and profoundly deaf'.

'I have always voted Conservative, but feel that we have lost our way. The Prime Minister doesn't listen to those of us who didn't want to go into the EU in the first place,' she said.

Indeed.

31 MARCH

The big handover – at last

We've finally handed in the GO application for official designation. Now we just have to await the outcome. I was overseas on business, having felt I'd done everything I could, and left the final arrangements to Liz.

We packed our Leave.EU bus full of supporters and drove to the Commission's office to deliver it, accompanied by the GO campaign truck, which, judging from the photos, looked great.

I had wanted to include some material about the behaviour of Elliott and Cummings. I think the way they've conducted themselves over the past few months shows they are utterly unworthy of the massive responsibility of running the official Leave campaign. In the end, though, Boneglove and others convinced me that we should maintain the moral high ground and say nothing about all this.

Let's play the ball, not the man!

PART 4:
APRIL–MAY 2016

APRIL 2016

1 APRIL

The real April Fools

I could hardly believe my ears when I heard the EC changed the deadline from 5 p.m. to midnight to accommodate the incompetence of VL.

Apparently, Elliott's application was a shambles. An early attempt to just rush *something* in by five seems to have ended in farce, with the flunky tasked with sprinting round to the EC building not quite making it in time and bouncing off the glass doors, which had been locked fast. They eventually made their submission just a few minutes before the new midnight deadline, but it had to be a bodge job. Ours is meticulous. It'll pay off.

The EC weren't the only April Fools today. The Education Secretary Nicky Morgan has popped up with an embarrassing speech designed to persuade young people to back Remain.

It reminded everyone what a strange, out-of-touch bubble-dweller she is. She described today's teenagers as 'the generation of eBay' – founded twenty years ago – and explained that they communicate using strange things called 'the Facebooks and the Twitters'. Presumably, we are to believe that these would go into meltdown if it weren't for Brussels. She even started rambling about the supposed threat to inter-railing, which, as we were quick to point out, has sod all to do with Brussels and began the year before we joined the Common Market. She really did say all that.

April Fools, the lot of them. They've gone from Project Fear to Project Farce. Who needs satire?

I'm in the States – it's beautiful in Miami, very hot.

3 APRIL

Farage has gone over to Amsterdam to do something for the campaign – or that's his excuse. I told him not to go crazy. I just did a five-mile run and my new fitness drive is going well. Nigel replied that he wouldn't make 100 yards at jogging pace.

4 APRIL

BPop life support

Chased the office for an update on BPop Live, as we need to focus on getting tickets going out and cash coming in. I wish I hadn't. Total embarrassment. There has been a meeting with Paul Ashford, editorial director for the *Express* titles, along with his editors at the *Express*, the *Star* and *OK!*. Louis Brown from Metropolis, the promoters, also popped along and was waxing lyrical about how great it was all going because Sigma, Electric Swing Circus and a load of other amazing acts were going to reach the youth vote like never before. The *Express* lot were keen to do whatever they could to help and had ideas for exclusive artist profiles, advertising, ticket giveaways – the works. Our press release had talked about 'some of Britain's hottest artists'.

They were all getting quite carried away, fantasising about a kind of Union Jack-themed Glastonbury, with Kate Hoey on the mic yelling, 'Good evening *Birmingham!*' to deafening chants of '*Brexit, Brexit*' from the crowd as Nigel got down to the drum and bass. Then, right in the middle of the meeting, Wiggy gets a text from the press office: 'Sigma's pulled out.'

Our crew nodded and smiled their way through the rest of the ordeal and then retreated to a nearby pub to regroup. It turned out Jim Waterson from BuzzFeed was ringing round asking the bands for comment on why they support Brexit and why they were playing at an 'anti-EU Nigel Farage rally'. Predictable really.

Under the slightest bit of pressure they all panicked and declared they'd be having nothing to do with it.

The bad news kept coming. *The Times* picked up the story. *NME* ran an article saying 'Bands playing anti EU gig say they don't support Brexit'.

A couple of days earlier they were all enthusiastic. Now you can't see them for dust. Electric Swing Circus – out. One of the band, Tom Hyland, said they were 'not pro-Brexit' and 'generally pro-EU'. DJ Luck and MC Neat – out. Their spokesman said they 'didn't even know it was about that [the referendum] to be honest'. Enough, enough, enough.

But no, there was more. Ella Eyre – out. 'She isn't playing and never confirmed,' said her publicist.

By the end of the day we were left with the '90s dance duo Phats and Small, who didn't care where the money was coming from as long as they got paid.

Somehow, I doubt their one big hit 'Turn Around' – from 1999 – will carry this thing on its own.

Louis talks the talk, but when it comes down to actually producing results, he turns out to be as much use as a handbrake on a canoe. He'd kept going on about how keeping the performers happy was his chief concern and primary responsibility. What performers?

Now he was panicking.

'How can we get the artists back on side?' he asked lamely.

'Don't know, mate.' Wiggy told him. 'That's supposed to be your job. We don't even have contacts for these guys.'

I've got a Plan B: just have Nigel, Boris and The Who.

5 APRIL

The Panama Papers

The German newspaper *Süddeutsche Zeitung* has been leaked millions of files from a Panama-based law firm revealing how the rich use offshore tax regimes to avoid tax.

The Guardian is so desperate to link it to Brexit that they've tried to implicate me. They've found my name listed as a shareholder of a firm called PRI Holdings and now I've got the press on my back. They actually worded it quite carefully to say I have an offshore company, which is true, that owns a business in South Africa. What's that got to do with Panama?

As it happened, I was thousands of miles away on a boat in the British Virgin Islands and had absolutely no idea what was going on.

I picked up a message from Pierce, who was muttering something about 'Panama Papers' and asking me to come on his LBC show.

'Panama what?' I asked, when I finally got a mobile signal.

At first I denied having anything to do with it as it just didn't ring any bells. However, I got someone at the office to look into it and discovered that we did actually use a law firm to set up a couple of companies for a project that didn't end up happening. It was all years ago and the firms were just sitting there dormant, which is why I'd forgotten about it.

Pierce's producer asked me where I was calling from and when I said it was the British Virgin Islands – the offshore haven of all offshore havens – she was very amused.

Pierce called Wiggy, only to discover he was in Belize, which is also somewhat dubious when it comes to its tax regime. He asked where Richard Desmond was, as he couldn't get hold of him.

Bahamas. Meanwhile, Ashcroft – whose name was also dragged in to the exposé even though he had nothing to do with it – was in Belize. *The Guardian* probably missed a trick there – they could have done a very funny graphic about shady men in sunny places.

Wiggy and I now have to try to salvage something from the wreckage of BPop. He's going to check if the artists owe us anything for cancelling – if they had even signed anything – and if so how much. It may be better to take the loss on hiring the venue, hold a rally anyway and see if the cancellation money covers the cost.

We have comprehensively overspent on the campaign anyway – got to review the numbers on Monday.

Andy blubbered that whenever we go abroad the shit hits the fan.

Kate asked if a Huffington Post story about me being the next chairman of UKIP is right. Not likely. But I like the tease.

So much for a holiday.

6 APRIL

Boneglove keep demanding more resources and pissing people off. They think they should be in control of everything, like all their kind. Bloody Tories – echoes of Vote Leave.

Extremely reluctantly, I have written to Elliott to tell him that against my better judgement I've instructed Mishcon to drop the litigation against him. But I did let him know just how much damage he's been causing:

> With two months to go the last thing we want is ongoing litigation that takes away the focus on the campaign. I hope on the 14th the Electoral Commission will make the right decision but I think I can say that your hubris, arrogance and ego has done more to help the IN campaign than any other person.

That was the nice version.

7 APRIL

Dave's dodgy dossier

Cameron is spending £9 million of taxpayers' money on a grubby piece of propaganda – which he describes as an 'information leaflet' – on why we need to stay in the EU. It's going to every home in the country.

This is outrageous. The referendum rules give each side one funded mailshot, but as those rules haven't kicked in yet, he's abusing his position to raid the public purse so Remain can have another freebie on the house.

Cameron is shamelessly loading the gloves because he knows his case is so weak. The leaflet makes no pretence at being balanced. It includes the shop-worn claim that 'over three million UK jobs are linked to exports to the EU', with the strong hint that three million people can expect to lose their jobs. Wiggy banged out a statement labelling it 'pure fiction'.

Jack Montgomery and Jordan Ryan knocked up a mock propaganda poster with the Prime Minister as 'Kim Jong Cameron' for our social media effort, which has been picked up by the Russian state television channel RT and some of the big political websites. It's already been shared over 10,000 times and reached nearly a million people online, so we've obviously struck a chord.

Cameron is treating the Exchequer as his political piggy bank, while we're doing this the hard, honest way.

Our supposedly neutral civil service should never have let Cameron drag them in, but they're in hock to the Brussels racket. Judging by the reaction to 'Kim Jong Cameron', though, it's going to backfire.

10 APRIL

Out for the count

Sometimes Europhiles do our job for us. My new hero is a German toff I had never heard of till today. Count Alexander Lambsdorff, the Vice-President of the European Parliament, has said Cameron's so-called 'special status' deal with Brussels is worthless. According to the Count, it's 'in no way a document of the EU, but a text of hybrid character, which is unspecified and not legally binding … the whole thing is nothing more than a deal that has been hammered out down the local bazaar'. Fantastic!

I want everyone to see this damning assessment of Scam Cam's dodgy deal. The words come from somebody in a position to know. The Eurocrats' idea of 'special status' for Britain is subjugation with benefits.

12 APRIL

The Electoral Commission discredited

Just when we thought they couldn't get any more biased, someone at the EC has given the nod to VL that they've got the designation – two days before the official announcement.

First they extend the deadline, then they give them the designation, then they leak it. It's the clearest proof we've seen in this farce of establishment mates fixing things for each other.

There is no reason to doubt it is true. The alarm bells started ringing earlier this evening when we noticed a tweet from Steve Bell, a Tory apparatchik who serves as president of the party's National Convention and is tight with Elliott and Cummings.

'Congratulations to Vote Leave on winning the official designation', was his message.

I'm now almost resigned to this being a complete stitch-up – what more evidence do we need? Still, we're not going to take it lying down, and issued a punchy statement questioning the credibility of the whole process.

> From the very beginning a number of Vote Leave officials and supporters (Douglas Carswell MP in particular) have

been saying the decision had been taken and this premature tweet suggests this might the case.

Steve Bell has to fully explain himself.

It's worth noting Vote Leave has arranged eight events on Friday with cabinet ministers to take advantage of the announcement and is holding a dinner with Boris Johnson tonight.

I know the Conservative Party is one of entitlement but celebrating two days early takes the biscuit. As an example of my generous magnanimity I've just put in a telephone bid at the fund-raising dinner for a game of tennis with Boris.

Mark Fullbrook's been in touch, saying we should consider a judicial review, as the decision has clearly been taken without a formal board meeting. Too bloody right we should.

13 APRIL

Shafted

It's official. We've been shafted. The designation has gone to Elliott. The Electoral Commission announced it today. It is a blow to us, but it could be an even worse blow to Britain's chances of leaving the EU. It's also a travesty. GO is the genuine cross-party people's campaign. Vote Leave is run by Tory wonks and fronted by Tory Cabinet ministers, with Gisela Stuart tossed in for window-dressing. They can never reach the Labour voters we need to convince.

Farage was much too early to concede, tweeting peace and love to Vote Leave.

'I congratulate @vote_leave on getting designation,' he announced.

I texted him saying I was 'v disappointed in your statement', but he didn't reply.

Faisal Islam asked if we are going to challenge the designation in court. Yes, I told him, it is 'clearly political corruption'.

If there was one thing that could make the day worse, it was the Norths chipping in. I cracked and told Pete to fuck off on Twitter. We've since had an angry email from Richard telling us: 'Face it – your application was thin [we sent the EC over a dozen boxes of documents], amateur and deserved to lose'.

That family really are poison-pen merchants of the worst kind.

Thank God for Mr Can-Do, Gerry Gunster. He's so positive. He emailed me saying: 'You can still claim victory on June 23 with or without the designation. We need to act like we are still the lead [campaign group]. And if you build a following of millions and millions you can do it.'

He is right. We are the ones with the mass support and as far as those people are concerned, it's us taking the lead, not VL. We won't let that change.

To show that we weren't going to let this get us down, Wiggy and I posed for a cheesy selfie, grinning with our thumbs up. But the truth is we're both depressed. We're off to drown our sorrows.

14 APRIL

Woke up feeling like death. We went on something of a bender.

I don't like to lose, so we sallied forth with some trusted confidants to numb the pain of defeat in the best way we know.

We started at Hertford Street, but the drunker we got, the lower our standards sank. Wiggy wimped out before things got too debauched, which was a little uncharacteristic. Before I knew it, I found myself in a strip club with my South African friend Kobus Coetzee, who was making me even more depressed by saying I should just abandon the whole campaign.

'I don't know why you want to keep going if you're not getting designation,' he drawled. 'It's like coming to a party without a date.'

He thinks Wiggy and I should concentrate on making money, not spending it, but some things matter more than pounds and pence.

The more he harped on, the more whisky I drank. Last orders

were no obstacle – we just kept finding somewhere else. I'm sorry to report that our last stop was a sleazy gay bar in Soho, the only place still open for business at 5 a.m. I finally staggered back to Claridge's at 6 a.m.

A couple of hours later I was woken by a call from Nigel wanting lunch. I wanted to die. I groaned something like 'Isss not happ-ennnin,' but he wouldn't stop talking.

It turned out I'd sent him a few slightly drunk messages last night along the lines of 'Never forget you are a frickin' hero!'

My head was splitting so I told him to call Wiggy, who was taking the loss even worse than I was. Then I switched off the phone and went back to sleep.

Eventually everyone convened in Claridge's at around 4 p.m. – me, Wiggy, Nigel and Andrew Reid, one of our lawyers. I was barely hanging in there, but managed to pull myself together enough to have a reasonably serious conversation. We had to discuss whether we were indeed going to take the decision to a judicial review.

Nigel was firmly against. 'You've got to let it go now,' he said firmly. 'If we challenge the designation we are just going to look like sore losers.'

Tice agreed.

'Bad optics,' he said grimly, lips pursed. Politicians can only ever think about 'optics'. Tice is turning into one of them.

Reid was much more bullish. He'd talked to Mishcon and there could be an open-and-shut case because of some shenanigans at the EC. Apparently someone who'd initially withdrawn from the room when they were making the decision because of a conflict of inter-est ended up casting the deciding vote.

We were buoyed by this and keen to keep our options open, so we issued a statement suggesting we were going to fight it hard. But then everyone on Twitter, even people who usually love us, started piling in, telling us we were stupid for even considering it. It also emerged that Mishcon's advice was not as clear-cut as we'd assumed. They were now saying that overturning the decision could mean the whole referendum schedule being derailed, which would have caused complete panic and we'd have got the blame. We backtracked and told the press we were waiting for our lawyers' views, but we'd already decided to fold.

I am doing my best to look on the bright side. In a way, we can be even more powerful now. We don't have to pander to Cabinet ministers, never mind the tedious Boneglove duo, and can run the campaign the way we want. Official approval is not our style anyway. Let the insiders stick together. We're on the outside, where we belong.

Andy Wigolo

The Electoral Commission weren't the only people who had it in for us today. When I was at my grisly worst, Andy emailed me one word – 'HELP' – above a long missive from Dominic Kennedy at *The Times*. And, oh God, it got worse. The gigolo story was back to haunt us.

Basically, Kennedy had been on a general muckrake, trying to find everything he could on just about any foreigner we'd ever known so he could make a fuss about 'overseas influence' on our campaign.

He was planning to run a load of nonsense about me being married to a Russian who has 'MI5' in her car number plate – obviously a spy, then. Jim Mellon lives on the Isle of Man (shock!), Wiggy works for the Belize government (blimey!), and so on.

Then, he managed to dig up the gigolo saga – and what a tangled tale it is.

Back in the mid-1990s, Andy worked for a massively off-the-wall late-night TV programme called the *James Whale Radio Show*. They decided to do an 'investigation' into 'the male escort industry' and Wiggy was duly dispatched to pose as the man for hire. The slight problem was that it meant moonlighting from his day job running a think tank, where he got to hobnob with the senior ranks of the Conservative Party. The *Sunday Mirror* heard what he was up to and did what any self-respecting tabloid would do: dispatched a foxy female news reporter to honey-trap the honey-trapper.

That weekend, Wiggy duly found his grinning mug all over the paper under the headline 'Tory Mr Fix-It Is £1,000 Sex Stud' – although he likes to claim the reporter was given a freebie.

In the normal scheme of things he likes nothing more than regaling an incredulous audience with this yarn over a few drinks. He thinks it gives him a certain mystique. But seeing the 25-year-old story in black and white in tomorrow's *Times* is another matter. It's not a great look for business or for the campaign, and it's certainly not going to amuse his wife Cath, who can do without getting scandalised side-eye at the school gates. We had to act.

The result is that another fat bill from Mishcon de Reya will be heading our way. Wiggy had to spend half the afternoon briefing the lawyers on the phone in very serious tone. Mishcon's had been his lawyers when the story first rolled round and were fully aware of the details: no, he'd never been a £1,000-a-night escort, and no, he hadn't been paid vast sums of money to take the virginity of an Arab girl as her 16th birthday present, as the original *Sunday Mirror* 'scoop' suggested.

In the end, Mishcon fired off an urgent missive to *Times* editor John Witherow, making it clear the whole thing was nonsense and threatening to sue.

There is a curious sequel to the gigolo saga which I suspect *The Times* won't run tomorrow.

During that same colourful period in Wiggy's life, a young *Times* journalist by the name of Michael Gove falsely accused him of hawking stories about sleazy Tories to the tabloids. This was at the height of John Major's ill-fated 'back to basics' campaign promoting traditional family values, so tittle-tattle about politicians with their pants down was gold dust.

Gove stuck the allegation into a biography he was writing of Michael Portillo, seen by some as the party's great hope at the time. This time Wiggy did sue – and won. The publishers had already printed the book and the whole thing had to be pulped, at a personal cost to young Gove (or so Wiggy claims) of £10,000.

Given Gove's Vote Leave affiliation and the *Times* connection, it didn't take Wiggy more than two minutes to put two and two together. He's convinced this whole story is a Cummings/Gove job.

Farage rang this evening, ostensibly to cheer him up, but really just to tease.

'I'm going to start calling you Deuce Wigalow,' he threatened, referring to the title character of a 1999 comedy about a rent boy. I think the nickname is going to stick.

15 APRIL

Witherow was not remotely rattled by the Mishcon letter and *The Times* has published the story anyway.

He is a stubborn bastard from South Africa, a grump with a bit of swagger – I come across his type all the time on the Veld.

The headline was about Jim – 'Millionaire backer for Leave does not have right to vote'. They stirred in some predictable bollocks about me and Katya: 'Banks is the son-in-law of a former state official in Russia ... His Russian wife, who was once targeted by Special Branch, uses the numbers 007 in her email address', though they left out the bit about the number plate.

None of it matters, but it does make Wiggy look dodgy. They ran all his denials but made them sound pretty flaky. I suspect Andy squared everything with Cath last night because he seemed fairly relaxed, though he may have been putting a brave face on things.

A flea in the ear

Whether it's party leaders whose time is up or backbenchers who defy the whip, the Tories like sending 'men in grey suits' to sort things out.

Today Vote Leave tried the same technique on us.

My heart sank when I heard that the dismal Leader of the House of Commons Chris Grayling, the greyest of the grey, wanted to come to Lysander House to talk about how we can work together in the next few weeks. When I see him on TV, he has the same effect on me as one of those Dementors from *Harry Potter* – I can feel all the life just draining right out of me. How much worse will the effect be in real life?

He duly appeared this morning and I did my level best not to show that being in his presence was easing me little by little into a mini-coma. Within about thirty seconds, it became apparent that his mission was to whip us into line. When I clicked, I was delighted. It was an opportunity for some mischief.

'You're very close to Nigel Farage aren't you?' he asked, by way of an opening gambit.

'Yes,' I replied.

'Well, we've all got to work together now on the campaign,' Grayling instructed, and drearily recited the Vote Leave mantra: no talking about immigration. He droned on for a while, making it clear that Vote Leave won't be campaigning on the issues that really interest people, just regurgitating a free-market spiel about the wonders of globalisation and how Europe is holding us back.

After five minutes of this, I was entering what people who meditate call the 'Delta' stage, when your brain waves become so slow you are essentially asleep. I let it all wash over me, smiling occasionally, just to reassure him I was still awake.

Finally, he stopped talking, at which point I suddenly jolted back to life. By now he was already looking at his watch, as if he had another appointment. So, just to piss him off, I made him sit for two and a half hours while I gave him a taste of his own medicine, jabbering on about anything and everything I could think of.

I started with Conservative education policy, a conversation I succeeded in stringing out for an eternity, before moving him on to detailed discussions about the challenges facing other departments.

It seemed to put him in reflective mood, and he began complaining about the travails of his job.

'You don't know what it's like to be a minister,' he said at one point. 'You can't get anything done. You try to cut anything and they stop you… It's just not as easy as you think. You're just a businessman,' and all that patronising kind of stuff you get from politicians.

Eventually I ran out of steam and decided to let him go.

But the more I thought about it, the more annoyed I became that Vote Leave was now trying to dictate our approach.

We might yet have gone our separate ways on civilised terms, had it not been for his parting shot.

'Well, are you going to try and control Nigel? You've got to try,' he enquired, as I walked him to the car park.

'Absolutely not,' I replied, bristling. 'How dare you come to my office and tell me "Oh, you've got to control Nigel"?!'

'I just wasted my whole last three hours, didn't I?' he asked, looking greyer than ever.

'Yeah, pretty much!' I replied brightly. 'There's your car.' I gestured at the vehicle, like I was swatting away a fly. 'There you go, get out.'

So I basically told him to fuck off.

Texted Nigel straight away to tell him what had happened, informing him that I'd sent Grayling away 'with a flea in his ear'.

At least we now have confirmation – as if there has ever been any doubt – that they plan to airbrush Nigel out of this referendum campaign. Good luck to Vote Leave with that.

≈

Far from bringing Nigel under control, I have been giving him big ideas. I have told him I'm ready to put £10 million into the new plan. It's to develop a popular political movement along the lines of Beppe Grillo's incredibly successful Five Star Movement in Italy. Emailed him with my vision: 'Let's subtly delink from UKIP, build your brand and we will start building Leave.EU … In my business career the best things happen when you let go of the past. Hard for you, Nigel, but needed to move up a level!'

I got no reply except a thank-you – unsurprising perhaps.

I've been trying not to show it, but I'd be lying if I said I haven't been feeling quite down about the EC's decision.

Late tonight, I just let it all flood out in an email to Kate Hoey. 'It's difficult to stomach,' I told her.

People brought up of a certain generation tend to be shocked and the blatant corruption shown just isn't British.

Kate, if I have ever been more angry I certainly can't remember it. We politely showed [Grayling] the door and said there will be no contact with VL and we will run our campaign – our way.

On a personal note I want to thank you and all the Labour people for being decent [and] straightforward.

At least we can count on her.

16 APRIL

We put together a funny newspaper ad on the 'people versus the elite' theme, showing a money-grubbing, Tory-looking wannabe banker with a cigar and a top hat. It takes the piss out of the Remain campaign being in the pay of Goldman Sachs and JP Morgan, whose ad said we make billions out of the EU. But the *Mail* are refusing to run it. Strange!

In all the drama last week, I forgot to mention that Corbyn finally made an effort to persuade people he supports Remain. He was useless, mouthing his half-hearted support through gritted teeth. He was standing against an infernal-looking red backdrop, with the floor lights along the bottom creating a weird optical illusion that looked like licking flames.

'Poor Jez looks like he's in his own personal hell murmuring EU propaganda to appease Blairite MPs', we tweeted.

Everyone knows he's been a lifelong opponent of the undemocratic EU and, in private at least, he still is. This speech didn't fool anyone.

If Jeremy really wanted to make people support something, he wouldn't tell them to accept it 'warts and all'. Jez also brought up George Orwell's Ministry of Truth from 1984. Sure, he was talking about it being based on Senate House, the London University building where he gave the speech. But it reminded everyone of the EU. I suspect he was hoping it would. Amusingly, Labour HQ has done its own Ministry of Truth job on his website, throwing every nasty thing he's ever said about the EU down the memory hole.

17 APRIL

Lucy Fisher asked if we'd binned BPop Live. Looks like tickets are no longer on sale. Last time I checked, it's still staggering on.

18 APRIL

When Wiggy walked into the London office this morning he came face to face with a huge Photoshopped image of himself sporting nothing but a pair of tighty-whitey Calvin Klein underpants.

The boys in the press office had Photoshopped his grinning mug onto some bronzed Chippendale with a gleaming six-pack, superimposing the words: 'Andrew Wigolo. It's his business doing pleasure with you.'

A heartbeat later, in walks Tice. Confronted by this ludicrous image of our head of comms (and having been on the receiving end of his teasing often enough), he roared with laughter, which just goes to show how far he's come in the past few months.

Our Belizean bombshell struggled to retain an appearance of dignity and good humour – this is one funny picture we won't be tweeting, for a change.

An awkward triumph in Stoke

A final sell-out rally for GO this evening, this time at the Victoria Halls in Stoke-on-Trent. Hundreds of people turned up. In public, it was a triumph. Behind the scenes, there was so much grief the wheels nearly came off.

We trailed it in the papers, Sky carried it live and it was number one story on the BBC's *News at Ten* and featured on ITV too.

It shows how strong our support is on the ground that with only three days' notice our events team can rustle up a gig like this. Our rivals think about it, have lots of meetings, think about it a bit more, have another meeting… We just do it.

That said, the event did involve Grayling: for us, it was an opportunity to arrange Nigel's first public collaboration with a Cabinet minister; for Grayling, it was an opportunity to try to stay relevant now that VL was pushing him aside for racier, sexier Tories like Boris Johnson and Michael Gove (groan). It had all been arranged prior to our little spat, so the atmosphere was somewhat delicate.

I had no plans to be civil to Grayling just because we had this one final event to get through. So when he and Nick Wood had the brass neck to come over to me after the event, wanting to shake my hand, I turned my back.

'Why do you have to be so aggressive?' Nigel demanded, when they were out of earshot.

'Nigel, I'm being aggressive on your behalf. These guys are just out to shaft us,' I replied defensively.

The poor bugger drew a short straw and somehow found himself having to share a car with Grayling all the way back to London. Must have been a fun ride.

≈

Osborne has issued his most ridiculous forecast yet of what will happen after Brexit, shambled together by his supposedly impartial researchers. After an orgy of fantasy number crunching, they have predicted that, abracadabra, the British economy will be 6 per cent smaller in 2030, equivalent to £4,300 per household, if we vote to leave than if we stay. It's laughable that a man who can't forecast six months down the line believes he can peer fourteen years into the future. He claims that leaving will be the 'most extraordinary self-inflicted wound', but our press team have been lampooning him as 'Mystic Gideon' and drawing attention to his less-than-clairvoyant record of predictions.

Every time he opens his mouth it helps us.

19 APRIL

Put my foot in it a bit after hitting 'Reply all' on some ranting correspondence from Jayne Adye, the slightly loopy director of the 'Get
Britain Out' group for Toby Blackwell.

Periodically, we bring people from all these smaller outfits together to try to co-ordinate efforts.

Unfortunately, the meetings are usually a waste of time, with endless pedantic wrangling over the minutiae of the previous meetings'
minutes and circular discussions about hare-brained schemes.

After today's tedious session, our head of press Brian Monteith
had Jayne on his back, complaining that the agenda was too basic
and the minutes for the previous meeting were not transcribed in
enough excruciating detail for her liking.

'Jayne is one of the few people that would make me vote IN,'
I told Brian, accidentally cc-ing all my contacts.

Shortly afterwards, I received a hysterical missive, quite dispro-
portionate to my minor offence.

> Arron
> Thank you for your strange email below!!!
>
> PLEASE Note – I was not so unprofessional to 'Reply to All'
> following your further insulting email! IE after all the others …
>
> I am not sure what you meant Arron – especially as you
> copied your insulting email to the whole Board.
>
> I am NOT FOLLOWING SUIT IE I am not copying
> your UNProfessionalism as I have deleted recipients outside
> OUR close group with Toby!
>
> I am acting under the instructions of Toby!
>
> It seems you are insulting me yet again – not for the first
> time.
>
> How many of your leaflets ended up in bins Arron – or
> loo paper…
>
> They did not get you designation and I raised a VERY
> understandable query:

Leave.EU LOST the designation.

Is the meeting following the lost designation still going ahead?

No Agenda or revised Minutes received.

If this makes you want to vote to Remain IN the EU Arron – Good Luck to you – I never understood why you were in this OUT camp anyway – apart from raising your own personal profile once 'you' felt Hague 'insulted' you.

You do not understand politics OR real people Arron.

So please stop insulting me – and praising me when it suits your own end game!

See you tomorrow Brian.

Jayne

Touched a nerve, I think. Whoops!

21 APRIL

Movie tussles

Martin Durkin and the team doing *Brexit: The Movie* have come back to us. Surprise, surprise, they want more cash. Apparently Vote Leave, who they previously claimed not to be tied up with, have now 'let them down'. So Andy and I are forking out another £55,000 out of our own pockets as we want it done right. We're going to book slots in cinemas and get newspapers and political websites to run excerpts. We're working with the *Express* and the *Star* to produce a CD giveaway with every copy of the papers. If we get it right, it will be the main broadcast of the campaign.

But the old problems haven't gone away. Durkin's lot don't seem to want to talk about Nigel or about immigration. Ominously, Dan Hannan, Douglas Carswell and Steve Baker are closely involved, and those three are obviously elbow-deep in Cummings, Elliott and the rest of their gang.

Our point man on this is Jack Montgomery from the press office, who says Durkin's lot are hardcore *Atlas Shrugged* types and thinks they're going to use our money to preach a libertarian sermon. He's trying to get them to see sense.

'We're not going to reach the people we need to reach if you start going off on one about how Brexit is an opportunity to deregulate the banks and flood the country with cheap Chinese steel,' he warned them.

Hunter DuBose, a caricaturish American with a toothsome grin fixed permanently on his face, assured Jack that they knew this would have to be 'almost a film they wouldn't enjoy themselves', with immigration and the like featuring prominently, but we think it's bullshit.

I called Martin personally to make sure he'd got the message.

'We're not funding a Vote Leave movie,' I stressed.

'No, no, no, it's not like that at all. They've let us down so much,' he protested.

He assured me all of our concerns will be addressed.

I pushed him to show us a rough cut, but was fobbed off. Ready to be pleasantly surprised, but starting to feel doubtful.

～

Boneglove are in trouble. Seems they've been coining it from the campaign! They have declared in the House of Commons register of interests that they've profited to the tune of £40,000 from running GO. I am livid!

They are shameless about it, though. They say the money was used to pay Bone's firm for vital services (which were actually carried out by Victoria and the team) and to pay Pursglove for his supposedly exhausting role as chief executive.

Apparently the little twerp's time and efforts were so valuable that the Electoral Commission would raise questions if we didn't assign a monetary value to them, and they were doing us all a favour by putting their hands in the till. What sort of fools do these second-rate nonentities think they are dealing with?

I have put out a statement headed 'Clarification on Peter Bone and Tom Pursglove's troughing', saying I am 'extremely shocked and disappointed'. Apart from that, we need to keep it low-key to avoid damaging the campaign. Privately, Wiggy and I are seething.

Tice, who put a great deal of stock in GO and Nick Wood's hollow operation, was also feeling less than collegiate.

> Peter and Tom,
> I don't think there is any point in GML continuing and propose we shut it down asap. Its brand is now tarnished and whatever remaining semblance of chance for fundraising from myself and a few others is gone.
> Irrespective of the value of what you did, setting up GO which I was not involved in, the optics are appalling and can be dragged up by the press at any moment, questioning what Arron and I knew and that we must have approved it. They are currently all over us.
> All of us have put in a huge amount of time whilst having other jobs and some of us given substantial sums. It was believed that you were doing this out of principle as an MP not for additional reward. No one apart from you at GO seemed to know about this.
> With thanks and kind regards
> Richard Tice

Nigel and Kate are just as angry. Infuriatingly for UKIP, people are now trying to tar Farage with the Boneglove brush. UKIP has had to put out a statement saying he's received nothing from GO.

It looks like what happened is that GO got fifty grand from a Tory donor and a few small direct donations. We paid all the bills direct so Boneglove simply pocketed the £50,000 and called it accountancy and management fees. They have told Farage they put the money back into the campaign – presumably only after being challenged, as the payment hasn't cleared yet. Bloody scandal.

22 APRIL

Back of the queue

Obama is here and it's exactly as predicted. Roped in by Dave to prop up his campaign, he has laughably declared that we'll be at the 'back of the queue' if we leave the EU and try to negotiate a trade deal with the US, plus all the usual guff about how we are at our best when we are 'helping to lead' in Brussels, with the EU making us a 'bigger player'.

So much for the so-called special relationship!

The journalists twigged straight away that Americans don't even use the word 'queue', they say 'line'. The media are all over Cameron, clearly suspicious that Downing Street wrote the script.

Either way, Obama will be out in a few months and what he's saying now will be long forgotten. Neither Clinton nor Trump will begin their term by pissing off their most important ally.

Most Americans have no idea what being part of the EU involves. They think it's just everyone hugging it out and trading.

We've been trying to enlighten voters on either side of the Atlantic with various articles and press releases. We're encouraging people to try to imagine what would happen to a presidential candidate who went to the American people with a plan to join a Pan-American Union which could overturn the judgments of their Supreme Court, establish a commission with the power to overrule Congress, and open their borders to Mexico, Colombia and all the rest. Absurd!

~

I've been laid up in bed with a bug, but was woken by a text from Matthew Parris, the *Times* columnist, about an article he's writing on 'party realignment and the idea UKIP might become a movement'. He's a pretty drippy Cameroon Tory, but he said he thought the idea was powerful and 'my purposes in talking to you are not hostile'. Called him back to chat.

23 APRIL

Times, three times

I think I am developing an unhealthy interest in my media profile. Three appearances in one newspaper today – definitely a record for me. I must admit, I'm proud. Lucy Fisher reports that Nigel is thinking of rebranding or relaunching UKIP because of some comments I'd made about how it needs to change after the last general election.

There's a passing reference to me in another article, plus the piece Parris telephoned me about. He used to be my least favourite kind of smug metropolitan journalist. Now I love him.

He began his column with a line I gave Lucy a few months ago, that 'I've got a weird feeling that British politics will be realigned after the referendum'.

Parris says that the kind of rebranding I am arguing for, which would transform UKIP into more of a popular movement than a traditional political party, could end up destroying Cameron's type of Conservatism.

He says my views are 'worth noting', 'his reasoning often cuts through the froth' and that I am the 'Holy Fool of the UKIP establishment'. Not sure about that last bit, but I'll take it as a compliment. Chuffed.

25 APRIL

The taxman won't leave Tice alone

Tice is still bogged down with HMRC.

He's had to spend an age putting together all the records they've demanded, and is fuming. He's more convinced than ever that it's a conspiracy, and wrote to them last month demanding to see his file under the Data Protection Act, as is his right.

He reckons that if he can see all the correspondence, he'll find No. 10's fingerprints all over it.

After five weeks sitting on his request, HMRC finally wrote back to him today, refusing to hand over his file. A revenue officer from their 'Wealthy Mid-Sized Business Compliance Unit' cited a list of feeble and totally unconvincing 'exemption' provisions which supposedly allow them not to release the information. He's going to appeal.

Tice's business empire – 'mid-sized'. Must remember to tease him about that.

27 APRIL

Farmer Tice

Tice and I had an uproarious couple of hours in the bosom of Westminster at the Treasury Select Committee. We had been summoned by its leaden yet formidable Tory chairman, Andrew Tyrie, who wanted to test the cases of all the leading organisations backing Leave and Remain. They are looking into the economic costs and benefits of the UK's EU membership.

The day didn't start too well, with Katya flat out in bed after putting her back out moving a box.

Nigel texted me wishing her well and telling me to keep my cool in Parliament. I also got a message from Christopher Hope at the *Telegraph* saying I was 'up in front of the beaks'. I told him I was feeling very collegiate.

I was right to be relaxed. Tice and I had a great head start because Cummings had been so rude and supercilious when he appeared last week, slouching in his seat like a sullen schoolboy with a nasty sneer stretched across his face.

They thought he was mad as a hat stand. (At one point, he came out with some bizarre line about Tyrie sitting at home in his slippers with his wife.)

I hear Elliott, meanwhile, has been refusing to appear in front of the committee at all. It meant they were inclined to sympathise with our point of view.

I couldn't help feeling that Tyrie rather enjoyed reading out some of my less flattering quotes about VL, especially my line about Matthew's aspirations to be 'Lord Elliott of Loserville'.

Once I got into my stride, I began enjoying myself too, especially when Rachel Reeves, the Labour MP who was once labelled 'boring snoring' by *Newsnight* editor Ian Katz, tried to get me to say interest rates will go up in the event of Brexit. I told her they were likely to stay near zero because in the UK 'everything is buggered' thanks to government incompetence, which certainly made the stenographer sit up.

Reeves had not seen fit to consider that interest rates near to zero (or even negative) are not the normal state of affairs in a healthy global economy, and was first bewildered and then miffed, trying everything possible to defend Cameron and Osborne's economic record, which was a curious approach for an opposition MP.

Numpty-in-Chief was an MP called Helen Goodman, who had the insufferable manner of one of those schoolmarms so used to talking down to children that they become unable to stop themselves from condescending to adults as well.

She asked me some tedious question about how other countries might respond to Brexit, and I confused her with a slightly off-the-wall answer I thought might humanise the issue.

'The only thing I would say on Obama is I took my son to his piano lesson on Monday night and the piano teacher said to me, "You are someone to do with Brexit, aren't you? I do not like that Mr Obama coming over and telling us what to do,"' I replied cheerfully.

'Mr Banks, I am not asking you about your child's piano lessons,' she replied, all hatchet-faced. 'I am asking you about your views on foreign investment.'

There was some suppressed sniggering behind me – probably Wiggy.

'We are allowed a little bit of levity, surely. It is not do or die, surely,' I replied, at which there was an audible intake of breath from Tice.

He was only sitting a few inches from me, and I could tell from his tense body language that he thought I wasn't taking the encounter sufficiently seriously. Gathering myself, I launched into a proper defence of the economic case for Brexit.

I argued that our EU membership isn't vital for either foreign investment or financial services. I told Goodman I knew from my own business experience that London's status as an English-speaking global hub with a legal system people can trust is really what's at the heart of our success.

I noticed that Goodman was beginning to look very pleased with herself.

'Well,' she announced with a triumphant smirk. 'You've brought me to the exact point that I was hoping you would come to. You do seem to have a lot of financial experience.'

She paused for dramatic effect, then began listing some of my companies.

You could see the Goodman train wheezing down the tracks. Here we go, how can rich executives like us possibly claim to be running an anti-establishment campaign?

Now she had her eyes on Tice.

'Mr Tice has been director of Valley National Banking Corporation—'

'No I haven't,' Richard interrupted. 'I've never heard of it.'

Goodman gazed about the room in a show of mock exasperation.

'Well,' she sneered, 'it's in the CV which you've submitted to the committee.'

Richard was confused. 'Valley National ... ?'

'The CV that you have given to us says that you are chief executive at Quidnet Capital Partners.'

'Correct.'

'You've been a partner of Tice Farms.'

Richard was very still for a second. When he did speak his tone had changed.

'That's not a CV that I've submitted to you,' he replied coldly.

That was it. Bang, hiss, clank. Great big chunks of metal flew off the Flying Goodman.

She shifted uncomfortably in her seat, glancing round the room. One of her colleagues on the committee passed her a note.

'Oh, it's information from Bloomberg,' she mumbled, attempting to compose herself and breeze on regardless.

Farmer Tice was having none of it, hammering home our advantage.

'Let's be very clear. That is not accurate,' he said simply.

'So… you haven't been director of CLS Holdings?' she croaked.

'I have been chief executive of CLS Holdings. I don't know what you've got in front of you, but it's not from me and it's not from our organisation. There's no such entity as Tice Farms. I've never heard of the banking corporation which you're referring to.'

Goodman was now looking utterly lost.

Richard leaned forward on the desk, savouring the moment.

'I was chief executive of a multinational listed property company between 2010 and 2014, which included operations in France, Germany and Sweden as well as the United Kingdom. It's now a FTSE 250 business. So yes, it was a billion-pound business, and I took it from a share price of £4.70 to almost £14, tripling it in four years. I'm quite proud of that track record.'

He had pre-empted and shot down Goodman's predictable punchline in masterly fashion. She came back, doing her best to patronise (which came easily), but was not up to it.

'Well, you've both been very successful financially,' she tried to conclude, lamely. 'So I just wonder why Mr Banks said that his campaign would be won against the establishment of international bankers, multinational corporations, tax dodgers and so on?'

'I started my businesses with a desk and two telephones,' I chipped in.

At this point, Wiggy, who was sitting just behind us in the public gallery, slipped us a note. He'd just had a text from Raheem Kassam, who had got to the bottom of Goodman's cock-up.

'She's taken the info on Richard from Wikipedia. Mixed him up with a New Jersey farmer who died in 1910.'

Brilliant. A committee of serious parliamentarians can't do a basic Google search.

Guardian sketchwriter John Crace was laughing so much Tyrie had to tell him to keep his gob shut.

Our only friend on the committee was the cartoonishly toffish Tory Jacob Rees-Mogg, who thanked us for our 'noble, patriotic service, backed up with your money being where your mouth is'. I told him about a passage in my old economics book about how wages went up 40 per cent after the Black Death, because the working-age population was so reduced. My thought was that less immigration would also mean less competition for jobs and higher wages.

Not in the best possible taste, but it amused Rees-Mogg, who replied: 'Even George Osborne has not yet suggested we will get the Black Death if we do not remain in the European Union. That may be what is coming in the next few weeks.'

At the end, Tyrie declared that it had been an 'entertaining' session and came up to us to thank us personally, as did Rees-Mogg. As we walked out, the policeman on the door tapped me on the shoulder and said it was the best committee session he'd ever been in – and he looked like he'd seen a few.

In the car on the way back home, I checked the media write-ups. Crace had already written his sketch, which greatly enlivened the schlep back up the M4.

> Given enough time, there's a fair chance the leave campaign would vote to leave itself. After weeks of trying to get both Vote Leave and Leave.EU into the same room, the Treasury select committee bowed to the inevitable. All attempts at mediation having failed, Andrew Tyrie … finally granted a decree nisi. Though not before hearing mitigation from one of the fratricidal parties.
>
> 'Yeah but no but yeah but Vote Leave is just the Eurosceptic wing of the Tory Party and Lord Elliott of Loserville is just

a loser and the electoral commission was a stitch up and Dominic Cummings is basically a bastard and my Mum says she saw Govey nicking some sweets from the canteen,' said Arron Banks, the insurance millionaire and co-founder of Leave.EU, which came off second best in the custody battle for recognition as the official leave campaign.

Love it. Baftas all round.

≈

Andy and I have received detailed instructions from Gerry about our trip to Washington. We've been given a run-down of what to wear: jacket and tie for the *Washington Post* and *Variety* magazine gala on Friday; black tie for the main shindig, the White House Correspondents' Dinner, on Saturday; jacket, no tie for brunch with Politico, the news website, on Sunday, followed by 'golf attire' for the Chevy Chase country club in the afternoon; then John Bolton, who was George W. Bush's ambassador to the UN, wants us to put our ties back on for him on Monday.

Gerry's next job is going to be as my valet.

28 APRIL

Better late than never. John Mills has finally seen sense and resigned from VL to concentrate on Labour Leave. According to Brendan Chilton: 'They have treated him particularly badly and have placed him in an impossible position.' At last. If only he'd done it before the designation. Still, good luck to him.

Gerry is excited about the number of requests for interviews we're getting for our visit. He says nobody from the Brexit side has yet done a trip to the US. Unbelievable.

Unfortunately, Nigel doesn't feel he can come. He's sorely tempted, but it's the local elections next week, and he says he can't be carousing around Washington DC when he should be out knocking doors.

29 APRIL

We hit Washington

Gerry might as well not have bothered with all his clothing instructions. As we boarded the flight to DC, I realised I'd forgotten the most important thing: my dinner jacket. I've put on so much weight during the campaign that I only have one tux left that fits and it was at the cleaners.

I was facing the shame of dining with the leader of the free world and Hollywood royalty dressed in slacks and a moss-green woolly jumper.

Thankfully, Gerry's people were on finest Jeeves form and when we arrived they found me a tailor who whipped me up a bespoke number in under an hour.

The White House Correspondents' Dinner is nicknamed the 'nerds' prom' in DC, and it's a big deal. Though it doesn't actually take place on Capitol Hill, the President and First Lady always attend, and it is an annual tradition for the President to give a funny speech.

The haggling for tickets begins 364 days before the event, while flunkeys at the Washington Hilton are still rolling up the red carpet from the last big bash. The place is always packed with media power players, pollsters and lobbyists and usually attracts a few movie stars.

Like the Oscars, it's not just a dinner, it's a whole series of parties spanning three or four days.

Our own itinerary kicked off with a swanky reception at the *Washington Post*.

Thanks to my wardrobe malfunction, we didn't make the main event, but we were on the guest list for an after-party.

There was champagne, sushi and spectacular views of the DC

skyline, and one of the *Post*'s senior executives gave us a tour of the building.

A few years ago the paper was bought by Amazon boss Jeff Bezos. I can't pretend to have understood all the detail about 'bots' and social media algorithms, but they seem to be doing a great job dragging of this very traditional dead-tree title into the twenty-first century.

I was about to collapse into bed when I received a very miserable text from Nigel saying he was 'at the end of the road'. I'm worried about him. I know he doesn't mean it but the pressure of the past year is taking its toll. He gets such a battering in the media and while he's very resilient, the constant accusations of being a 'racist' do get to him sometimes.

30 APRIL

Front of the queue

Wiggy went crazy at the dinner, running round taking selfies with every celeb he could find.

Buoyed by an early success with Whoopi Goldberg, he zoomed around the function room pursuing his targets like a dog on heat.

To begin with, he did at least observe some social niceties, introducing himself and attempting to engage the object of his desires in polite small talk. Before too long, however, he got carried away by the atmosphere and descended into shameless selfie grabbing, sidling up to unsuspecting targets, thrusting his phone in their face, and pegging it before they had time to object.

This technique proved quite successful, but he lost his nerve with Helen Mirren, who fobbed him off with a disdainful twitch of the nose. To his chagrin, he also bombed with a Victoria's Secret model in a slinky red dress.

'No pictures,' she said curtly and turned on her heel, leaving him staring forlornly at her perky derrière.

We ran into Steve Hilton, Cameron's former policy guru, who is a notorious Eurosceptic. He lives in California these days, but his name still counts for a lot in political circles in the UK. He kept his powder dry, but let slip that he was deeply unimpressed by Obama's failed intervention. Word is he might be planning to make a pitch of his own into the campaign.

Gerry had done us proud with a decent table in the outer middle but we still could have done with binoculars to see Barack and Michelle. The heavyweight on our table was the Governor of Florida, Republican Rick Scott, and before I got too squiffy we had a serious conversation about the referendum campaign. I tried to get Wiggy to join in but he kept bobbing up and down, gawping at celebrities, so I left him to it.

Around four hours later we staggered out, silly with drink and dazed by the scale and the glitz of it all. There was talk of an after-party at the Colombian Embassy, which sounded very promising, but we couldn't find the venue and, after twenty minutes of leading our driver into three-point turns and one-way streets, decided to call it a night.

Probably for the best.

MAY 2016

1 MAY

I felt very groggy this morning and was relieved to see that the main event on our itinerary was brunch at someone's house. I assumed it was a casual get-together with one of Gerry's mates and was looking forward to not having to try too hard to impress.

As the driver dropped us outside a spectacular colonial-style mansion in one of Washington's most exclusive districts, however, I realised this was not going to be coffee and cookies in someone's front room. We were at the private home of Robert Allbritton, son of the late Texan billionaire Joe Allbritton, who owns the international news website Politico, and we were about to be thrust into a scene out of *The Great Gatsby*.

I knew very little about Politico, the doyen of political nerd news websites, but it was immediately clear that Mr Allbritton knows how to throw a party. In the garden was one of the fanciest marquees I've ever seen, thronged with beautiful women, and men who looked like Tice. Everyone oozed money and success.

Wiggy skittered about, thrilled at the opportunity for more selfies, while I tried very hard to ignore the lavish catering and Kate Hoey fretted about being in too many photos with Republicans.

As we stood in a huddle, sipping Bloody Marys and surveying the scene, I made the mistake of mentioning that I'd spotted one of the Watergate journalists on the other side of the room. He was locked in conversation with Alan Greenspan, former chairman of the American Federal Reserve.

Almost before the words were out of my mouth, Wiggy had whipped out his phone and bolted. The truth was that he had no idea what the Watergate bloke looked like and there was an embarrassing case of mistaken identity with Greenspan. I tried not to laugh as I watched him struggling to engage the bewildered economist in a conversation about Deep Throat. I managed to intervene just in time to stop him tweeting a picture with the wrong caption.

I was pleased to be introduced to Reince Priebus, chairman of the Republican National Committee, and to the chairwoman of the Democratic Party. We discussed the challenge of engaging people who tend not to vote.

Everyone wanted to talk about Brexit and there was a lot of indignation and embarrassment about Obama's 'back of the queue' threat to America's closest friend and ally in so many wars. The general feeling was that objecting to our bid to regain our sovereignty could hardly be less American.

Almost all the Republicans with whom I spoke think Trump has the Republican nomination sewn up. Few are willing to predict he'll be taking the Oval Office next January, however.

Whether or not he makes it to the White House, it's great to see outsiders shaking up the political elite.

2 MAY

Exposed

Wiggy and I had a meeting at the US State Department. We had a pleasant chat with Conrad Tribble, a senior guy in their European division. Knowing the Americans like to be prepared, I asked him about their contingency plan for relations with the EU if we vote to leave.

'There is none,' he replied simply.

'What?' I replied, confused.

'The British government has told us not to bother with it. They say Brexit can't possibly happen, so not to worry about it.'

We explained all the reasons this could very well happen. He was patient and curious, but it was clear that the briefing from the Foreign Office was essentially: 'Jog on, nothing to see here.'

As we talked, I could see Tribble looking increasingly worried. At the end, he thanked us, before saying: 'You know, this is the first proper briefing on Brexit we've really ever had.'

It's our job to make sure it won't be the last.

≈

Something has happened to Tice. He's gone native. He bears almost no resemblance to the Mr Collegiate we once knew.

He emailed the team today asking if they could 'come up with a punchy picture/logo of the EU stars flag with a Kalashnikov and Semtex bomb inside it?'

He thought it could 'become a key image & part of our new guerrilla battleground'.

My eyes were drawn to the word 'punchy', which is what I say when I mean something really outrageous.

'Test new slogan or variants thereof: Britain in Europe: weaker, less secure, more vulnerable,' Tice instructed.

Wiggy was thrilled.

'Richard's gone rogue!' he declared delightedly, bashing out a quick response to egg him on.

'You OK? clearly making you come over to the dark side – Go Richard Go.'

The metamorphosis is complete. He has turned into us.

3 MAY

BPop revival

BPop has been resurrected! It has risen, phoenix-like, from the ashes, and this time, it's better than ever. It will be a proper Brexit event called BPop Leave. Some proper names are interested now. Alesha Dixon will headline. The others, I'm told, are 'oldies, but goodies' from the golden ages of rock and pop. Apparently we might get Soul II Soul.

There are still murmurs of dissent from London. 'Risen from the dead like a shit Jesus,' one of the press guys was overheard muttering. They reckon these new acts will crumple like tissue paper as soon as the press catches wind, and Jack Montgomery is trying to persuade Wiggy to turn it into a Trump-style rally with one strong musical act at the end. But our irrepressible head of comms is bouncing with enthusiasm and convinced we can pull it off.

We were thinking that BPop Live as the organising brand was perfect, but the *Express* people have said that to give it extra punch we should consider calling it 'BPop Live presents "Rock the Vote" referendum festival'. It is quite a mouthful, but the thinking is that it is more neutral and a much better way of selling the concert in the papers and magazines. Also, Richard Desmond and Paul Ashford at the *Express* feel that as the event is so close to the referendum, calling it Rock the Vote is a good way of pitching the concert to bands, who are more likely to sign up to an event designed to get out the vote than an event promoting Brexit.

Nigel has suggested that Jeremy Kyle would make a great host, if he's available. If not, maybe Michael Caine, Sol Campbell or Joey Essex? Wiggy wants some Brexit cheerleaders and has suggested asking Stringfellow's nightclub about lending us some girls. We also want a gospel band or something like that to sing the national anthem. For the finale, we are still working on Roger Daltrey to perform after the final speaker.

The pièce de résistance could be the venerable Mikhail Gorbachev, who we're close to confirming. Nabbing someone like that will give the event real gravitas and win one back after Obama's intervention.

One slight problem is the dreaded Electoral Commission, which is keeping an eye on how much we're spending. We won't be able to mention Leave.EU in any correspondence or publicity material, in case we find ourselves in hot water for busting official campaign spending limits. The question is whether a concert designed to encourage young people to vote qualifies as 'campaign spending'. Liz is trying to get them to chill out and has met them for a chat.

The Bill and Tony Show

There are rumours that Tony Blair is planning to up his efforts to 'help' the Remain campaign. Apparently he's going to rope in his old mate Bill Clinton.

According to reports, the former President is going to fly over on Hillary's behalf to tell us all off for contemplating saying goodbye to Brussels. Poor Remain. First they're backed by the man who conned us into a disastrous war and then they get the ex-President who happily lied about his fling with an intern and bombed a hospital in Sudan to distract the country from it. Lucky them. Two more fantastic liars will fit in well at Remain HQ.

≈

Tice has had another letter back from HMRC turning down his appeal for his own file. Surprise, surprise. What could they possibly have to hide? He's not letting it rest and is now taking it to the Information Commissioner under the Freedom of Information Act.

These days, our formerly mild-mannered friend is like the Incredible Hulk. 'When Richard Tice grows angry or outraged, a startling metamorphosis occurs. The creature is driven by rage.'

4 MAY

Good news – Jeremy Kyle thinks he might be available to host BPop Live. He's also quite cheap. He got back to us saying he'd do it for £5k. Meanwhile, John Mills wants another fifty grand from me for Labour Leave to print 1 million leaflets for the closing weeks of the campaign. He's still being sabotaged by VL, who haven't honoured the promises they made. They've kept their hands on the Labour Leave website, via which donations are sent. It's a disgrace, but I don't want to waste time chasing them when there are more important things to do.

We're planning four big rallies for the last few weeks of the campaign: Cardiff, Leeds, Peterborough and the Odeon Leicester Square. Let's win this thing.

6 MAY

Tory election spending – a national scandal

It's not just Thanet any more. Seven police forces are now investigating the Conservative Party for fraud in the general election and in various by-elections. There are now twenty-nine Tory MPs in the frame.

They are accused of bussing in activists to marginal seats and failing to declare the costs. *Channel 4 News* and the *Mail* have got evidence of stuff like this happening in thirty-three seats if you also count the ones they lost. We're supposed to be Great Britain, not a banana republic.

8 MAY

I'm still recovering from the US trip, so got a bit behind. I asked Wiggy for an update and he gave me a pithy summary: 'Brexit movie … aaahhh … security dickheads … Grassroots knobs … Nick the c*** Wood … Need I go on?' He's suggested Gloria Gaynor as a possible replacement for the concert, as it looks like Soul II Soul are having second thoughts. Groan.

Mark Fullbrook's getting flak for Zac Goldsmith losing the mayoral election to Sadiq Khan on Thursday. It's interesting that Lynton Crosby wanted nothing to do with it. Wiggy said Mark's a bellend and it's his own fault for not coming to work for us.

Brexit: The Turkey

In between insulting Mark, Wiggy's brought me up to speed with the full horror of *Brexit: The Movie*. The producers finally let us see what they've been doing, and it's a mess. No wonder they've been fobbing us off.

The whole thing is exactly the sort of free-market wet dream I feared, with supporting commentary provided by the cast of Vote Leave. They wheeled out so many weirdo, dead-eyed academics and pet journalists to make the case that it almost looked like a conspiracy to damage the cause.

There is literally no mention of immigration and Nigel barely gets a look in. The production team missed a bunch of open goals: nothing on the money we pay to the EU, nothing about the euro wrecking Greece, or ISIS infiltration through the migrant influx. Nothing about TTIP either, although we suspect that's because they can't wait for it.

Meanwhile, they tout the rapid destruction of the steel industry as one of the benefits of leaving the EU, when we have been saying for months that thoughtless EU energy policies and restrictions on state aid are to blame for its sorry state!

Wiggy and Nigel went to Millbank to watch it with the production team.

As the credits rolled, Hunter DuBose, our American friend with the unsettling fixed grin, turned to them.

'Well, what do you think?' he asked brightly.

'Andy, I can't say anything,' Nigel muttered, which was code for 'I'm completely fucked off.'

'I think it's shit,' Wiggy replied bluntly.

'…Oh.'

'Seriously,' Wiggy fumed, 'you can't put our name to this. You're going to get monstered and we are not touching it with a bargepole unless you make some very major changes,' Wiggy instructed.

The team slunk off and Wiggy had Jack from the press team prepare a clinical dissection of this horrible turkey before personally injecting an extra dose of bile and emailing it to DuBose.

> In my view you will have a big problem taking this on tour and engaging the key % of the audience that we will need to persuade. It feels more like a documentary not an inspirational film.
>
> It's a Libertarian deregulation-fest view of Brexit … Strong start on democracy … Film then gets mired in quicksand for what feels like 20–25 minutes on the subject (and history) of regulation. This section includes … a cringe-inducing segment on the Normans bringing regulation to England…
>
> The pace of the film slows way, way down [with] this rather self-indulgent libertarian history lesson, and the EU itself is not mentioned at all. There are a few potential howlers, including a reference to the joys of 'unregulated' toys. The likes of Nick

Clegg only have to point to one example of a cheap foreign toy made from toxic plastic or highlight a case like Claudia Winkelman's daughter bursting into flames [the presenter's child was injured when a Hallowe'en costume caught fire in 2014] and we lose the general audience immediately.

We then move on to trade and tariffs. There are some huge gaffes here, with the film explicitly pointing to the steel industry as an example of the sort of business which would go under in a post-Brexit world...

We also get an awful section on how Asians 'who are good at maths' are outperforming lazy European producers (sleazy Italians and onion-wearing Frenchmen in costume) ... but the EU protects them from competition. This segment will almost certainly lead to accusations of racism – despite the fact the film ends up not mentioning immigration at all. Lose–lose in terms of messaging.

There's something to this argument, but the execution is absolutely dreadful, and they actually chose to illustrate how great free trade would be by showing a picture of someone making cheap clothes in a sweat shop.

Immigration ... is literally not mentioned once, besides one of the talking heads saying, 'if we were offered a trade deal but it featured something we didn't want, like open borders, we wouldn't sign'. This is despite the fact the film's proposal purports that it would be aimed at undecideds and that immigration was identified as their number one issue. Sold a false prospectus, in my view.

Talking Heads

... No real people or businessmen get a look in besides some fishermen early on, John Mills and a Tate & Lyle rep.

Nigel is in there, but fairly infrequently. The unhelpful (and now old) clip of him lambasting Van Rompuy [former

President of the EU Council] is included. It seems he has only been featured at all as a sop to us and UKIP, who are/ were needed for funding, publicity, etc.

Sorry if it's a bit strong, I'm sure you will get a different view from others but this is how I see it.

They've promised to come back with some changes. Wiggy's next job is going to be film critic.

9 MAY

The BBC's *Today* programme has been to Barnsley with the local Labour MP, Dan Jarvis, who's campaigning for Remain – and they could hardly find anyone who agreed with him.

I think this is significant. The bookies and commentariat still think the odds are heavily against Brexit. Get out of central London, and the mood is very different.

Osborne's latest ruse is to predict house prices will drop 18 per cent after Brexit. The reaction from young voters is: 'Great, maybe one day we can afford somewhere to live.' Another helping hand from the Chancellor. He looks pale and rattled.

The movie man sulks

Durkin has come back to us after Andy's demolition job on his life's greatest work. They've cut a little bit of the libertarian rubbish (Hunter DuBose dressed up in ludicrous renaissance fair garb and pretending to be an evil, regulation-mad guildmaster is out but the interminable history lesson beginning around 1914 stays in). They have added nothing about immigration. We never wanted editorial control, but this is ridiculous. They're too squeamish to touch the number one issue for undecided voters, but they're happy to burble inanely about 'Asians who are good at maths'.

I probably should have known better. After all, this is the same guy whose CV includes a film offering sex advice from the animal kingdom (really) and a documentary on extreme ironing (a 'performance art', in which participants get a kick from ironing their undies in remote locations).

I'm withdrawing all the support I was putting in personally – the advertising, the *Express* CD, the big cinema bookings, the lot. This has thrown Durkin into a panic.

'You'll ruin my career,' he bawled.

What a drama queen. Wiggy and I have sunk £130k into this flop, but the money's a side issue. We both feel we've been taken for a ride, and that they were only interested in our chequebooks. I am glad that my other contribution to the movie – an interview – ended up on the cutting room floor. I do not want to be associated with this dog's breakfast.

Nigel's going to hold his tongue and attend the premiere anyway. Says it would be 'churlish' of him not to go.

'You two can afford to have a tantrum about this. I can't,' he said firmly.

This film could have been sensational. We would have made sure it was shown up and down the country if it was on point. Instead, Durkin and co. will get their time in the sun for one night only, in front of an audience no more expansive than the clapped-out Eurosceptic aristocracy and their crusty patrons. Perhaps it's all they really wanted, but what a waste.

It's war

Run for the hills, emigrate to Australia, or at least invest in a bunker. When we win the referendum and leave, the PM has warned us, World War III will break out.

Yes, that's right. Angela Merkel's panzers are revving their engines on the Polish border as we speak. In Paris, François Hollande is already writing out the French surrender document.

OK, he didn't actually use the words 'World War III', and his people are trying to claim his words have been twisted. But the message could not have been any clearer: 'The serried rows of white headstones in lovingly tended Commonwealth war cemeteries stand testament to the price this country has paid to help restore peace and order in Europe. Can we be so sure that peace and stability on our continent are assured beyond any shadow of doubt?'

He can hardly claim that the EU has kept the peace. He neglected to mention the years of bloodshed in Yugoslavia in the 1990s, which started when the EU openly encouraged Croatian and Bosnian separatists to break away from the Federal Republic. He must know that these apocalyptic comments will be lampooned. Call the men in white coats.

10 MAY

Our showbiz careers are jinxed

Our barrister Francis Hoar has been trying to calm the Electoral Commission down about the funding of BPop and the Brexit movie. We screwed up last week by wrongly telling them they're being funded by Leave.EU, and they are in a flap about us busting spending limits.

Hoar explained that Leave.EU isn't putting money into either event. I've lent cash personally for BPop which I'm hoping to get back through ticket sales. Tragically, we also put our own money into the film. There's no restriction on this.

After the appalling way they treated us during the designation saga, they should wind their necks in.

Donald and the snake

We've got our biggest gasp of outrage yet from the leftie media, and we're savouring it. It all started with Trump. He has taken to reciting a poem based on an Aesop fable, about a woman who takes in a poisonous snake she finds dying on the side of the road. She nurses it back to health. The snake then bites her. As she lies dying, she asks the snake why it bit her when she'd saved its life. The poem ends with the snake cackling and saying, 'Oh, shut up, silly woman. You knew damn well I was a snake before you took me in.' It's a very thinly veiled message from 'the Donald' about the dangers of open borders and unlimited migration, so we created a little film overlaying his speech with snippets of the violence that has broken out in European cities following the migrant crisis.

It didn't even do particularly well by our standards, getting around 50,000 hits. (Even a dry video of that Eurosceptic corpse Sir Bill Cash berating Cameron over his failure to secure treaty change got a million or so views.) But that wasn't the point. The idea was to whip up a bit of media outrage to keep the focus on immigration. We can always count on *The Guardian* to oblige and, sure enough, they ran a story, full of synthetic rage, under the headline: 'Leave.EU condemned for "xenophobic" Donald Trump video'.

Right on cue, the self-appointed spokesman for political correctness Chuka Umunna comes out to condemn it as 'vile and disgusting ... racist ... down in the gutter'.

Tubby Two Belts Soames and invisible Tim Farron from the Lib Dems added their voices to the chorus, accusing us of running an 'inflammatory' campaign. All this played straight into our hands. We know voters worry about the impact of uncontrolled migration on their communities, and the row only helps keep the issue front of mind.

11 MAY

Premiere

Tonight was the premiere of *Brexit: The Movie* at the Odeon, Leicester Square. I'm off to South Africa for a few weeks tomorrow, so I wanted to spend the evening at home with the kids, a far more appealing prospect than spending an evening watching some libertarian bore-a-thon.

Diplomatic as ever, Wiggy summarised our feelings in an elegant message to Durkin.

'You're disgraceful. And a liar.' Boom.

Later I watched it all on a video link. As everyone arrived, you could see the tourists in Leicester Square rushing towards the red carpet, expecting to see Johnny Depp, instead of which they were met with a grinning Farage, who seemed to be getting very friendly with the ITV presenter Lizzie Cundy. Presumably he'd had a few, which is understandable, given how he was going to be spending the evening.

At the end, Durkin leapt onto the stage to give an Oscars-style thank-you speech and omitted to mention moi.

I was not the only one to notice. As Durkin attempted to close out his simpering little soliloquy with an insincere 'I hope I haven't left anyone out', our press guys shouted out in unison: *'What about Arron Banks?'*

Pay rise for them.

'Ah, OK, yes,' Durkin grimaced. 'And we'd like to thank Arron Banks and Andy Wigmore.'

Watching it at home, I turned to Andy:

'What a bunch of c***s.'

I just wanted it to happen, and have been willing to fund anyone and anything that helps the cause. If done correctly it could have been absolutely brilliant, which is why it is so disappointing.

There was a fantastically nasty write-up on the Vice News website, dripping condescension on the audience of 'potato-headed men' with 'leathery wives', who clearly weren't left-wing or London enough for the reviewer's liking.

But they nailed the problem with the film:

A ramshackle European umbrella factory is represented by two skinny men in white vests and suspenders who spend their time pawing at a woman in a red dress; their Chinese competitors have straight backs, expressionless faces, and are very good at sums ... The victims of EU regulation here aren't ordinary workers but businessmen and bosses.

Bullseye.

12 MAY

Bullshit on a bus

Vote Leave are launching their battle bus today. The vehicle itself is a bit of an eyesore: bright red with an enclosed top to stop them having to get too close to the oiks. Worst of all, it makes the daft promise that we will get back £350 million a week from the EU if we leave and can spend it all on the NHS. The number is a blatant lie. It doesn't account for the rebate that is lopped off our bill before a penny goes to Brussels. We've been trying to run a clean and honest campaign and put the spotlight on Osborne and Cameron fiddling their figures. These exaggerated claims undermine the credibility of our entire case.

I got my own back on VL today with the donation figures released by the Electoral Commission. Serious bragging rights for me and I lost no time in showing off to Elliott, Cummings, Wheeler etc.

So, for all the big talk the EC numbers are in!

Lightweights
Patrick Barbour £500k
Stuart Wheeler £200k
[Peter] Cruddas £350k

Heavyweights
Arron Banks £5m
Peter Hargreaves £3.2m
Public £500k
Pathetic effort – we matched the government. You did – fuck all!!

Believe me, we will set this campaign alight in the last four months.

Arron

Nigel is under unbelievable pressure and is feeling it. His schedule is absolutely rammed and taking him all over the country, so I've told him 'just whistle' if there's anything I can do. Andy and I only take the piss out of him because we love him. He can call any time.

13 MAY

Time to audit the elites

Osborne's mates at the International Monetary Fund are chipping in for Project Fear. The institution's dodgy French boss Christine Lagarde says a vote for Brexit would have 'pretty bad, to very bad' consequences for us. They've released a report talking about 'severe regional and global damage', and a 'protracted period of heightened uncertainty'. The IMF predicts a stock market crash, a sharp fall in house prices and a 'technical recession'. Anything else you want us to chuck in?

Lagarde said she could think of nothing positive to say about Brexit, which guarantees that people here won't take her warnings seriously. In any case, no one should pretend she is an impartial judge. She is a groupie for the single currency and the IMF is in the pocket of Brussels. It backed the euro, didn't see the financial crisis coming and inflicted horrendous austerity on Greece to bail out the currency and its own banker friends. That was despite the very serious objections of some of its non-European members.

Lagarde herself has been under investigation for more than a year for her role in a €400 million corruption affair in France when she was Finance Minister. Her home was raided by police. I knocked out a statement suggesting that Lagarde was 'as credible as the Wolf of Wall Street when it comes to financial probity'. It's time to audit the elites and start judging them on the basis of their performance, not their undeserved prestige.

14 MAY

Tice has been wondering if we should call for election monitors to stop vote-rigging in fraud-infested areas like Tower Hamlets. May be better to raise it now rather than look like sore losers moaning about foul play if we don't win.

I like the idea of international observers. It would make Britain look like a tin-pot dictatorship, but, with Cameron splurging taxpayers' money on propaganda leaflets and the unelected Jean-Claude Juncker as our President (what a sobering thought), sometimes it feels as if we're not far off.

15 MAY

Nigel did a good job on Robert Peston's new Sunday morning ITV show. I wished him good luck last night and he seemed much bouncier than he has been of late. The producers wanted him to wear the metro-liberal uniform of crisply ironed open-neck shirt, but he refused to go on without a tie. The inimitable Jacob Rees-Mogg, an MP we both like, was also properly attired. We have high standards on our side.

The weather in South Africa is foul and I'm coming down with the flu.

16 MAY

Loony O'Leary

I'm glad Michael O'Leary isn't a pilot. He's all over the shop and prone to crashing in interviews. The Ryanair boss only recently suggested post-Brexit Britain would be a great place to get a cheap holiday because of the fall in the pound. Now he's changed his mind. In two days. He's fallen into line with the rest of the international mafia and is crediting the EU with lower air fares and more competition.

This is the man who once complained the EU was always either 'suing him, torturing him or criticising him' and that no new idea had come out of Brussels since 1922. 'Brussels is the Evil Empire and the Berlaymont is the Death Star' was his warning to young entrepreneurs.

Jack and Jordan dug out the footage, tarted it up with a suitable *Star Wars* theme ('Ryanair boss embracing the Dark Side?') and distributed it far and wide on social media.

Every day, another corporate or self-proclaimed expert comes crawling out of the woodwork, and every day we pick them apart. If BSE thought they were going to crush us under sheer weight of institutional prestige, they must be reconsidering now.

I wonder what Osborne has offered O'Leary? A peerage? For all his loud-mouth bluster, he's a corporate schmoozer at heart and loves the EU with all its sweetheart tax deals for big companies. Thankfully, he's from the Republic of Ireland, so he doesn't have a vote.

19 MAY

Thanked by Theresa May

Theresa May has a long memory, I will give her that.

Wiggy bumped into the Home Secretary at the Dorchester Hotel at the summer ball of Care After Combat, a charity run by Jim Davidson that gives practical help to forces veterans to get their lives on track.

The place was seething with Tories, none of whom would talk to him or even shake his hand.

He sent me a panicky semi-literate text saying he was wandering around friendless.

'Fuck me Michael Gove Peter Bone Tom Pursglove Elliott and

Teresa [*sic*] May all here as well as david Davis [*sic*] who wants to come to the republican convention…'

I had forgotten he was going and had no idea what he was talking about.

'Where are you?' I demanded.

'Very uncomfortable,' he rambled confusingly. 'They are not talking to me and refused to shake my hand, apart from Theresa May.'

He was clearly in a distressed state. He was hoping things would get easier when everyone sat down to eat, but to his chagrin he found himself sitting opposite Gove.

They spent the rest of the meal trying to avoid eye contact and pretend they weren't both thinking about the Wigolo affair.

The only person who was nice to him was the supposedly cold fish Theresa, who thanked him for the poll last autumn that showed her in such a good light on immigration.

What a pity she came out for Remain.

20 MAY

The Nigel and Boris show

He's off! Nigel has begun his nationwide battle bus tour to target the places Gerry Gunster has identified as being full of 'persuadables'. If all goes according to plan, he may have a new chum called Boris at his side.

Our charabanc is way classier than Vote Leave's aptly nicknamed 'blunder bus'. It's a big, double-decker Daimler in purple livery, dubbed 'The Flying Aubergine' by our events manager Victoria Hughes, who organised everything.

The side is emblazoned with Nigel's grinning face and the slogan 'We want our country back'. No dodgy numbers on the NHS, no closed top to hide from voters. Nigel wants to wave to everyone as he goes.

Open, accessible and (Nigel has promised) the 'best drinks cabinet anywhere in the country'.

After all the antics of the designation, VL seems interested in Boris and Nigel doing some kind of joint tour. We're willing to bury the hatchet – and not just in Dominic Cummings's head. We've always said we'll work with absolutely anyone to get out of the EU, and that still stands.

It's like Churchill said when pushed about working with Stalin during the Second World War: 'If Hitler invaded Hell I would make at least a favourable reference to the Devil in the House of Commons.'

Boris has privately agreed to do five campaigning events alongside Nigel in the last few weeks. They'll get on stage together and then go for a series of walkabouts through towns up and down the country.

This is a fantastic idea. The media will love it: two of the country's most popular politicians putting country before ego. We've always suspected that Boris isn't a real Brexiteer, but he won't be able to bluster with Nigel breathing down his neck. He must realise this will burnish his credentials when he goes for the leadership.

Crocked

While all this is going on, I'm laid up in bed in Pretoria. I thought a few days ago I just had a heavy head cold or flu.

But it's a proper health scare. Blood pressure gone haywire at 170/98, the works. I've been pumped full of liquids and multicoloured pills. I'm slowly getting better, but the doctor says it's stress and lifestyle. No more booze and fags, and lose weight. Now that sounds stressful to me. Miserable.

Kate told me to take it easy, and Tice says he's keeping an eye on Wiggy, so I'm trying, not very successfully, to rest.

Jim Mellon is in a tizz about a column in *The Times* saying Remain is going to win and we shouldn't be having this referendum. 'Matthew Parris should be put down. His article today makes my blood boil,' said Jim. Of course I immediately forwarded the text on to Parris, who replied that he does enjoy winding us all up. He sent his love to the Witwatersrand.

The real stress is watching the campaign from afar and the Tories being smashed to bits on the economy, while the four million Labour voters we need are just ignored. That's what I want our tour to achieve. The polls show Remain 10 points ahead. I am positive, but they are sweating back at base.

Luckily for my blood pressure, Tice didn't copy me into a no-holds-barred letter he sent VL. He thinks it could be 'game over' if they don't step up a gear.

He laid it on thick in his letter to Gisela Stuart, the Vote Leave chair.

> Halfway through the official designated period, with less than 5 weeks to go, it is increasingly clear that the Vote Leave campaign of Boris and Gove, masterminded by Elliott and Cummings, is failing.
>
> I have not heard anyone on our side say, or write, that it is a well-run campaign with a clear strategy. It is turning into a depressing blue on blue male ego battle, between Boris and Dave, with a splash of Michael, which is turning off Tory voters and leaving the rest utterly cold. Most of the campaign appears to be based around £350m a week to spend on the NHS ... the wrong number on the wrong thing.
>
> The polls are now turning against us and the markets think it is all over...
>
> An admission needs to be made by the Vote Leave non exec leaders that Boris and Gove need less exposure, whilst Elliott and Cummings need to go.

Things are definitely afoot again. Malcolm Pearson, who has slunk off to Scotland in despair, told me mysteriously but happily that a top-secret plot is afoot to take Cummings round the back and shoot him. If it hadn't been for him and Elliott owning the holding company for Vote Leave, Bernard Jenkin would have been able to get rid of them both long ago.

I'm feeling better and will be back in business tomorrow.

22 MAY

Farage axed

Wiggy's flown out and we're off to the diamond mines. I am trying to look after my health, but you can always trust the BBC to up the blood pressure.

They've axed Nigel from the Wembley stadium debate just before polling day. This cannot be allowed. Instead they are giving the places to Boris, Andrea Leadsom and Gisela Stuart. Two Tory ministers and their pet Labour MP – a straight VL line-up. By way of compensation, Nigel will be offered some BBC youth debate in Scotland where he can be assured a small audience and a hostile studio. He'd have a warmer reception in prison.

This calls for war. My plan is to publish the personal emails and phone numbers of everyone involved in this establishment stitch-up and get our supporters to demand that the leader of the only UK-wide genuinely anti-EU party be included in what could be the most important televised debate of our lifetime. My targets are Robbie Gibb, Elliott, Cummings, Carswell and VL's head of press, Robert Oxley. I would include Tony Hall, the BBC's director-general, if I had his number, but I can't get hold of it, so we'll have to make do with his email.

Andy didn't like this one bit when I mentioned it. He spent months cultivating Robbie and is worried someone may have a go at us under harassment or breaching data protection laws.

'They're public representatives, public campaigners and public broadcasters; why shouldn't the public be able to let them know how they feel?' I protested.

We decided to go for it – a letter to all our subscribers, and public posts to our Facebook followers.

I caught Andy in the dining room making a sneaky call to Mishcon de Reya to get some legal advice and quickly put a stop to his nonsense. 'No calls. Just get it all out there.'

They are all in for a big surprise.

∼

Great news for us and awful news for Dave. His one-time bestie and guru Steve Hilton has come out for Brexit – as he hinted to us he would when we saw him in Washington. He has written a really punchy piece in the *Mail* saying that Brussels has been 'corruptly captured' by elites and Britain will be 'literally ungovernable' as a democracy if we stay.

23 MAY

Gibbgate

Well, that certainly kicked the hornets' nest. We published the phone numbers, and the party started. Hall's and Gibb's mailboxes both crashed in minutes. Gibb was straight on the phone to Andy, in his trademark hurt-not-angry tone.

'I can't do my job, I just can't,' he railed.

Andy was chain-smoking on the deck outside, sheepishly trying to placate him. It was a good thing I warned him not to give up smoking a year ago. While he was getting his ear chewed off, Nigel was frantically trying to reach me.

Wiggy looked a bit shaken when he finished with Robbie.

I laughed: 'Oh well, Andy, another bridge burned. And nine missed calls from Nigel – that might be a new record.'

Finally we thought we'd better ring him back. He likes Robbie and we knew it wasn't going to be pretty.

'You've gone too far!' he bellowed.

I put him on speakerphone so Andy could hear, though, given the volume of the shouting, it wasn't really necessary.

'What next? Are you going to adopt ISIS tactics and blow up Television Centre? Throw bricks through their windows?'

Meanwhile, Chris Bruni-Lowe, Farage's right-hand man, was dealing with a fire-breathing Douglas Carswell. Old Popeye's battery had been run flat by at least 2,000 calls. Rob Oxley must have been delighted by his sudden fame, but he pretended to disapprove.

'Angry phone calls only last a few minutes, true class lasts forever', he tweeted sanctimoniously.

Having thrown the grenade, I was thoroughly enjoying watching the explosion. But Nigel was furious. He told us there was 'no upside' to our mischief and complained about having to run around cleaning up our mess.

Eventually, we reluctantly removed the contact details from Facebook. Our supporters were getting very passionate, bombarding our friends at the BBC with ALL CAPS texts about the 'BIASED BRUSSELS CORPORATION'.

We'd made our point.

Mystic Gideon and his Magic 8 Ball

A month to go and another laughable set of so-called forecasts from the Treasury.

Apparently, if Britain votes Out, 800,000 jobs will be lost, there will be a massive recession, soaring food prices and a house price slump.

If Brexit is really going to be so dire, then why did they have the vote in the first place? Of course it's not going to be anything like this and they know it. Even the Europhile *Guardian* says the Treasury's numbers don't just need a pinch of salt; 'these so-called scenarios need the whole salt mine'.

Osborne's Treasury will pump out whatever he wants. He announced his nonsense in a suspiciously well-staffed B&Q with a totally useless pun: 'Do we really want a DIY recession?' Groan. I'm sure Mystic Gideon would rather we all forget that he was forecasting a budget surplus by 2014 but still the deficit is at £69 billion. The man has all the predictive capability of a Magic 8 Ball, and we haven't sugar-coated that assessment in our press releases.

The truth is that a post-Brexit economic boom will bring thousands more jobs.

The Electoral Commission is still snooping around on BPop. They've demanded all our correspondence about the event by 1 p.m. tomorrow or else. Or else what? I told Liz to ignore them completely until 23 June. 'I have plans for these muppets when I'm back,' I said.

24 MAY

BPopcalypse

Wiggy's no Simon Cowell, that's for sure. Hot on the heels of Gibb gate, BPop is turning into BPopcalypse. It's like *Groundhog Day*. Alesha Dixon has pulled out, claiming she's shocked at finding out the gig has something to do with Brexit. Presumably she is under orders from some PR knob end, as she knew exactly what this was about from the start.

Andy's phone lit up as, once again, act after act dropped like flies: 5ive, East 17 and a whole lot more. The press are gleefully sticking the boot in. 'Leave.EU's BPop Live gig makes us want to leave the planet', 'BPop Live sees even Leave supporters begging for it not to go ahead' and 'Is this the worst political gig of all time? The answer is yes, 100% yes' were among the more generous headlines.

The unflappable Andy, the life and soul of the party, has finally slumped. The last I saw of him today, he was outside chain smoking, unshaven, head bowed, looking like a deflated balloon.

Liz was less than impressed by my 'fuck you' attitude towards the EC trying to shut down this already doomed project, and fired off the following to Andy.

> I know you don't give a shit but I do. If it's been mentioned
> on Radio One that it's anything to do with [Leave.EU]

then you have gone against any instruction on this. I will be stepping down from Leave.EU as I will not take responsibility for something I have clearly told you not to do.

You will need to sort this out. It's a jail offence.

We both laughed – a little nervously.

25 MAY

Tice gave me a read-out from a parliamentary meeting last night. Gove thinks it's neck and neck, IDS thinks it is going OK. 'They are away with the fairies,' said the Artist Formerly Known as Collegiate. 'Thinking of joining you in SA so depressing here.'

I agreed with him. They are in a bubble. It's obvious from Pretoria we are being hammered.

I've decided to stay out in South Africa for longer so I get my health back. I'll be in the UK for the closing weeks.

Perils of an open-top bus

Nigel is loving waving at everyone from his open-top bus, larking around like he's on a Premier League victory tour with the fans running about below. It's proving a great success. He's being mobbed in all the Labour areas and drawing much bigger crowds than the VL bus.

It's not a risk-free strategy, though. We all had a good laugh at him today when he got whacked in the face by a tree branch in Sheffield.

Then, as he passed the railway station, he yelled out to one man, 'Are you for Brexit, sir?'

'Bloody well am,' came the answer.

Nick Clegg would have been appalled. Go Sheffield!

26 MAY

Pouring in

This could be the jolt our campaign needs. The official Office for National Statistics immigration report came out today and it's a slam dunk. Net migration was at 333,000 in 2015, the second highest figure on record. Almost half those people came from the EU and there isn't a damn thing anyone can do about it. It will be impossible for either the Remainers or VL to pretend immigration isn't a key issue.

Tomorrow, at least, the playing field levels. It's the start of purdah, when the civil service has to go neutral on the campaign. This means the prophets of doom in the Treasury won't be able to predict early Ragnarök – the end of the world in Norse mythology – if we leave the EU. This is the perfect time to start pivoting the debate away from the economy and on to immigration, where we are creaming the other side.

27 MAY

The Treasury Select Committee has published its report. Tice sent me a choice excerpt about Cummings and Elliott: 'Their conduct has been appalling.' Couldn't have put it better myself.

30 MAY

Daltrey and the Donald

I'm not going to let the BPop dream die. We've been moving heaven and earth to recruit new acts. And some very old ones too. ACDC have said we could fly them out to Birmingham straight from their gig in Bilbao, and The Who are still in play. Roger Daltrey came out a few weeks ago saying about the EU: 'We need to get rid of this bunch of fucking useless wankers that are running it.' Classy.

Maybe we could even get Donald Trump? His people tell us he could be in the UK around then.

31 MAY

Farage rocks in Birmingham

There's a bloody good chance that if we win England's second city, we win the whole thing. It's looking good because Nigel had his best day on the bus so far when he hit Birmingham.

He was warned there could be protests and that the Unite Against Fascism nutters would be out in force. Instead, he was glad-handing in the streets and people kept coming up encouraging him to keep up the good work. We had second- or third-generation immigrants complaining about uncontrolled immigration. It shows we are sending out the right messages – and there's nothing racist about what we say. You don't see this kind of excitement for the VL bus.

I'm disgusted about how the BBC portrayed the day, though. Some Labour activist started yelling at Nigel about his attendance record at the pointless European Parliament, and told him he was 'blaming immigrants' for the country's problems. So the Beeb ran a headline saying 'Nigel Farage Heckled on Birmingham Walkabout'. They didn't mention the huge crowds of working people who turned out to give him support. It is the same phenomenon Trump has called out during his rallies: broadcasters will only cover these events when someone protests.

We're still trying to get the Vote Leave ministers to do some joint events. Nigel's getting on very well with Priti Patel, who's sympathetic to us from her old Referendum Party days. Even Gove and IDS are warming to his style after seeing the results he's producing. But Cummings is busy ensuring we don't get too close. The Boris/ Farage bus tour now looks unlikely to happen.

PART 5:
JUNE–JULY 2016

JUNE 2016

2 JUNE

The Electoral Commission v. BPop

The concert isn't turning out to be quite the star-lit extravaganza we hoped. The line-up currently boils down to 'three quarters of Bucks Fizz and an Elvis impersonator', as the *Mirror* put it.

We can't even use the Bucks Fizz name as they've lost the rights to the fourth guy after an endless court battle. We're not going to get Gorbachev either.

The *Mirror* isn't far wrong, but sod it, we've sunk so much cash and time into this venture it just has to go ahead.

We've sold close to 8,000 tickets and I don't want to let these people down.

The press office released a statement saying 'third time lucky for BPop'. They're hoping our Elvis guy 'won't be giving his rendition of "So Close Yet So Far" on June 24th'. It's now going to be more of an American-style rally with a bit of music thrown in for good measure. 'Andrew Marr on steroids', we're selling it as. We've got a string orchestra and a bunch of Union Jack flags, and are calling the event The Last Night of the Brexit Proms. The Beeb, humourless as ever, has sent us a 'cease and desist' letter claiming copyright infringement on the word 'Proms' and threatening to sue. They can join the queue.

Some journalists are actually starting to come round to the concert, telling us they really want it to happen. I know they just want some fun at our expense.

Meanwhile, the Electoral Commission has written to Liz threatening to prosecute us if we go ahead. They've decided to include the concert in our official campaign spending, which will take us over our legal limits. We've got until 10 a.m., Monday 13 June to respond. I intend to ignore it.

Cameron roasted

First major televised debate of the referendum campaign tonight, and Dave got a roasting.

Sadly, he didn't have the balls for a head-to-head debate with Boris, Nigel or anyone else. Instead, it was a live interview with Sky's political editor Faisal Islam, with questions and interventions from a carefully selected audience.

I was worried that Faisal might go soft, and was pleasantly surprised. He gave the Prime Minister the grilling he deserved, particularly over immigration. He must bitterly regret pledging to reduce net migration to 'tens of thousands' – something he can never achieve while we're in the EU.

I texted Faisal afterwards to say well done.

'Really good performance – I was expecting you to give him an easy ride. You need to go equally hard on Gove. Best Arron.'

He replied saying: 'Tsk! Easy ride? As if. PM should really do more interviews like this though – Thatcher used to do loads of long ones.'

Kate has forwarded a message from Elliott about an invitation to join a 'Brexit Express steam train' from London to York on 13 and 14 June. If I'm on the train with Elliott, it might turn into *Murder on the Orient Express*. One to decline.

3 JUNE

Enough experts

Shiny-face Gove had his own good grilling from Islam and the Sky audience tonight. He came off quite a lot better than Cameron, admittedly not hard. His most popular sound bite came straight out of the Leave.EU playbook: 'People in this country have had enough of experts.' The delivery was inexpert, but what he meant is that impressive-sounding institutions and organisations like the IMF often fail to get the big calls right. This lot pretty much all said we needed to join the euro, and failed to anticipate the global financial crisis.

5 JUNE

Did a turn on the *Murnaghan* show on Sky today. Was fine, but annoyingly they led on Nigel's comments about how staying in the EU could risk mass sexual attacks by immigrants. He said it was the 'nuclear bomb' in the debate. As Tice found out on *Marr*, you can do all the preparation you like, but it's today's headlines that matter.

8 JUNE

The Dave v. Nigel show

Cameron versus Farage on ITV tonight. Sadly, they were on one after the other, not head to head, but there was much media excitement.

We took him to the venue in style on the Flying Aubergine, which almost ended in disaster when the driver took a route that involved negotiating a low bridge. We came perilously close to getting stuck and were forced to divert.

He had been very tense all day, pacing up and down chain smoking, and insisted on a last-minute fag before the programme kicked off. We went outside with him for moral support, then all strode back in looking like something out of *Reservoir Dogs* – and promptly ran smack into Cameron and the Downing Street team.

His flunkeys looked horrified. They'd specifically told ITV they didn't want any backstage encounters and now they couldn't avoid us.

Trapped in a narrow corridor, Cameron tried to hide his dismay behind a rubbery mask of good cheer as Farage greeted him with a mischievous 'Hello, Prime Minister!' Wiggy immediately sprang into action to capture the super-awkward moment on his phone.

For all his nerves, in the end Nigel did very well. Judging from the online reaction, viewers particularly liked his call to rebel against big business, big banks and big politics, a line Nigel first used at UKIP's spring conference at the Winter Gardens in Margate last year. It went down a storm and he's stuck to it ever since. The Remain campaign are trying to sell the public the status quo, but the status quo doesn't serve everyone very well.

≈

I posted leaflets through the letter boxes in my village the other night and I've been chuffed to see some people have stuck them in their windows. I have a feeling the silent majority will turn up to vote Out.

9 JUNE

The EC cosy up to Remain

Half a million people have bombarded the Electoral Commission website trying to register to vote, and the system has crashed. What a joke. It's only used to getting half a dozen hits a day and they didn't think to crank it up so it could deal with a last-minute rush. There's no excuse. After all, they had a warning weeks ago when our supporters crashed the site ahead of the designation decision.

Now they've appealed to Dave and there's going to be emergency legislation to extend the deadline by two days – right in the middle of a campaign. In my opinion, it stinks. Backed by the Prime Minister, Remain is trying to register as many young people as possible who are not currently able to vote, because they think under-25s are more likely to be on their side. I don't like quoting European organisations but, for the record, this behaviour is against the Council of Europe's own code of good practice on referendums.

12 JUNE

Shifting diagnosis

Big wows today over a 'defection' from Vote Leave.

Remain is crowing because a Tory MP called Sarah Wollaston who had been backing Brexit has suddenly decided she wants to stay in the EU. The truth is that nobody outside the Westminster village has ever heard of her, but the media is acting like this is scoop of the year, partly because Wollaston is a doctor.

Up until now, she's been acknowledging that the NHS is under huge pressure as a result of uncontrolled migration and just can't cope with the surge in patients from overseas. Suddenly she's changed her mind.

She's told her Twitter followers, all five of them: 'As much as I enjoy a good conspiracy theory; I'm no spy, schemer, traitor etc. just examined the evidence & Brexit is bad for our health.' We never said anything about her being a 'schemer' and 'spy' – but I certainly wouldn't want her as my doctor.

I tweeted back: 'I hope you are a better doctor than politician. Getting halfway through an operation and doing the research.'

Wollaston's Damascene conversion seems to have been driven by Vote Leave's dubious suggestion that leaving the EU could free up £350 million a week for the NHS. She has a point. Elliott knows that figure is dodgy, but he persists in using it.

Nigel had dinner with Michael Gove a couple of weeks ago and begged them to drop it. He pointed out that the net figure is quite impressive enough, and has the benefit of being accurate.

Gove shrugged and claimed it was too late, as the figure was already 'out there'.

13 JUNE

No messing around

Ten days to go! I've decided that from now on, we should just focus on immigration. The media will attack us, but it doesn't matter.

We will do whatever we need to do to get people talking about it.

Today, that meant exploiting a dreadful incident in Orlando, Florida yesterday in which forty-nine people were murdered in a gay nightclub by a Muslim with an assault rifle.

We weren't ashamed to use it to remind voters of the dangers posed by open borders and we posted an ad featuring a picture of terrorists waving AK-47s under the headline: 'Islamist extremism is a real threat to our way of life. Act now before we see an Orlando-style atrocity'. Wiggy then tweeted that 'Freedom of movement for Kalashnikovs in Europe helps terrorists. Vote for greater security on June 23. Vote Leave.'

Everyone went crazy, just as we hoped. Nigel thought it was a step too far, but the truth is, he doesn't like being upstaged. He wants to be the one delivering shock and awe.

Yes, we've outraged some people – but far more think we're talking common sense.

Turning point

The polls have swung towards Leave, and the Remainiac media is starting to panic.

YouGov and TNS both give Brexit a seven-point lead, while ICM has us five ahead. Cue yet more hysterical twisting of facts and presenters breathing into paper bags and choking on their morning croissants.

Darren McCaffrey, political correspondent for Sky News, claimed that the pound took a 'beating' as a result of the latest surveys. It did have a slight wobble, but what he omitted to mention is that it remains higher than it was at the start of the week and higher than it was many months ago when Remain was in the lead. The truth is that sterling is in long-term decline, primarily because Osborne's been shredding the public finances.

Brexiteers pounced on McCaffrey on Twitter, producing multiple graphs demonstrating that the pound has generally become stronger as Remain's lead has shrunk. I tweeted the guy that if the pound had taken a 'beating', I was struggling to see it, as it was more or less the same as at the start of the campaign. 'Stunning indifference really'.

≈

Update on BPop. The Electoral Commission has given us two days to decide what to do. We now have until 5 p m on Wednesday. As Liz has been designated the responsible adult of the outfit, she will be personally liable if we defy them and go ahead with the concert. She's made it fairly clear she isn't willing to acquire a criminal record and is pushing me to pull the plug. I am mulling it over.

14 JUNE

BPop dead

I've decided to ditch it. I hate being beaten, but the EC won't budge, and it looks like they may actually try to send Liz to prison if we ignore their edicts. It's becoming a ridiculous distraction and is unfair on her, so that's it. BPop is officially dead, and there will be no further resurrections 'like a shit Jesus'.

I told Andy to put out an aggressive press release and he responded by labelling the EC 'crooked'.

> It is with great regret that I have to announce that the Last Night of the Brexit Proms aka BPop Live has been shut down by the Electoral Commission … This promised to be a truly unique event, with a live orchestra, a little tongue in cheek entertainment and speeches from Nigel Farage and other leading lights of the Leave campaign.

Francis Hoar thinks it's the right call.

Osborne's blackmail budget

Our omnishambles Chancellor has stooped to a new low. I thought the Treasury had done its worst after the ludicrous warnings about plummeting house prices and the £4,300 that every family will somehow lose if we leave the EU, but now he's threatening an 'emergency budget' if we win on 23 June.

He claims Brexit will mean a £15 billion cut to public services like the NHS and another £15 billion in tax rises including massive hikes in income tax and death duties. But he has been perfectly capable of ripping giant holes in the national finances without anyone's help. Now he is just chucking basic economic sense on the bonfire. It's a massive gamble on his part which has already backfired. The media is dubbing it a 'punishment budget' and political commentators are piling in saying he may have committed career suicide.

Ed Vaizey, a veteran of the Cameroon project, was given the unenviable task of defending this nonsense on the BBC and was subjected to a suitable mauling. By the time he had to face Andrew Neil, over sixty Tory MPs and the Labour Party had trashed the plan, warning they would never vote it through, so he was stuffed before he even started.

Neil claimed Osborne's initiative had 'crashed and burned on take-off', leaving Vaizey floundering around complaining about the interview not being balanced.

Fat cat, my arse

Remainers have been calling me a 'fat cat'. Ridiculous. I started my business from scratch. I'm not pretending I don't have a nice lifestyle these days, but anyone who comes to Lysander House can see I've got no pretences.

It all started when Corbyn gave a speech trying to claim Brexit will mean the end of the NHS. Given his reputation as a man of great principle, I've no idea how he got the words out of his mouth, because he knows full well it's rubbish. However, it's exactly the sort of codswallop that appeals to readers of the *Mirror*, and their belligerent leftie columnist Kevin Maguire duly got stuck in.

He dredged up a line from an interview I'd given ages ago suggesting that the rich should pay more for healthcare by purchasing top-up insurance, thus saving money for the NHS – an idea one might have thought would appeal to the left. But right now anything Brexiteers say has to be shouted down, and he started tweeting that I want to 'end the NHS' and 'force patients to buy insurance', adding nastily that I might make a few quid from such a policy.

'Must feel great being lined up with Goldman Sachs, JP Morgan, big business and Cameron. Proper Labour values,' was my response, along with a press release headlined: 'Fat cat, my arse'.

Even the *FT* believes plans are being laid for Turkey to join the EU. They've run a story saying the Foreign Office is helping to clear the way for further membership talks. Cameron's protests are as thin as a Communion wafer.

15 JUNE

Battle of the Thames

Trafalgar, Jutland ... the Battle of the Thames. We've written our own chapter of Britain's great naval history. A glorious summer day of messing around in boats that turned into pure, madcap anarchy. Just what this campaign should be. Trafalgar meets the Wacky Races.

It started off when we were approached by a group of fishermen, mostly Scottish, who wanted to converge on Parliament in their boats to highlight the devastation the EU and its Common Fisheries Policy has caused to their livelihoods. We can only rescue their communities if we have control of our own waters and don't have to let the whole of Europe dip its nets in them.

I quite fancied the role of Admiral Banksy, with my faithful cabin boy Wiggy. It wouldn't come cheap, though. The Scottish skippers wanted us to cover the running costs so the expedition didn't leave them out of pocket – £10,000 per boat for the biggest trawlers, 250 grand in all for seventy boats, though in the end fewer than that turned up.

I decided the free coverage would be worth a hell of a lot more than that. So the signal went out from Port Catbrain for the fleet to gather, and I shelled out. I co-ordinated with Jim Sillars, a former deputy leader of the SNP, to take out a load of adverts in local papers in the Scottish fishing ports. I've now funded people from pretty much every party apart from the Lib Dems.

Down came our salty sea dogs. We had some pretty big trawlers – one with its EU flag decal painted over with a skull and cross-bones – right down to a little fishing smack from Southend with St George's cross bunting. Everything covered in lots of bunting and banners, it was a cheery flotilla.

The first hint that we might face some resistance was when the Harbour Master of the Port of London got on the blower to Wiggy and gave him an earful. We were only allowed four large and eight small craft past the Thames Barrier. It was a bit of a shame as we'd brought more than thirty boats down, with some coming hundreds of miles. But with a fleet like that all milling around at the mouth of the Thames you couldn't beat it for drama.

Kate Hoey started to get cold feet as the fleet was cut down to size by the Harbour Master, asking if she might be able to jump ship mid-voyage, as she thought it was going to turn into a non-event.

Wiggy and I were ambling about trying find the open-top bus hired for the occasion to take the gang down to the river. We weren't sure the journos wanted to be on oily trawlers all day, so I planned to put my flag, or rather Nigel's, in a rather plush wood-panelled Edwardian river cruiser.

We finally caught up with the bus as it trundled to the river past St Thomas' Hospital to be met with a tongue-lashing from Nigel.

There was no jovial 'run up the Jolly Roger' banter from him, as there was from the rest of the crew. He was pensive, worried it was all going to backfire, and annoyed that we were really looking forward to it.

'This is not a booze cruise,' he muttered irritably. 'We've got to be sensible and well behaved.' He was less the Brexit Buccaneer, more the health and safety inspector. Meanwhile, Kate was getting increasingly riled about the number of cameras pursuing Nigel, and the two politicians were now openly scrapping for attention.

'Look at him! He's such a show-off,' she complained.

Somehow, we managed to get everyone aboard without coming to blows. Farage orders notwithstanding, we got Kate a G&T to simmer her down and started on the booze ourselves.

Some of the fishermen had heart-rending stories. The skipper on the little boat beside us, which came from Southend, had cancer and only had six months to live, but he was hoping his son would succeed him, and he would have a brighter future if we left the EU. Gesturing to the rest of the fleet, Nigel began giving an impromptu speech about how they have been failed by the EU and must now eke out a living with the odds stacked against them. Barely had he mentioned the poor fisherman before Michael Crick began having a pop at me for being rich.

'How much are you worth, Mr Banks?' he shouted.

Clearly I was onto a loser with that one, so I got personal too.

'How much was your suit?' I retorted cheerfully. 'You need to get a new suit.'

We were all drifting along happily, when suddenly there was a phenomenally loud BOOM.

A Boomtown Rats Boom, as it turned out, as a pleasure cruiser full of metropolitan types bore down on us from astern, with Bob Geldof capering about at the railing with a megaphone and a sound system that was loud enough to have been lent by one of his chums at the Notting Hill Carnival. It was blaring out hits like 'The In Crowd' from 1964. We aren't in the in crowd? Fantastic, bring it on.

I'll give credit to the other side, it was a great ambush. There was a Remain boat with Charlotte Church on board and another carrying Boris Johnson's Europhile sister Rachel. The leftie group Momentum also had a little flotilla.

It was about the time of Prime Minister's Questions at midday and the battle on the river in front of Parliament was in full flow. Plenty of MPs in the Chamber were distracted, with even that smoothest of Remainers Chuka Umunna tweeting that he was watching events on his iPhone rather than paying attention to the latest Cameron *v.* Corbyn tedium. Some MPs decided to skip PMQs altogether to watch the fun and Kate began to cheer up as her colleagues waved to her from Parliament's terrace overlooking the river.

Geldof was yelling full throttle at us. 'You're a fraud, Nigel.

Go back down the river, because you're up one without a canoe. Or a paddle,' he bellowed in his Irish tones.

At one point, he lurched into fluent Brussels-speak: 'You were on the European Parliament fishing committee. You attended only one out of forty-three meetings.' Not sure you've quite nailed it with the new lyrics there, Bob.

Wiggy and I were finding the whole thing hilarious. Not so our elder statesman.

Nigel stood stoic and tried to grin and bear the fusillade of brogue coming at him from off the port bow – Geldof's boat was now overtaking us. Nigel was staring at us and muttering, 'Don't react, don't react' and trying to play it cool, before adding: 'He was a crap pop star and he's not even British as far as I understand. He's from the Irish Republic, he hasn't got a say in the matter.' Kate quietly stared Bob down – Ulster *v.* the Republic. A Sky News helicopter came whirring in overhead.

Geldof and his luvvie crew looked like they were pissed as farts, sticking fingers up, shouting 'wanker' and making vulgar gestures. It's quite incredible what contempt these people have for those who are trying to scrape a living against the odds. It was too much for some of the more principled lefties on the boat. A few of them got off, and one of them tweeted: 'On a boat with Bob Geldof and its awful. I may vote remain, but don't support jeering at fisherman worried about their livelihoods.' She followed that up with: 'as someone who was on Bob Geldof's boat, and left with others in protest, I can tell you It Is everything wrong with strongerin'.

Nigel is not short of courage, but today the Nelson touch distinctly failed him. Sometimes, his response to the latest broadside boomed out from the Good Ship Geldof was to rush down below.

It was only the ciggies that stopped him losing it totally today.

Things livened up even more when the boat from Southend began spraying Geldof's vessel with its firehoses and Bob yelled back.

'You're all London. All of you. Not one of you is from Southend or Essex,' he rambled.

We had a great moment, one of the pictures of the day, when Kate and Nigel put Kate Winslet and Leo DiCaprio in the shade with an impromptu *Titanic* pose in the prow of the boat.

Later in the day, there was a very funny map going round that someone had drawn to look like a chart of a naval battle with the different fleets in red and blue. It was headed 'Situation at 1 p.m.' and showed wind direction and everything.

We had a bigger fleet and a bit more credibility with our fishermen, but they had a much better sound system and prettier crews. Sums up the whole campaign really. There was no doubt who'd won by the time the boats dispersed back down the Thames. Salty sea dogs 3, sneering softies 0. We'd won a mass of free publicity, highlighted a great cause and put fun and energy into a great cause. Nelson would have been proud.

16 JUNE

The murder of Jo Cox

Yesterday was a mad bright day on the river. Today it all went dark. The murder of the Labour MP Jo Cox has shaken us all to the core.

It started as a normal enough day. Katya had talked me into taking a few hours off to go to Ladies' Day at Ascot. She hasn't got a clue about horses but had a spookily successful day one year by betting on the horse numbered two in every race. Against all the odds, her nags kept winning and, as she had an accumulator, she returned home with a lot of cash in her pocket.

Ascot's not really my scene, but I had agreed to tag along. She's not seen much of me during this campaign, and I thought an afternoon away from my desk wouldn't do any harm.

I woke up feeling under the weather, however, and she ended up going with a girlfriend instead.

The morning news bulletins were dominated by the 'punishment budget', until Nigel unveiled a UKIP billboard designed to switch the agenda back to immigration. It showed a tidal wave of refugees tramping along a road across Europe, under the words 'Breaking Point'. The message was that the EU has failed us all and we needed to regain control of our borders.

Nigel had been jittery about it.

After a photo opportunity unveiling the billboard, he rang me to ask what I thought.

'Have I done the wrong thing?' he asked anxiously.

I was adamant that he had not. I thought the poster was just stating facts. Similar pictures have been appearing on the front of newspapers for months. I knew it would divide opinion, but that was the point. We're not afraid of a row.

Entirely as predicted, it all kicked off, with sanctimonious lefties and establishment types piling in to accuse Nigel of 'vile xenophobia'. A handful of Kippers joined in, as did the leftie writer Bonnie Greer, who made a fool of herself by likening Nigel to the Nazi Hermann Göring. Nigel kept in regular contact and I encouraged him to hold his nerve.

I was still not feeling great, and taking it easy at home, occupying myself sending invitations to a party we're throwing at Millbank Tower on referendum night. Win or lose, it's going to be a good bash.

I was also thinking about how we should spend the final week. I emailed the team emphasising that we must keep our sights firmly on Labour supporters. They will be the key to victory in this campaign.

I was so absorbed in all this that I didn't pay much attention to developing news about an attack on a Labour MP until I realised it was serious.

Michael Crick tipped me off that Jo Cox had died following a terrible incident in her constituency, although this would not become public until later in the day. It was clear that the rest of the day would not be business as usual. She had been shot and stabbed, a shocking incident at any time, but particularly in the heightened atmosphere of the referendum campaign. My heart sank when Crick told me that her husband and young children had been on one of the Remain boats on the Thames yesterday. Worse, she also devoted much of her life to campaigning for refugees. The timing of the Breaking Point poster could hardly have been worse.

Wiggy, Tice and I talked about how to respond, and all agreed we should suspend campaigning activities immediately.

When the terrible news of her death was announced, I knew this was going to have profound implications for the rest of the campaign. We issued a statement expressing shock and sympathy for her family, and spent much of the rest of the evening discussing how it might affect the next few days.

In no time, Remainiacs were trying to suggest that Brexiteers were somehow responsible. I turned down a suggestion that we should hold a press conference to counter these claims. Offensive as they were, the last thing I felt we should do was fuel the debate. So we're sitting tight, reflecting that two little kids have just lost their mum. Puts everything in perspective.

17 JUNE

Taking the flak

Vote Leave is in panic. They think Jo Cox has changed everything.

Priti Patel texted Jimbo this morning, fretting that we might do something to make things worse.

> We at VL are naturally very sensitive about the next few days and also how we are viewed and perceived in the light of what has happened. We've had so many comments levelled against us so we want to avoid any misperceptions about the campaign and are holding off from major activities rallies/poster launches etc. Farage has had noise around his poster and really wanted to touch base to make sure that the 3 groups are talking to avoid any activities that could be viewed as insensitive? Let me know your thoughts as this is now a balancing act. As ever x

Jimbo reassured her that even we know when to shut up.

I still can't believe what's happened. It just shows that you can never control events.

Gerry says he once ran a referendum campaign in Maine in which he was winning with 56 per cent going into last weekend. (They vote on Tuesdays over there.) A horrific storm hit the day before the election, and he lost by 12,000 votes.

'The volatile nature of these campaigns is nasty,' he says.

Just as we feared, the left has been making hay, accusing Leave campaigns of stoking up hatred and fear. Zealots on the fringes of the Remain campaign are desperate to depict Jo as a martyr to the cause.

Nigel warned me they would push this for all it is worth. After years of being painted a racist, he knows how it goes. I spoke to him four or five times today, as I do most days now. He veered between saying it won't make much difference to the outcome and being very despondent and saying we have lost momentum just when things were going in our direction.

He went to lay flowers in Parliament Square. It was the right thing to do, but I was annoyed that he gave a long interview about her straight afterwards. I thought it was unnecessary and just whipped things up. For all his rebellious streak, he gets caught up in the Westminster and media bubble and doesn't always know when to step away. I have an outsider's perspective and told him that I don't think this whole thing will affect the way very many people vote.

Sent an upbeat email to Malcolm Pearson, Tice, Elliott and a load of others with my prediction:

> I think people have pretty much made their minds up and the sheer amount of background noise means nothing will get through.
>
> I think we will win on Thursday.

All the same, we can't return to campaigning tomorrow, as I'd originally hoped. Everyone is still too upset, and it just doesn't feel right.

～

Hot on the heels of Osborne's blackmail budget threat, his old friends the IMF have been scaremongering again. Lagarde says jobs, growth, investment and financial markets will all suffer if we vote to leave the EU. Apparently the global economy will suffer too.

This stuff will have no impact. It's just the same noise, rows of people in suits worried about their own power and pay packets.

People have made up their minds. I think we'll win. Roll on the 23rd.

18 JUNE

Keeping this brief, as it's very late, but I'm fuming about a piece John Prescott has written for tomorrow's *Mirror*. Old Two Jags has done what a lot of people are secretly itching to do but don't quite dare. Adding two and two together and reaching eight, he's suggested that Jo's death somehow strengthens the case for staying in the EU.

'Next Thursday, let hope trump hate and vote with Labour to Remain,' he says.

What a load of tripe. In a rare display of discipline, we've decided not to hit back, but it just shows what we're up against. How much longer before this brigade start wearing badges saying 'Vote Remain for Jo'?

On a more positive note, I was at a friend's 50th birthday party tonight and the mood was overwhelmingly for Out. A lot of the guests were Tories but have turned against Cameron. Very interesting.

19 JUNE

Thank you, Jezza

We're getting some interesting intelligence about the scale of support for Brexit in the Labour Party. Officially, only ten Labour MPs have come out for Leave, but our contacts at Labour Leave think at least forty-three would vote Out if they could.

Corbyn, like the IMF, is a gift that keeps on giving. It's obvious to anyone watching that he doesn't give a toss about staying in. He was asked today whether there was anything that could be done to cap free movement while we remain in the EU. His reply?

'No.'

The Labour leader's mad, but he's not stupid. He knows he's doing next to nothing to help the side he's supposed to be on. Apparently he was planning to stay neutral until Hilary Benn threatened to lead a shadow Cabinet walkout if he didn't whip the party into supporting Remain. Wet Hilary is not exactly a chip off the old Benn block.

Nigel's on the *Today* programme tomorrow. Wiggy and I have been encouraging him to say the Breaking Point poster was a mistake. It was meant to be an attack on the system, not people fleeing their countries, but it was deliberately misinterpreted.

My advice to him at 10 p.m. tonight: 'It takes a big person to say you made a mistake ... It's a bold move and allows you to talk about immigration in the last three days. Also massively sets the agenda and destabilises their plans. PS. Always do the unexpected.'

He replied: 'I will try but not easy.'

'No one said it was ever going to be easy!' I texted back.

Incidentally, we've done some polling on Cox. The tragedy doesn't seem to have made any difference to voting intentions on Thursday.

20 JUNE

A bust-up with Iain Dale

Nigel did well on *Today*.

'Great performance – right tone,' I told him. I suggested we get together for lunch on Thursday. By then it will be as good as over and I can't see any point in spending the day rushing around.

I survived my own media encounter this morning with Iain Dale on LBC. He tried and failed to pull a fast one on me over Jo Cox.

I actually have a bit of respect for Dale – he does his interviews well. He'd been trying to get me on the show for a while. I kept putting it off, but lately he's had Osborne and the head of the London Stock Exchange, so I thought, 'Why not?'

As I was waiting to go into the recording studio, I got talking to his producer and happened to mention the polling we've done on Jo. I assumed our conversation was off the record, but she tipped off Dale, and the minute we were on air, he bounced me into discussing the findings.

We never intended to make the material public and, in any case, it was never a 'Jo Cox poll'. We'd simply stuck an extra question onto a survey we were already doing. All the same, Dale tried to suggest it was somehow in 'bad taste'.

I didn't give an inch, saying I didn't see anything wrong with it at all. We spent the rest of the interview knocking lumps out of each other.

I'd barely left the studio before journalists began calling asking us to release the poll.

Sanctimonious politicians on all sides of this debate might like to pretend the question of whether this terrible tragedy might affect the referendum outcome has never even crossed their minds, because they're too busy feeling devastated for her family. It's bollocks. They all want to know – and there's nothing wrong with asking.

21 JUNE

Bending it like Beckham

We've upset Posh Spice. Quite a coup. It started when her hubby David Beckham put out a wishy-washy statement backing Remain.

The great statesman told us we should be 'facing the problems of the world together and not alone'. Wiggy immediately remembered how much mileage the Spice Girls made out of the Union Jack during their Cool Britannia days. So he dredged up an interview Posh had given *The Spectator* magazine in 1996 and fired the quotes straight back at her: 'The Euro bureaucrats are destroying every bit of national identity and individuality. We must keep our national individuality.'

We added the caption: 'Should have listened to the missus, David.'

This didn't go down very well in the Beckham household. Within minutes, her people were on to us, sniffing that we'd been twisting her views. They put out a statement accusing us of trying to 'put a spin on quotes made twenty years ago' and saying she believes 'in a future for her children where we are stronger together'. Brooklyn and co. are not exactly going to struggle for a crust or two, so I'm not sure why she's dragged them into it. Meanwhile, we were being bombarded by Beckham fans on the phones, email and Twitter, accusing us of misrepresenting their heroine. I told them she was quite capable of twisting her own words and labelled the whole saga 'Bend It Like Beckham'. She's threatening to sue. She can join the queue.

An old soldier tells it like it is

Tubby Two Belts Soames has been invoking his grandfather again. Never one to pass up an opportunity to exploit his distinguished ancestry, he's been busy claiming that if Winston were alive today, he'd have 'listened to his allies' advice' and voted Remain.

I can't look at the man without remembering how one of his former mistresses described the experience of having sex with him: like having a wardrobe fall on you with the key sticking out. He's lost a lot of weight lately, but he still looks like an angry pufferfish.

As I watched him on TV, harrumphing about Churchill, someone in the office handed me a letter we'd been sent by a 95-year-old war veteran. He'd sent us £30.

I wish it was £3,000 but being on a pension it's all I can afford. I am pushing 95. I am an old soldier from the last war. I remember the French and Belgians in 1940, what we called the surrender monkeys ... who we saved.

My father was an old contemptible in France in 1914. He always said you can't trust them and they proved him right. We were never thanked. Best of luck, Leave.EU.

Take that, Two Belts.

Project Fear, Norwegian Edition

Our online videos have been doing fantastically. We turn out original content and promote Nigel wherever possible, but what people really seem to like is clips of Remain campaigners being taken down by 'neutral' interrogators.

Our first choice for this is usually the fearless Andrew Neil, though we pounced on a brilliant clip of Jeremy Paxman pulling his classic 'rubbery horse face of mock indignation' (as Malcolm Tucker aptly put it) at our European Commissioner, Lord Hill, while demanding to know if he had 'ever been elected to anything'. (Answer: no.)

We were concerned that the Corporation might start agitating for these to be taken down, especially after our run-in with Robbie Gibb, but it turns out Neil's team have been enjoying the extra exposure. The BBC *Daily* and *Sunday Politics* even sent us a Twitter message today, suggesting our supporters might be interested in a short interview they conducted with an anti-EU campaigner from Norway.

Indeed they were. Millions of people have now seen the footage we captured of a lovely Scandinavian blonde talking about how the version of 'Project Fear' her countrymen were exposed to during their own EU referendum – massive job losses, foreign investment evaporating overnight, and all the rest – proved to be totally unfounded after they stood firm and told the establishment to get stuffed anyway.

Farage plays Clacton…

Today was the last hurrah for the battle bus. The old girl is begin-ning to look as if she's been in a war zone, and has been making an alarming clunking noise.

Wiggy and I thought we should finish with a flourish, or rather a giant 'fuck you' to Carswell, so we took her to his constituency of Clacton.

Nigel didn't want to come – anything to do with Carswell brings him out in hives – but we talked him into it.

'This is it,' I said firmly. 'We've avoided Clacton until now, but like it or not we're going to go and park the bus on Clacton High Street and you are going to give the speech of your bloody life, right in Carswell's home territory.'

He wasn't happy, but grudgingly agreed.

We pulled into town around 11 a.m. and were greeted by a cheer-ing throng. Immediately, Nigel was surrounded by people asking for selfies and autographs. He told them he's 'saved the best until last, and Clacton is the best'. It was one of the biggest crowds we've seen, and they treated him like a hero, which is just what he needs, after the last few days.

Getting there turned out to be easier than getting out. As we were leaving, the bus snapped an axle and ground to a halt. Another Carswell assassination attempt? Sadly, we can't pin it on him. She's clocked up about 15,000 miles in less than a month and has finally conked out.

Tice is planning to buy her as a rather large memento. The own-ers have agreed to let her go for three grand. God knows where he's going to put her. In the garden?

… while Boris plays Wembley

The Wembley debate was just what I feared. Vote Leave fielded Boris, Andrea Leadsom and Gisela Stuart. Boris could hardly bear to mention the word 'immigration' and moved as swiftly off it as he could. Remain fielded Ruth Davidson and the head of the TUC, along with Sadiq Khan, the Labour Mayor of London. Khan overplayed his hand, coining the phrase 'Project Hate' for our side, which was insulting and will backfire. In the final few minutes, however, Boris did produce a corker, declaring that Thursday could be our 'Independence Day', winning him a standing ovation from the audience. One of our sound bites, by the way.

~

I set the call centre a target of contacting 10,000 people today to test the mood. It was ambitious, but if they get round that number, we should have a very good indication of the way people plan to vote.

22 JUNE

Suspense

Very exciting results from our 10,000 poll. We're doing another tomorrow. Other polls have the result on a knife edge, but ours indicate Leave will win. We're on 51.5 per cent to 48.5 per cent. Close, but enough!

We've thrown everything at this. I've been totting up the facts and figures, and they're pretty impressive, though I say it myself: 20 million leaflets, 10 million letters, 9 million views for our best video, a million social media followers and reaching 15 million people every week. We're almost done.

There is a strange quiet in our operation now. I don't think there's a lot we can do but wait. We'll be on the streets turning out the vote tomorrow, but I'm not planning on sweating it. The job is done.

Nigel is on edge, and I'm not surprised. He's been building up to this moment for the last twenty-five years of his life. He thinks the Jo Cox murder has cost us the referendum.

I tried to cheer him up by telling him about our encouraging private polls, but it cut no ice. For all the bravura, at heart he is a pessimist.

Kate's been getting a lot of flak from elements in the Labour Party about Jo Cox.

However, she's just forwarded me a lovely email she received from a friend, which shows other people have more sense.

> Dear Kate
> Whatever stream of undeserved emails you are receiving concerning the use of the dreadful murder of Jo Cox as emotional blackmail, I support & respect your sincerity and know you do not support xenophobic nonsense. There is nothing I have ever read or heard of yours that demonstrate the slightest hint of racism – more power to you.
> I wish you well, be strong; You have eloquently put your case and you have the support of many.

It was her birthday yesterday and I forgot. I am terrible at remembering these sorts of things. I sent her a belated message and congratulated her on the incredible work she's done for this campaign. I apologised to her that her links to us meant the broadcasters had kept her out of the TV debates. She has been a real star.

23–24 JUNE

Farage despondent

We've done it! It has actually fucking happened. Independence Day. All the pain, the aggro, the time, the money, the rows, the bitching, the tension, everything that was thrown at us – it has all been worth it. The British people have spoken, and we've won. I'm still trying to get my head around it. I was always optimistic, but just can't take it in.

In the morning, bookmakers and pollsters were saying Remain

had it in the bag. I was feeling fairly positive, but everybody on the team was very tense, and there was a very strange feeling in the air, partly because of the weather. In what felt like an omen, there were dramatic electrical storms during the night, and some of London is underwater. By the time I had breakfast, the sun had just about broken through, but it was still very muggy.

I'd organised a special lunch at Nigel's favourite Italian restaurant, Zafferano in Lowndes Street, and had bought him a present: a first edition of Ernest Hemingway's *For Whom the Bell Tolls*, signed by the author. I couldn't believe my luck when I found it last night as I was window-shopping in an antiquarian bookshop. I love rare books, and it seemed so appropriate, because the bell was very definitely tolling for Nigel. Whichever way the result went, it would define his place in history. It was pricey, but I couldn't resist it. I gave it to him at lunch, but he was so preoccupied I don't think he really took it in.

I'd invited Heffer as a thank-you for all his support during the campaign, but sadly he couldn't make it because of flash floods. True Brexit weather! So the line-up was Wiggy; 'Posh George' Cottrell, who runs Nigel's private office and came armed with three packets of fags; Chris Bruni-Lowe; and myself.

The lunch was long and boozy, and between us we polished off several bottles of red, none of which improved Nigel's mood.

'We're going to lose. I can feel it in my waters,' he kept saying.

Bruni-Lowe wasn't making things any better, acting as if it was already all over.

'I can smell it and I'm never wrong,' he said gloomily.

Personally, I still thought we were going to win, but when you're surrounded by people running up the white flag, you start doubting yourself.

'What if we win?' I asked quietly.

Posh George and Bruni-Lowe looked scornful.

'We've got the polls to say we'll win and I can tell you we are going to win,' I told them.

'Your polling's wrong,' Bruni-Lowe replied dismissively. 'It's rubbish. Your methodology isn't right. I don't know how you came up with those results.'

We parted ways around 5 p.m. to prepare for the long night ahead.

A few minutes later, Nigel texted me to thank me again for the book. Perhaps he thought he hadn't been effusive enough.

'I can't believe your present. So generous. Thank you.'

I told him I'd just had a bit of good news from the mines in South Africa.

'Diamond found with a blue hue ... FYI, blue diamonds can fetch between $45,000 and $65,000 a carat. We need to find his bigger, deeper colour brother!' I reported cheerfully.

I had booked into Claridge's for a couple of nights, and went back to the hotel to change before heading to our Millbank office, which is in the same building our party was due to take place in. I told Nigel he should be there at 10.30 on the dot, because he was expected by the press.

Throughout the evening, I kept calling him to exchange bits of intelligence and tell him to stop being so dismal.

'Our poll is way, way bigger than anyone else's,' I said encouragingly. 'I think we're going to do this.'

He wouldn't listen. Years of political disappointment had conditioned him to expect the worst. He didn't dare to believe it could be different this time. I told him we'd polled another 10,000 in the last twenty-four hours, and once again it showed a narrow victory for Brexit. In all, we've spoken to 20,000 people in the last few days – many times more than other pollsters – and the margin is narrow, but clear. But Nigel was sure a high turnout had done for us.

Around 9.40 he received a call from Sky News asking for his prediction. He'd been talking to some hedge fund contacts in the City who'd spent a fortune on exit polls, which suggested victory for Remain.

'I think Remain just edged it,' he told Sky flatly.

The minute the polls closed, his comments went viral. Television channels announced he'd conceded defeat.

I was livid and couldn't understand why he'd done it. After all, not a single vote had been counted. How could he know? My mood wasn't helped when YouGov released a poll just after 10 p.m. with a 52–48 per cent lead for Remain, the exact opposite of our finding.

'What on earth did you do that for?' I asked him. He was in no mood to explain.

Even as we spoke, the signals from the City were changing. The torrential rain appeared to have depressed London turnout, and some of his hedge fund contacts were now messaging him saying it looked as if Leave might just be ahead. He tried to update to Sky, but no one was listening.

Party time

Altitude, the venue for our party, is at the top of the Millbank Tower overlooking the Thames. That building has been the setting for many a political drama. It's where the Prince of Darkness himself, Peter Mandelson, schemed his way to victory for Tony Blair in 1997 and, over the years, it has housed both Labour and Tory head offices.

A few weeks ago, someone from the venue rang our office asking if we wanted to go ahead with a provisional reservation of the bars and function rooms on the 29th floor for referendum night. We were bemused. We hadn't actually made any enquiries about the venue, but soon twigged who had: Vote Leave. We hastily signed on the dotted line.

We were a bit worried that nobody would turn up, so I told Wiggy to invite everyone he could think of. By 11 p.m., the place was heaving, probably because it was the only Brexit bash in town. Vote Leave had decided not to have a party, and Elliott had left town for Manchester, where the official declaration was due to be made.

Wiggy was very agitated because Nigel had vanished. By 11.30 p.m., with hacks getting increasingly impatient, I had still not heard from him and was getting quite annoyed. It was embarrassing: we'd laid on a big party, gathered everyone, and the star of the show had gone AWOL.

By the time he finally appeared, I was fuming and so was he.

Surveying the massed ranks of reporters and cameras, he started having a go at me.

'Why have you invited so many foreign reporters?' he grumbled ungratefully.

'Well, you wanted a platform! Here you are: 400 journalists, every major paper and TV channel! Kay Burley and the rest of them, right in the centre of London. And still you're kicking off,' I snapped.

I was so annoyed I had to go outside to let off steam. By the time I'd simmered down, it was carnage inside. Nigel was being jostled by photographers and reporters, and people were shoving, shouting and being knocked over. My strop over, I tried to take some of the pressure off him by giving some interviews myself.

A little after midnight, the first result came through: Newcastle, which had been expected to produce a strong showing for Remain. Instead, it was almost a tie, falling 50.7 per cent for Remain and 49.3 per cent Leave, on a difference of less than 2,000 votes. Shortly afterwards, the score came through for Sunderland, which had been expected to vote narrowly for Leave by around 6 points. The northern working-class city rejected Brussels by 22 points. Following all the pessimism, suddenly there was a note of caution in the media commentary. Political commentators and pollsters still thought Remain had won – but might there be an upset?

As more results flashed up on TV screens, the atmosphere at our party underwent a dramatic change. The night had begun miserably, with Nigel missing, Wiggy and I arguing with Bruni-Lowe, and all the atmosphere of a wake. Now the mood was electric: there was all to play for! With every new area that voted Out, or voted to Remain by the narrowest of margins, our whoops and cheers grew louder.

Nigel, Wiggy and I retreated to an air-conditioned room off the main function suite for a breather. It was all so intense. We allowed a handful of people we trusted to join us. Nigel got in trouble with the management for smoking, but politely instructed them to sod off.

Around 2 a.m., we all moved downstairs to a bar called Reels that was well set up with television screens, where we could watch the results coming in. The adrenalin and the alcohol were doing their work. Excitement was at fever pitch.

By around 3 a.m., we were pretty sure we'd won, but Nigel couldn't risk calling it. He'd already had to do one handbrake turn, admitting his earlier declaration of defeat had been premature, and would have looked even more of a clown if he'd had to do a second.

But when the result for Birmingham came in and we'd won by a whisker, we knew we were home and dry. The BBC and ITV both decided to call it for Leave and wanted to go live to Nigel.

Quick confab. Nigel: 'Yep, we've done it. Time to claim it.'

And so, at 3.44 a.m., he took to Twitter to declare:

'I now dare to dream that the dawn is coming up on an independent United Kingdom.'

I have never seen him so happy or so emotional.

Surveying the media mob, he tried to collect himself.

'I don't know if I can hold myself together,' he whispered.

'Course you can. Get out there,' I instructed.

A second or two later, in a mad crush of microphones, cameras and long lenses, he finally gave the speech he had waited a quarter of a century to deliver.

> If the predictions now are right, this will be a victory for real people, a victory for ordinary people, a victory for decent people.
>
> We have fought against the multinationals, we have fought against the big merchant banks, we have fought against big politics, we have fought against lies, corruption and deceit. And today, honesty, decency and belief in nation I think now is going to win.

Nigel is a true British hero. It's his life's work and the most phenomenal political achievement of our time.

Wiggy and I had one last surprise for him. We had arranged for a ballsy full-page advert in the *Telegraph* for the morning after the referendum, thanking our followers and paying tribute to him for his incredible efforts. It had a picture of him next to the full version of that Teddy Roosevelt quote from 1910: 'It's not the critic who counts; not the man who points out how the strong man stumbles. The credit belongs to the man who is actually in the arena, whose face is marred by dust and sweat and blood.'

Which is Nigel to a T. He loved it.

'I can't believe you've done that. I mean how on earth could you put a congratulation notice in the paper when you didn't even know the result?' he said delightedly.

What he hadn't noticed was 'win or lose' in very small print above the words 'Thank You, Nigel'.

But I had always been positive.

The morning after

As the party wound down, Wiggy and I left the cleaners tidying up the knocked-over glasses and general debris and stumbled out into the dawn sunshine, clutching a couple of bottles of champagne. We came across an old bloke at a cash machine trying to get out as much money as he could. He told us he thought there was going to be a run on the banks.

We headed to Chris Bruni-Lowe's flat, just near the House of Commons, and cracked open the bubbly before making our way to Westminster for victory interviews. The atmosphere was extraordinary: cabbies and lorry drivers blaring their horns as they thundered past the Houses of Parliament; the world's media camped on College Green; TV news anchors bellowing into mics.

The rest of the morning passed in a blur.

We watched Cameron's resignation speech in UKIP's poky Westminster office on a crappy TV that kept cutting out. Then we all trooped off to the Ritz for a celebratory breakfast. The hotel lobby was decked in Union Jacks. Fred Barclay, who along with his brother owns the hotel (as well as the *Telegraph*), joined us for a feast of champagne and kippers – what else? When his phone went off, the ring tone was 'Land of Hope and Glory'.

Through the knackered haze, I summed it up in a text to Nigel tonight: 'In the last day we have won the referendum, fucked Cameron, fucked Corbyn, caused a second referendum in Scotland, caused discussion of a united Ireland; Holland and Denmark now want a referendum.'

Unbe-fucking-lievable.

25 JUNE

I sat down for a breather today, and now I've come back down to earth a bit, I tried to do a proper analysis of how this war was won. It's important to do this, as no campaign in this country will be the same again. I set it all out in an email to Christopher Hope at the *Telegraph*.

> The landscape of British politics has been changed forever with the People voting Out on Thursday.
>
> The consequences of this decision have not only led to leadership challenges in both main parties but have started a potential domino effect across Europe with other countries facing referendums.
>
> Goddard Gunster, the US strategy firm hired by Leave.EU, has been approached by parties in Italy to run a similar campaign there, where public demand is growing for a referendum.
>
> ...
>
> The internal Leave.EU supervised by Gunster's poll called the result at 52% leave to 48%, released at 10.01 p.m. The only accurate poll issued in the last week.
>
> The use of big data for the first time in any election in the UK left Leave.EU [with] a massive advantage [over] both official campaigns.
>
> The social media campaign ... was a huge success, providing a platform far bigger than the ones built up by either

the Remain campaign or the official Vote Leave group, with 100,000 followers on Twitter and 800,000 supporters on Facebook, where the weekly post reach often broke twenty million people.

This was achieved through having a strong focus on audience engagement, with a broad range of content designed to appeal to different types of voter ... we were able to update this material in real-time to improve its appeal, driving engagement even further, building crowds...

The end result was not just a fantastic tool for direct outreach, bypassing the broadcast and print media entirely, but an extremely useful database which enabled us to better understand the concerns of the voters.

Goddard Gunster were able to mine this database to conduct in-depth demographic polling and recommend precision target-messaging, while focusing our greatest areas where the Leave movement had to make its greatest inroads to tip our campaign over the line.

Nigel Farage's nation-wide battle bus tour, for example, while dismissed as a bit of an eccentric romp by the media, was directed at those areas we had identified as holding large numbers of 'persuadables' – and persuadables identified as being most likely to be open to the UKIP message rather than the very staid, Tory messaging of the Vote Leave group.

We saw the proof in the pudding on 23 June, when Leave romped home in predominantly Labour-voting, working-class areas and a 20,000-sample macro poll conducted by Leave.EU managed a bang-on referendum prediction of 52/48 in favour of Leave, while the establishment pollsters at organisations like YouGov who had thrown the kitchen sink at getting this right after the general election fiasco got it wrong yet again.

Using – new to the UK – social-media polling technology developed in the US and dismissed by the established polling companies, the Leave.EU team had at their fingertips the confident ability to understand exactly what was on

people's minds, where they lived and how they would
vote. Each day headlines on social media were changed to
reflect the individual moods of their audience as much as
20 times in a day. But perhaps the most potent weapon that
Leave.EU used was simple and always ignored by so-called
sophisticated polling organisations – they listened to the
chatter on social media and responded.

This has been about responding to people and the issues they care
about. If I think about how I've changed over the years, it's quite
similar to Nigel. We both came up through the Thatcher revolution and were big fans. Now, the priorities are different. They are
about people. We both loathe the way things are stitched up by big
businesses and politicians, the corporatism. We loathe the lack of
honesty and lack of personality of politicians.

Extraordinarily, it appears we're turning into left-wingers.

26 JUNE

Remainiac panic

The Remain campaign's media groupies are howling. They are so
shocked by their defeat that they are trying to make it look like
Brexiteers have unleashed a wave of racist attacks across Britain.

Adam Boulton from Sky claimed he and his family had witnessed
foreigners being asked: 'When are you going home'? three times.
He complained that racist incidents were being aimed at EU citizens living here. I just replied: 'Poor media luv, I bet you didn't have
a single friend who voted out. X.' Boulton had a very priggish comeback: 'I don't have one who would think yours is an appropriate
response to racism'. Others called me unpleasant and illogical. Some
even said that maybe – just maybe – their children could be taunted,
even though they hadn't actually been abused. Sheer, desperate
madness.

═

I sent Elliott a congratulatory email. But I couldn't resist warning him not to get into the 'bitter enemy category – it's an unpleasant place to be'.

He told me he didn't consider me a bitter enemy. What a petal.

27 JUNE

An epidemic of hurt feelings

The wailing and gnashing of teeth from the Remain side has tugged at my heartstrings. I have announced that I would like to extend my 'heartfelt apologies' to those I may have hurt. I am not laughing. I am being generous in victory.

So far we have clocked eight cases.

Nasa *v.* Leave.EU in court would have been fun but I'm sorry, Nasa, if you thought I'd used astronaut Tim Peake's quote 'out of context'. Oh, Superdrug, we quoted your founder accurately, but we did use your logo without permission. Soz. Gary Lineker and Victoria Beckham, it was funny – bring it on, luvvies.

Dearest Electoral Commission, you were the legal division of the In campaign – so bite me. And last and least, the Information Commissioner's Office, who had a go at us for sending information to voters – whatever.

To those I may have missed: I'm sorry, I'm sorry, I'm so, so sorry To all of you: We've discovered a great home remedy. It's called 'grow a pair and get over yourselves'.

Keep calm and carry on

Four days. That's all it took. Four days for everything to quieten down again. Some apocalypse. Seems Remain's scare stories sat on the bestseller list for a far shorter period of time than the publishers hoped. The FTSE's fine – actually higher than it was twelve days ago. New jobs are being created, the companies that said they'd pack their bags have recovered from their hissy fits. What's not to like? Yet mainstream media like the BBC are still running around like headless chickens trying to persuade everyone it's like we're in the middle of World War II. They should just keep calm and carry on.

Computer says no

There is something funny going on with our IT. Our website is down, along with several other pro-Brexit sites, in what looks like a denial-of-service attack. Early indications are that the source of the mischief is mainland Europe.

It's flattering that our little organisation is attracting international cyber-warfare tactics, though it is a bit unlikely that the Chinese or the Russians are to blame this time.

We have picked up quite a few enemies along the way in this campaign, but we haven't got time to sift through all of them to find out which democracy-hater is behind this one.

≈

Gerry Gunster's sent me and Wiggy a 'You guys rock' email. We need a press release to do a big drumroll for Goddard Gunster, highlighting the accuracy of the polling, their messaging, understanding the voters. They are stars.

I feel washed out now, but we need to think about what the future holds for UKIP.

29 JUNE

Bad losers all over

The Remain lot really are terrible losers. It is getting embarrassing. Today hundreds of them gathered outside Parliament and there was another mob in Trafalgar Square, protesting about the result. They made fools of themselves and their cause, carrying pathetic 'let's hug it out' placards and hurling abuse at Brexiteers.

That old sourpuss Anna Soubry, who is in the denial phase, almost broke down as she told the crowd how members of her family had wept at the result, prompting her fellow MP Nadine Dorries to tweet that she'd seen Soubry leave the Commons bar before talking to the crowd and 'she was inebriated not emotional'.

Soubry was telling the crowd not to accept 'hate' – as if anyone has asked them to!

She then went on a loopy tweet-fest, screeching that Nigel 'does NOT represent the British ppl' and accusing him of creating 'division & hate by preying on prejudice & fuelling fear'.

A load of bollocks. In bullish mood, I messaged her saying she was a loud-mouthed loser. Someone on Twitter came up with a far better description, calling her a 'Poundshop Thatcher'.

I have not one jot of sympathy for these sore losers. They are the scumbags who tried to pin Jo Cox's death on us and show zero interest in the death threats levelled at Nigel.

Feeding off the Remainiac media, squealing fools like the Labour MP David Lammy and microscopic leader of the microscopic Lib Dems Tim Farron are saying the result should be overturned by Parliament. Tony Blair, that foreign policy genius, has suggested a second referendum.

This was the biggest democratic decision in British history, backed by more than 17 million people, who these elites now say should be ignored. Shocked establishment types are shrieking because they can feel the power slipping away from them. Enough already!

A dose of steroids

Ideas zipping round from the great and the good like Nigel Lawson and David Owen about where we go from here with the EU. Lawson thinks we should forget trade negotiations with the EU. He also says, quite rightly, that it would be 'dishonourable' to trade away control over immigration, which we campaigned so hard on. Don't give Europeans any favours over non-Europeans, he reckons.

Owen also favours pulling out of the single market, as the campaign promised, but thinks we should give trade talks a chance. He wants to move fast on Brexit: 'The British government needs to table a European Communities Act 1972 Repeal Bill on a timetable to become law by December 2016. Within it there could be a possibility of an extension only for one year and that dependent on real progress on a bilateral trade negotiation.' He said we need to be 'out completely from the EU whatever happens by December 2019'.

My view is simple: we should stay tariff-free and let the EU do what they want, then introduce an immigration cap of 50,000 with a £5,000 deposit from all newcomers. The economy would explode. Singapore on steroids.

30 JUNE

If the Tories do one thing well, it's betraying friends. Daggers glinting in the dark, blood on the floor. Boris and Gove were meant to be the Brexit dream team, but Gove is obviously sick of playing Jeeves to Boris's Wooster. He's not just betrayed him, he has stuck the knife in deep, announcing this morning that he's standing for the party leadership by himself because Boris is 'not capable of … leading the party and the country in the way that I would have hoped'. All hell has broken loose and my old friend Mark Fullbrook is hopping mad. He had been running Bozza's campaign, which is now in tatters. Poor old BoJo had to bow out, having lost half his backers and the confidence of his running mate. It's very entertaining, but one of the many reasons people loathe politicians. I never wanted to work with Gove and I'm glad we didn't have to. He is not to be trusted.

Shell-shocked Cameroons are rallying round Theresa May as the best prospect for fudging us out of a real Brexit. She says she wants to be judged on her record as Home Secretary. That's a mistake!

Her record on immigration is beyond shocking. In six years at the Home Office, she completely failed to bring the numbers under control. The Tories promised they would bring net migration down below 100,000 a year and it's three times that.

The other Remainer in the running is a bedwetter called Stephen Crabb, who's even softer than May on immigration and the single market. The only two I'd trust with carrying out the people's wishes are Andrea Leadsom, the Energy Minister, and Liam Fox, the former Defence Secretary. Received wisdom at Westminster is that Fox is too right-wing for the general public, but he has been totally solid on Brexit from the start.

Leadsom is an unknown quantity, but seems the most exciting option. She was impressive in the debates and had a great referendum campaign overall. We've decided to get behind her. We've now got a million supporters, many of them Tories. We could make a real difference.

I have a massive hangover and am heading to bed early. I'm still considering where UKIP goes from here. Told Nigel he needs to overhaul the party structure, make Tice chairman, take a break and come back for 2020.

JULY 2016

4 JULY

The battle of Essex

Nigel resigned today, prompting a smiley-face tweet from closet Tory Carswell.

I have been hoping for months that he might be expelled from UKIP for gross disloyalty, but the party's ruling body, the National Executive Committee, has stepped back from the brink.

Jamie Huntman is on the warpath, calling the decision 'weak, weak, weak'. He thinks it's 'game over' for the party and says he has local members who are 'inconsolable' that Nigel rather than Douglas has gone. The leader of the UKIP group on Basildon Council calls Carswell a 'sanctimonious p****' and Nigel 'the greatest politician ever'.

Huntman wants us to get together to talk about how to stop the 'disloyal clique' of 'Carswellites' who he fears will turn UKIP into a 'beige establishment party'. He said he wouldn't employ them to sweep his timber yard (he owns one) and that 'my parrot talks more sense'.

I told him to relax – and that I may even stand for the leadership myself. Cue much hilarity from Raheem Kassam, who used to work for Nigel and fancies his own chances. He told me I 'couldn't smash a sugar glass window', some tongue in cheek reference to me not being tough enough, I suppose. Yeah, right.

Lucy Fisher texted tonight asking if I might stand. I told her I might think about it. Bit of mischief.

5 JULY

The grey woman pulls ahead

Theresa May has pulled ahead in the Tory leadership contest, winning the first round with MPs by a country mile. She's already making speeches about Brexit as if she's PM.

Leadsom came second, and Gove's still in play.

I've tweeted that if May wins, 'UKIP will be back [on] steroids. She has been an awful Home Secretary & as PM she will be dull'.

Dull is dangerous. I don't trust her. Once MPs have had their votes and the final shortlist of two goes out to the membership, they may not take kindly to a Remain PM. Members voted 70–30 to leave.

Exposed

Wiggy and I have been trying to get back to business, but keep getting distracted. I had the perfect excuse today in that the bank manager wanted to see me, so I left him to it in the office.

He was outside, having a fag, playing with his phone and generally trying to put off doing any work, when Pam, our operations manager, came rushing over.

'We've had a security breach,' she shouted, as if we were GCHQ, not a call centre in Cribbs Causeway.

'What are you talking about?' said Wiggy.

'Look, out there! In the bushes!' Pam shouted excitedly. 'There are people hiding in the bushes!'

Sure enough, there were two suspect characters knocking around in the shrubs.

Wiggy got straight on the phone to our head of security.

'Your guys are shit. We've got two intruders on the property and you didn't even notice,' he said.

Apparently the interlopers had been wandering around the office asking folk if they were 'happy with the way they'd ruined the country in getting people to vote for leave'.

Never one to eschew a drama, Wiggy called the police. Meanwhile, our unexpected visitors took up position outside Topps Tiles.

Noticing that they were armed with long lenses, Wiggy did what he always does in the presence of any kind of camera, and struck a series of poses to keep them entertained.

Naturally, the second the police arrived, the suspects scarpered. While the cops set off in pursuit, we looked at our CCTV, which revealed that the pair had waltzed into the building, cool as cucumbers, by tailgating some genuine visitors.

A few minutes later, the officers returned and informed us that the suspects were in fact undercover reporters. It transpired that they were low-rent comedians from an outfit called Hat Trick Productions.

We thought we might as well have some fun at their expense, so we fired off a press release with pictures of their faces, and a video of the incriminating CCTV footage, to make it a little harder for them to go incognito next time.

Nice guys that we are, we also tipped off Elliott, as their next stop is most likely the offices of Vote Leave.

≈

Gove has crashed out of the Tory leadership contest in spectacular style. Nick Boles, a smarmy Tory MP who did as much as the Justice Secretary to assassinate Boris, got caught up to dirty tricks, trying to persuade colleagues to vote tactically to keep Leadsom off the ballot paper. It all backfired and he ended up looking a tit. Clearly he and his puppet master have spent too much time with Cummings.

The Tories aren't the only party with a traitor problem. I texted Paul Nuttall to say that Carswell may have escaped so far but I have a letter on my desk that is going out to all his 64,000 constituents explaining what a prick he is. Paul urged me to have one last go at just trying to get along, and offered to mediate. I almost never fall out with anyone, but Carswell did his best to undermine Nigel all the way along. I'm irreconcilable.

8 JULY

Motherhood and apple pie

The shit has hit the fan over an interview Leadsom's given *The Times*.

Poor Andrea made the fatal error of mentioning that she's a mother, when Theresa May unfortunately isn't. She compounded the mistake by elaborating on how her children have affected her life, and pointing out that they give her a very real stake in the future.

She might just as well have labelled Theresa barren, for all the hysteria. Everyone is piling in.

Personally, I couldn't see the big problem, and ended up having a Twitter spat with Harry Cole from *The Sun*, who accused me of defending 'direct slurs' on May. Ridiculous that *The Sun* of all places is siding with a few uptight Labour women who are disgusted by mention of the M word.

Our supporters are right behind her.

10 JULY

Leadsom's campaign is lurching from disaster to disaster. She seems to be surrounded by amateurs and is getting terrible advice. It now turns out that she did the interview in a noisy café and didn't even bring a tape recorder.

We've tried to reach out, but she and her 'people' seem to have retreated to their bunker. Have we backed the wrong horse here?

I've been on *Marr* talking about Brexit, Tory leadership etc.

Gunster said my appearance was 'excellent and very statesman-like' though rather spoiled the effect by adding that it was 'one of my better ones'. He told me to turn off my phone and get some rest.

Angela Eagle, the shadow Business Secretary, has announced a formal leadership challenge against Corbyn. Thankfully, she's political D-list. This won't go anywhere.

11 JULY

Leadsom has pulled out. Big shame. It means May is going to be PM. The Mexican stand-off is over, the men in grey suits have dragged the bodies away, swabbed down the floor and she is the last one standing. There will be no chance for the party's members to have their say.

I still think Leadsom could have won if she'd brazened it out. This was a storm in a tea cup, but she lost her nerve. Which probably proves her critics right: she wasn't ready. In the Labour leadership contest, Angela Eagle has been shouting from the rooftops that she's a northern working-class lesbian. The Westminster class love it. Dare to admit you're a married mother and proud of it, and you're finished.

The Leadsom business has at least given us a glimpse of what Leave.EU supporters could do. Just look at what Momentum has achieved on the left by getting behind Corbyn.

I told David Wall (who backs May and was chaperoning her at the Dorchester earlier in the year) that I have been chatting to some of the really big donors on our side. We're ready to put the Tory Party to the sword so we can stop the establishment murdering Brexit. Wall tried to hose me down, telling me to give May time. She says 'Brexit means Brexit' and I suppose we should give her a chance. But she did so little as Home Secretary that I am sceptical.

I told Wall that we might form a new centre-right party with new faces – something that lets Nigel return to frontline politics in due course. It'll be properly run with a national network of agents and a solid structure. Leave.EU has a million online followers and a huge database. Over the summer, we'll work on it.

12 JULY

Labour's fucked. The Corbynistas on the NEC have decided their man automatically goes on the ballot for the leadership contest. I couldn't hide my delight. Now the party will lose even more working-class votes. Its narrow-minded, pseudo-intellectual leadership simply can't comprehend that their voters disobeyed them and voted for leave. We stand to gobble up 40 per cent of their supporters. Will Straw got all pissy about the NEC decision and tweeted that it was a victory for UKIP. I tweeted him back that we were far more pleased when we found out that Will would be running the

Remain campaign. He's right about Corbyn, of course. He's our greatest ally. Long live Jezza.

No jungle for Nigel

Doesn't look like Nigel's going to be short of things to do now he's quit as leader. In a moment of weakness, a few weeks ago, he agreed to star in an advert for my car insurance company Go Skippy. I've promised it will be tasteful! Now that everyone wants a piece of him, we'll make it worth his while.

Given the demand he's in, we're probably a bit lower on his list of priorities than before the referendum.

He told he that he's turned down 'a monster sum' – supposedly £250k – to appear on *I'm a Celebrity … Get Me Out of Here!*

'If you want to go eat kangaroo bums in the jungle, go ahead,' I told him.

It's not going to happen. For one thing, he knows that 16 million Remainers would jam the phone lines trying to vote him off. For another, he couldn't go three weeks without a fag. But mostly, he just knows it would be a giant embarrassment. No amount of money could compensate for that.

A new start for Leave.EU

Nigel, Wiggy, Tice and I are still thinking about the future. We can't let all the energy just fade away. We need to make sure the network of supporters we've amassed keeps changing this country for the better. They've achieved an unbelievable amount already and Leave.EU has been a success beyond anything we ever imagined. It has shown what ordinary people can do if they band together against their supposed 'betters'.

We've got this great movement for change with a huge social media reach and committed grassroots activists, so what do we do with it? If May is pulling the wool over our eyes and Brexit doesn't actually mean Brexit, there will be a huge vacuum for a serious anti-EU organisation to occupy. It's early days, but we are thinking about something like a right-wing Momentum, the group that has driven the Corbyn phenomenon. It's been done in other countries: Five Star in Italy and Podemos in Spain. We nearly saw the start of something with Leadsom.

I've asked Liz to draw up three potential scenarios. We could create a brand-new political party; a Momentum-style movement that's not a party; or just continue to fund a reformed UKIP, with a return for Nigel at some point in the future. Nigel is putting a bit of a downer on all this. He's ruling out coming back at the helm of a new party, saying it's 'crackers' to try to fight a turf war with UKIP over its vote share. He's pointing out the immense amount of work it took to build UKIP from the fringes to become a real threat to the establishment. After all he's done, I don't think he has the energy for that fight all over again. Time to wait and see whether UKIP can properly reform itself and deal with the likes of Carswell before we try to challenge it directly.

If Diane James wins, which we hope she will, we're going to stay on good terms with the party. But I've genuinely been shocked at the duplicity of the Carswells of this world. He's part of a potentially fatal disease within the party. It needs major surgery – or it will die.

Wiggy's the keenest voice for a new party. He knows I've caught the political bug and am tempted. Exciting times ahead, regardless. I've got a feeling my time in politics has only just begun.

13 JULY

The new broom

Dave has left the scene humiliated and Theresa May is in No. 10. I am not clapping my hands, but it's good to see she is having a proper clear-out. Osborne, of course, had to go. He got no consolation prize, no chance to resign – he was just sacked and booted onto the back benches. The wonder is that he ever thought he could cling on.

It's good to see a trio of Leavers in the key Cabinet jobs for dealing with Brexit. Boris as Foreign Secretary, David Davis with a new department for leaving the EU, and Liam Fox in charge of international trade.

Now let's see if this is divide and rule or if May means it.

18 JULY

Trumped

I'm properly ill. Not just man flu. We're taking Nigel to Cleveland, Ohio for the Republican National Convention tomorrow and, on doctor's orders, I'm missing the trip. I basically collapsed and thought I might be having a heart attack. The doctor was shocked at what had happened. My blood pressure was 180/120, which is medical code for sit down, don't do anything or you'll burst a blood vessel. The campaign has really taken its toll.

I've had a load of tests and, thankfully, there's nothing physically wrong with my heart. To hammer home his diagnosis, the doctor took out his notepad and wrote the word LIFESTYLE in capital letters. The long lunches and fancy dinners, the stress of constant media interviews and attacks, long nights of drinking and cigars have not done me any good.

Am gutted to be missing the trip to the States. Wiggy and I wanted to take Nigel as a kind of victory lap. He has quite a following out there and it would have been a hell of a way to cap the campaign. Instead, I'm in bed.

19 JULY

I'm doing what I'm told and have my feet up, but Wiggy's keeping me updated on the convention. He's set off with Nigel, Tice and

Posh George. I think America will be the setting for another victory for outsider politics against the establishment – the crowning of Donald Trump as the Republican Party nominee for President of the United States.

20 JULY

They got into Chicago O'Hare yesterday from Heathrow, where something slightly strange happened: Posh George was detained and questioned at immigration. He was taken aside for a while. The gang didn't have much time to catch their connecting flight to Ohio and had to abandon him to his fate. Nigel thought it might be because he was carrying a lot of cash. Apparently he's from a very wealthy family and routinely carries around thousands of pounds.

He reappeared just in time to make it to the plane, and told them that he'd been stopped for carrying too many duty-free cigarettes. He seemed entirely unruffled: quite impressive for a 23-year-old.

Gerry met them at the airport and whisked them off in a typically gigantic American vehicle. Unfortunately, we'd left all the arrangements till the last minute, which had created a real headache with hotels. Cleveland is a small city and everything was packed. Posh George and Tice drew the short straw and were dumped in a crummy motel thirty miles out of town. Posh George caused a stink but Tice was his best collegiate self and acted as if he was delighted to find himself miles from anywhere. Andy and Nigel have checked into a nice downtown hotel.

They seem cheerful: apparently Farage keeps being stopped for autographs and selfies, and everyone wants to talk about Brexit. As a bonus, they managed to hook up with Ashcroft, who loves American politics and is also at the convention.

Wiggy says the place is heaving with wackos in silly hats and people sporting 'Hillary for Prison' badges and busty girls wearing pink T-shirts saying 'Hot Chicks for TRUMP'. Only in America.

21 JULY

Wiggy called and filled me in on yesterday. Nigel's schedule was jam-packed with interviews, mainly for various Fox outlets, but also with Jon Snow from Channel 4. After all Posh George's pestering, they managed to land him a room at the very swanky InterContinental, but he still wasn't happy. Apparently it wasn't downtown enough for the little toff.

In the evening, they met for drinks on a roof terrace at the Hilton hotel, overlooking the lakes. There was a rumour Trump was going to do a surprise speech, so they hotfooted it to the conference centre in the hope of a glimpse. They say the Quicken Loans Arena, where the convention is being held, is vast, with a full capacity of over 20,000. They waited for an hour but the rumour came to nothing. There was one Republican big cheese who gave a speech about Hillary Clinton's long list of crimes. 'She won't be put on trial, so I want you to be the jury.' He then read out a rap sheet a mile long and after each charge asked the crowd, 'How do you find her?!'

'GUILTY!' they yelled.

Way over the top!

They wound up having a very late-night dinner in an Italian restaurant, where they had a bizarre encounter with one of Trump's henchmen. It was after midnight, and they'd just finished their meal, when they got word via one of Wiggy's contacts that he is interested in securing Nigel's endorsement. Wiggy made encouraging noises and in the dead hours of the morning a bunch of heavies and a yellow-haired old geezer named Roger Stone, famous in the States as Trump's long-standing unofficial fixer, rocked up at the restaurant.

Stone is an old friend of President Nixon's and has a reputation in Republican circles as a real political dogfighter. He and Nigel had a long conversation in a corner of the restaurant, which ended inconclusively. Seems Trump was just sizing Nigel up.

22 JULY

Yesterday was Trump's big keynote speech. I wish I'd been there. Wiggy told me the excitement was fever pitch. Getting into the conference centre appears to have involved running the gauntlet of a mob of reporters, bloggers and hawkers plying Trump-themed tat. Everywhere he went, Nigel was pursued by a gaggle of journalists and women of a certain age desperate for a photograph. In the morning, Gerry, whose wife Kristi has a senior role running the convention, arranged for the gang to be given a private tour of the centre.

Wiggy says the security round Trump was quite something. Parts of the stage are bulletproof and they were told that Trump stands on a trapdoor which can be opened in a millisecond at the first sign of trouble, sending him plummeting out of harm's way.

In the heat of the afternoon, things got a bit edgy as Nigel was pursued down a street by a hostile blogger.

'How does it feel to be hated, Mr Farage?'

It unsettled him a bit and Wiggy and Posh George considered drafting in some security. Thankfully, he was distracted by a chance meeting with Newt Gingrich, the former Speaker of the House of Representatives and general Republican big cheese. Then, after a few late lunch drinks, he was in a better mood.

In the evening, they headed back to the convention centre for Trump's keynote speech, swatting off selfie-grabbers and reporters. Wiggy told me they spent half the evening circuiting the arena trying to get Nigel to various media engagements while blokes talking into their sleeves blocked their way. Nigel had a serious sense-of-humour failure as he and Posh George raced round like demented hamsters getting sweatier and sweatier.

Eventually, they made it to the various interviews, after which they all squeezed into the auditorium to watch the speech. Wiggy says the woman sitting next to him got so over-excited by Trump's trumpetings that everyone in the vicinity had to block their ears.

The good news is that he's bringing me back a present. On the way out, he nicked a huge Republican Convention-branded Exit sign. He says he's going to draw the letters 'Br' in front of it and keep it as a memento. The last I heard from him, it was the middle of the night out there, and he, Farage and Tice were in some dodgy downtown bar.

23 JULY

I'm feeling a lot better but Nigel's in shock. Posh George has been arrested! Nobody knows exactly what's going on, but it doesn't look good.

After spending the day mooching around Cleveland, the gang flew from Ohio to Chicago, from where they were due to catch a connecting flight to Heathrow.

As they were alighting from the domestic flight, five FBI officers cuffed him. They swooped the minute he set foot on the gangway and if Wiggy hadn't been standing right behind him, nobody would have known what had happened. All the other passengers were held back. It was swift and discreet, and he was hauled off without explanation.

Nigel was stunned. As his nickname suggests, Posh is extremely well connected (his model mother is an old flame of Prince Charles; his godfather is reputed to be a billionaire) and he was working for Nigel on the back of a personal recommendation from his aristocratic uncle, the UKIP-supporting Lord Hesketh. He was wealthy enough to give his time for nothing, and had proven hard-working and loyal. There was nothing to suggest any criminal connection.

As they waited to board their connecting flight, the gang wondered what they could do. Nigel felt terrible about abandoning the young man, but they were helpless.

Wiggy spoke to some contacts at the Foreign Office in an attempt to find out what was going on. They weren't entirely forthcoming, but he seems to have been arrested on suspicion of 'financial impropriety'. Wherever Nigel goes, drama seems to follow.

25 JULY

Posh George in the slammer

Nasty shock today as Nigel got Posh George's full rap sheet. It's not pretty. He's been indicted on twenty-one counts of crimes including money laundering, wire fraud and blackmail. Apparently, two years before he joined UKIP he was caught up in a sting by undercover FBI officers. He allegedly offered to launder drug money for them over the dark web, and they ended up transferring him £15,500 after a meeting in Las Vegas. Later, he tried to blackmail the agents by threatening to turn them in to the police unless they gave him a 130 Bitcoin, worth around £50,000 at the time.

Seems the family problems may run deeper than we thought. He's pleaded poverty and been granted a public defender, paid for by the US taxpayer. Not sure I'd want to rely on one of them if I was facing a decade in a US federal prison. Rumours are that he's had a gambling addiction and his family have cut him off. A sad time for everyone involved. He is very young, and I suspect he's been caught up in something way over his head.

Never a dull moment.

31 JULY

Full circle

Finally, some time to reflect. I spent the day sitting in the garden with Wiggy, looking back on the past year. The truth is we had no idea what we were getting into. At the beginning of the campaign, Nigel said that only time would tell if we were geniuses or complete idiots. The answer is we're neither. We got a lot wrong, but we got a lot right.

We went into it knowing we wanted to shake things up, but we didn't know how it would play out. We were up against far more powerful forces than we anticipated. We discovered pretty quickly that the Remain-supporting establishment and the stalwarts of the traditional media propped each other up, while Eurosceptic grandees were often too invested in the status quo to be as bold as required.

These people have spent years, sometimes decades, sharing the same television studio couches, dining in the same restaurants and quaffing champagne at the same events. Understandably, they value their relationships with individuals on the other side of the argument too highly to go for the jugular.

There were certain issues they all agreed should not be touched and certain lines that must not be crossed. As we discovered, they didn't appreciate outsiders forcing the debate. The attitude seemed to be that immigration ought not to be discussed in front of the children – i.e. the voting public.

Nigel Farage, the one politician in this country who has been consistently willing to give a voice to voters who bear the brunt of uncontrolled immigration, could not win the argument alone. He needed back-up, and we were his special forces.

Everyone else we brought into the campaign – Gerry Gunster, our messengers from the worlds of business, medicine and science, the young working-class guys on our press team – came from well outside the incestuous Westminster bubble.

Our style was very different from the conventional approach adopted by both the Remain campaign and the official Vote Leave campaign, populated as they were by has-been politicians, the sons and godsons of former ministers and ambitious backstairs crawlers with an eye on personal advancement.

Through a combination of social media and good old-fashioned campaigning, we were able to build a mass movement amazingly easily. Voters were itching to take on the establishment. They had differing agendas, but coalesced around Brexit not only because they believed in it but also because they wanted to teach the cosy elites a lesson: that the status quo does not serve everyone well.

These voters have seen the enormous change they can achieve if they come together. I think they are ready to make their voices heard on other causes. That's why I'm thinking about building a new mass movement, through new media, like Five Star in Italy.

Our campaign wasn't always easy. We were up against individuals and organisations who poured scorn on us day in, day out, while our supposed allies at Vote Leave tried to shuffle us off the pitch to maximise their own airtime.

With or without our Westminster friends, we changed the face of politics not just in Britain but across Europe. Our movement achieved something truly historic, which I think is just the beginning of something much bigger.

I wouldn't trade that for all the diamonds in South Africa.

EPILOGUE

TRUMP CARD

'Just a quick nightcap?' Farage suggested.

It was 4.30 a.m. in Cleveland, and he and Wiggy were the last men standing from our team. They'd watched Donald Trump accept the Republican presidential nomination. Now they'd wound up at a pretty iffy bar, where they were occupying an outside table so they could smoke.

They hadn't eaten all day until a pile of pizzas appeared on the table, but adrenalin had kept them going till the booze kicked in.

Little did they know at the time, but the drinks they were about to order would to lead to one of the most extraordinary political journeys in Farage's long career of extraordinary political journeys.

As I write this, we are weeks away from what could be an epoch-defining moment. It is a long shot, but Donald Trump, the man once dismissed as the court jester of American politics, with his improbable blond weave and his blunderbuss speeches, could yet win the presidential election. At times he has equalled his Democrat rival

Hillary Clinton in the polls. Whatever happens on 8 November 2016, Trump has shaken the assumptions of American politics to the core. The staid establishment of the Republican Party has been upended. We're witnessing the rise of outsider politics.

Few among the complacent elites of London, Washington or anywhere else have grasped just how shaky their hold on power has become. Individuals like Trump and Farage have given a voice to people who feel ignored by the metropolitan class, with its groupthink love of free markets and left-liberal values.

The outsiders have shouldered the disadvantages of globalisation and mass immigration on their jobs, public services and communities, while the international elite trouser the advantages. Traditional principles like patriotism are routinely and openly sneered at from on high.

These people can no longer be ignored. The power of social media has liberated disenfranchised individuals to come together in mass movements. When they're well organised, they can paralyse the establishment and shatter conventional wisdom.

In Britain, a left-wing movement without a single MP, Momentum, has created a following hundreds of thousands strong and brought the historic Labour Party to its knees. A Tory establishment that thought it had everything under control was humiliated by a national groundswell of anger about the EU that the elite is still struggling to comprehend.

UKIP started the ball rolling, but the world has moved on. With its remorseless infighting, and absence of a clearly defined mission, it is not fit to spearhead a great national movement in its current form. It's too traditional. Structurally, it is a mess, held together by rubber bands and by the extraordinary stamina of one man, Nigel Farage. It is clear that something new is required.

The way we built Leave.EU shows that it's possible to marshal mighty forces if you've got a great cause to pursue and you organise yourselves efficiently.

We have only seen the beginning and we can only guess at how outsider politics is going to end up revolutionising our country.

Back in Cleveland, Nigel and Wiggy walked into this bar for last orders and all of a sudden a huge cheer erupted. They turned to see twenty or so very drunk Republican suits, who seemed delighted to see Farage. Within seconds, he was surrounded by people asking for selfies, as he had been all day by Republican delegates.

Farage and Wiggy bought their drinks, then got talking to the delegates. It turned out some of them were from the office of Governor Phil Bryant of Mississippi, who's a big Trump supporter and believes he is the man who can save America. It seems that meeting Farage was the highlight of an evening celebrating the end of the convention. They appeared to know more about Brexit than a good many British voters and wanted the lowdown on how Mr Brexit himself had done it. There may be a scrum of politicians claiming credit for the result in Britain, but only one name has made it across the Atlantic – Nigel Farage.

That shows how successful our networking campaign in the US had been. A lot of the credit for that has to go to Gerry Gunster, our referendum guru, who proved so right so often through the campaign.

Amid the alcohol-fuelled joviality, it became apparent that Governor Bryant's right-hand man John Bartley Boykin – known as JB – was eager for us all to visit Mississippi, where Farage would have an opportunity to speak to grassroots Republican voters. Before they called it a night, he extended a verbal invitation, promising to follow up formally.

Farage had already been hatching a tentative plan to return to the States. There had been so much interest in Brexit during this whirlwind trip, and so many unofficial invitations from Republican senators, that he was considering a low-key speaking tour. American political observers were talking about the parallels between British and US outsider politics.

Now we had influential Trump supporters wanting to know about our strategy in case they could use some of the same methods.

'OK, OK,' Farage replied to Bryant's man politely. 'I'd love to come.' Ever the pessimist, he assumed it would never happen.

Instead, the following day, a formal invitation from the governor's office duly appeared in Wiggy's inbox, complete with suggested dates.

Wiggy resolved not to tell Farage until the trip took shape, but he did tell me.

'Brilliant,' was my reaction – and I was determined to come. I had missed out on the trip to the Republican Convention, but no doctor was stopping me this time.

A fortnight before we were due to set off, Wiggy finally told Farage. He sent him the proposed itinerary, which included an intriguing line: 'Attend fundraising event with Donald Trump – invitation to address the audience before Trump speaks.'

Farage rang us as soon as he saw it.

'Is this more Wigmore rubbish?' he demanded. 'This isn't going to happen, is it? There's no way they'll get me to speak before Trump. Who organised this? Stupid idea. Not going to happen.'

'Is that a yes, then? You're happy to come?' Wiggy asked, unruffled by the usual Nigelisms. We were well used to him.

'Yes. All right. It may be fun,' Farage conceded.

Whatever else it would be, he knew it would be that.

And so it was that the three of us arrived at Heathrow on 22 August for the journey to Jackson, Mississippi, in the Deep South.

After clearing security, Farage suggested a quick sharpener at the Virgin bar.

He presented me and Wiggy with what he called a 'filthy cappuccino martini', which was a new one on us.

Feeling a little light-headed after three glasses each, we boarded. Eleven hours and four bottles of red wine later, we landed.

'What's the plan?' I asked Wiggy.

'Sharpen up,' he instructed. 'We're off to the governor's house for dinner.'

'Christ,' muttered Farage. He dusted himself down and the three of us prepared to put on our best faces.

We knew Trump was in the area and Nigel was looking forward to being a guest of honour at a fundraising dinner for him. He thought he might be asked to make a few comments to the gathering, but nothing much.

At Jackson International Airport, a blacked-out car with security detail was waiting to collect us and whisk us off to meet Bryant and his wife Deborah at their home.

In the car, the governor's aide talked us through the planned schedule.

'So, Nigel. We have a packed itinerary for you,' he declared.

Nigel perked up.

'Firstly, if you're happy, you'll be interviewed on our state's largest talk radio station tomorrow, followed by a visit to the Capitol building, lunch with our top supporters and then on to the fundraiser at five. You'll speak before Trump – if that is OK – and then you and him will do a photo op.'

Farage looked at us anxiously. 'Is this a good idea?' he asked quietly.

'Absolutely,' I said. 'It's amazing, Mr Brexit meets Mr Trump.' Nigel laughed.

We pulled into an impressive colonial-era mansion, where we were met by the Bryants.

'Nigel, it's a great, great honour, thank you so much for coming, I am so pleased to meet you,' beamed the governor. They hit it off immediately.

At the end of a great Southern feast, where we told a few of our best Brexit war stories, Bryant announced it was 'time to retire into my man cave'. In real old-school style, the ladies said goodnight and the men went into the converted garage outside, which was full of motorbikes, old Chevy cars, comfy chairs, a full bar and the best tobacco the South could offer.

'Make yourself at home,' the governor ordered, and we needed no further invitation. The guests could not get enough of hearing about Nigel's 25-year battle against the EU and our victory this year.

It was at this point, when we were too exhausted to think straight, that the governor suggested that Farage take part in a second event with Trump the following day.

'Nigel, I would like you to be the guest of honour at the big rally we are holding tomorrow. Fifteen thousand Trump supporters, and the man himself is speaking.'

'I would love to,' Nigel replied happily.

The truth is, we bounced him into it. Wiggy and I had been in cahoots with the governor's team and had known about the second invitation all along. We hadn't told him earlier because we knew he would have either refused point-blank or changed his mind after thinking about it. For all the apparent bravura, he can be quite risk-averse.

Now he was here, he didn't think twice.

That night, none of us slept well. We gathered at 6 a.m. for break-fast and made our way to the radio talk show. It was exactly as we'd imagined: a larger-than-life presenter with an impressive following across nine states. We pumped out a cheeky press release with a teaser that Nigel would be taking to the stage with Trump. Within minutes, 6,000 people from the UK logged onto the radio show and our phones went white-hot.

'Who told everyone I would be on the same stage as Trump? It's a stupid thing to say, guys, it's not going to happen,' Nigel huffed, cautious as ever.

'Oh yes, Nigel,' piped up JB. 'You'll be introducing Trump tonight at the rally.'

The rest of the day was a blur of media requests and enquiries. Journalists were eager to know what time Nigel would be speaking. We had no idea. Eventually, Nigel got a call from Steve Bannon, recently appointed CEO of the new Trump campaign team, to ask what he was going to say. Nigel reassured them it would be positive, but couldn't tell them much more, because he didn't know himself.

Ahead of the fundraiser, out of earshot of the governor and his aides, Nigel rehearsed a few lines with Wiggy and me.

'I can't say I endorse Trump, can I? But I can say I'd never vote for Hillary.'

'Perfect,' I told him.

We were ushered into a holding room with other guests, gin and tonics in hand, when Trump came in.

'Where's Nigel?' he asked.

He strode over and gave Farage a bear hug, congratulating him on 'a great job winning Brexit'.

Nigel's speech to the fundraiser prompted a standing ovation. After his own speech, Trump called him back onto the stage, where he showered him with plaudits and drew parallels between the Brexit campaign and his own.

With no time to enjoy the dinner itself, we were then whisked off to the second event.

At the rally, 15,000 stoked-up Trump supporters were waiting for The Donald to appear.

Backstage, we hovered nervously, awaiting instructions.

Eventually, one of Trump's aides appeared to talk us through the running order, down to the last minute.

'Mr Trump will start his speech and, eleven minutes in, he will call Nigel on stage. Nigel will speak for six minutes and then leave. You all OK with that?' he asked.

It transpired that the Republican nominee was so enthused by Nigel's earlier speech that he wanted to introduce the UKIP leader himself, rather than the other way round.

Nigel absorbed this information, hurrying outside for a quick cigarette to calm his nerves.

'I don't know why I do this,' he muttered – but he was loving every minute.

Not everyone was happy, however. The new running order had left noses out of joint. It emerged that Farage had bumped Rudy Giuliani, the former New York Mayor, from his speaking slot. His team scowled at us, while we just kept taking selfies and smiling.

Finally, the moment came. Trump strode onto the stage, while Nigel, Wiggy and I hovered in the wings.

'This is nuts,' I whispered.

The Donald paid tribute to Farage's referendum triumph, portraying Brexit as a bid for independence. He vowed that his own presidency would bring the chance for 'American independence'.

Then he called Nigel on stage. Nigel told the crowd: 'We reached those people who have never voted in their lives but believed by going out and voting for Brexit, they could take back control of their country.' He ramped up his lines about Clinton: 'If I was an American citizen, I wouldn't vote for Hillary Clinton if you paid me.

'In fact, I wouldn't vote for Hillary Clinton if she paid me.'

The crowd went wild – and then, as suddenly as it had started, it was over.

After Nigel came off stage, the three of us went outside for a cigarette. We were standing in silence outside, no one wanting to speak first. Then who should come past but The Donald again, heading for his plane. As he left, he turned to Nigel, motioning to Wiggy and I.

'Those boys look like trouble. I'd keep an eye on them.'

Say what you like about the man, but he's a fine judge of character.

AFTERWORD

AUGUST 2016

Can't barrage the Farage

So much for a summer off!

Wiggy and I saw Nigel Farage raise the roof in Mississippi, but we had no idea he'd blown the proverbial doors off back home in Blighty. Our phones were red-hot to the point of volcanic from the moment we touched down at Heathrow – except it was a constant flow of excitable journos threatening to submerge us, not magma.

Farage genuinely believes Trump will win. The pundits and pollsters remain convinced Clinton is going to win a landslide despite Brexit – a phrase we're starting to hear a lot, the longer the promised Leave-apocalypse seems to be delayed – but he thinks our referendum has struck a chord with the American electorate.

Change is possible, Trump is telling them. The same sort of people who said Brexit couldn't be done – exactly the same people, in Clinton and Obama's case – are telling them it's not possible to accept anything but more of the same, but now they know that isn't true.

Luckily, we got some idea of what to expect from the baying hack pack while we were still waiting on our flight. Sitting in the bar at Atlanta airport, G&Ts in hand, we were confronted by Nigel's sun-tanned fizzog in all its HD glory on the jumbo-sized TV overhead (cheers).

Moments later, up pops Madam Crooked herself (boos) – and she's laying into Farage!

'Did she just call you a white supremacist?' I asked.

'Fuck, she really is having a proper go at me,' observed Nigel, incredulous.

'This is real,' Wiggy piped in – a big statement from a man who generally lives his life as though he were an extra in a 21st-century adaptation of a *Flashman* novel.

We must have looked a picture, gazing up at the screen, start-ing to realise just how big an impact Nigel's speech had had – and it wasn't lost on the bar's other patrons. Within a few minutes, Nigel was surrounded by people wishing him luck and thanking him. The fact that, after everything that had happened, we still hadn't been prepared for the reaction, was pretty surreal, when I think about it.

As ever, of course, our reception from the professional opinion-havers was significantly cooler than the one we got from the man in the street (or airport). Criticism of Nigel, Wiggy and I was at fever pitch – but a healthy sense of the absurd kept us from being too overwhelmed by our ridiculous adventure. Whether we liked it or not, we were now guerrilla fighters in the Trump insurgency – not a bad gig for a trio of Brexit revolutionaries with plenty of rounds still left in the tank, really!

Nigel's old friends Steve Bannon and Jason Miller were right at the top of the Trump campaign, and we kept hearing the man him-self repeating the Brexit comparison over and over again. It had really energised the campaign. Officially the establishment were still convinced he was doomed – but they were beginning to look nervous.

SEPTEMBER 2016

Never mind the bollocks

Back in the semi-real world of British politics, I've decided to back Diane James to succeed Nigel as UKIP leader. I'm looking forward to party conference; he's looking forward to getting his life back.

We've been making plans with him for a speaking tour in the US, and naturally the British press are hanging on his every word waiting for more Trump comments. He's got a spring in his step and rightly so – he's our hero, and we've started planning a big thank-you party for him in November.

I've been invited on BBC *Any Questions?* Not a gig I'm really keen on, but Wiggy is a twat and has managed to twist my arm after three days of gentle but persistent bullying. It's on the Friday after the UKIP conference – what could possibly go wrong?

We've decided to base ourselves in Sandbanks, a few miles from the UKIP conference venue in Bournemouth. Nigel is making one last speech and then the new leader will be announced – we are convinced Diane James will get it.

Indulging in a little pre-celebration dinner, we decided to take our drinks onto the terrace outside our hotel, turning a blind eye to an impending thunderstorm and undeterred by a wedding with 150 guests in full swing next door.

After a fair number of war stories and a fair amount of teasing, Nigel got it into his head that now was the perfect time for a paddle in the (eerily calm) sea. With thunder rolling in the background, we all stripped, piled our clothes on the shore and jumped in – of course.

Wiggy screamed like a banshee and immediately began complaining about the cold water, which was having a fierce disagreement with his immaculately brylcreemed hair, while Farage gave us his best rendition of 'Singing in the Rain'.

As if on cue, the heavens opened and a monumental lightning storm started lashing down on us. Wiggy, making an uncharacteristic attempt at being sensible, told us we would have to stay in the water or we might get electrocuted. We told him he was talking shit, and decided to swim to shore and made a run for it towards the safety of our drink and the terrace.

Slight issue: we had drifted about 300 meters from our clothes, so Bournemouth was treated to the spectacle of three drunken, over-weight, middle-aged nudists waddling up the beach in hysterics. Fortunately, the press were not on their game, or the episode could have been immortalised in print.

Back on the terrace, the wedding party turned out to be the only people in Britain with no idea who Nigel is, allowing us to carry on our naked piss-up in peace.

Go on Any Questions?*, give some silly answers*

Diane James won the leadership – really pleased for her. Farage's farewell speech was one of his finest – really emotional. He was kind enough to brief me for *Any Questions?* in Basingstoke afterwards, and I arrived early, feeling bullish.

We go live and the first question is about UKIP: how long until Nigel's inevitable comeback this time?

I assure Dimbleby that Farage is happily decommissioned, and underline my point by regaling the audience with an account of our skinny-dipping escapades. Not the actions of a man who is anything other than happy to be leaving!

Dimbleby – in a state of some shock, I suspect – halts the proceedings to confirm the details.

'Can we just record for posterity that you, Arron Banks, and Nigel Farage went skinny-dipping last night?'

'Yes,' I reply. The other panellists' eyes are like dinner plates; the audience is laughing. I spot Wiggy in the crowd – head in his hands.

Fuck, I think. Maybe this wasn't such an innocent anecdote after all.

Wiggy has to take his head out of his hands pretty sharpish, to fend off journos sensing a delicious story. Five missed calls from

Nigel – not looking to congratulate me on an assured *Any Questions?* performance, I suspect.

Never a man to let the situation keep him down for long, Wiggy is soon laughing his head off at exactly how deep the shit we are in is. We toss a coin to decide whose turn it is to get both barrels – my turn for the now-traditional bollocking, sadly.

'Why the fuck did you say that?' he demands. 'Fucking stupid!'

Wiggy is crying with laughter in the background – which really helps to cool things down, as I'm sure you can imagine. He's a fucking useless press officer, but he still manages to reassure me.

'It will play well – it makes Nigel look human,' he says. 'People know what he's like. He's not some PR creature like Call Me Dave, who can't even be spotted eating Pringles on an aeroplane without people thinking he looks like a dog walking on his hind legs.'

Naturally, it's fucking everywhere in the papers the next day – 'Farage goes skinny-dipping', etc. etc.

Wiggy, to his credit, was spot on. The press love it: Farage is the butt of many jokes, but they're affectionate and come with a heaping side of fulsome praise. As usual, once the positive coverage is in, the great man descends from 50,000 feet and actually laughs with us – I'm still a bit on the naughty step, but overall I think *Any Questions?* was a success!

OCTOBER 2016

Lone Woolfe attack

Diane James resigns – eighteen fucking days! Farage is back as interim leader (old Dimbleby looking smug somewhere, I'm sure) but he's determined not to be dragged back in for long. Fresh leadership elections are called and I decide I'm backing Steven Woolfe.

I head back to Bristol and Nigel heads over to Brussels to give the Eurocrats a richly deserved kick and have a bit of a showdown with the Carswell/Evans tendency in the UKIP MEPs group.

Wiggy calls me – I'll have to get back to him in a moment – and then he starts texting as well. Call Nigel, he insists, it's urgent.

Soon Nigel is on the phone. It's all a bit of a blur.

'He's dead,' he tells me.

'Who's dead?' I ask, not quite taking it in.

'Woolfe. He's dead.'

Silence.

'He's collapsed after a bust-up with Mike Hookem. He's hit him, and he's dead.'

I start laughing – not in amusement, but in disbelief. He can't be serious.

'It's not fucking funny – he's dead,' repeats Nigel. 'This is serious.'

I try to get sense out of Farage, but he's mumbling now: 'He's dead. I'm standing over him, they're taking him to hospital… I'll have to call you later.'

Shell-shocked, I get on the phone to Wiggy.

'What the fuck's happened?'

Wiggy sends me a picture of Woolfe prostrate in the European Parliament. He's spread-eagled on the floor still clutching his briefcase – it looks so literally unreal I burst out laughing and can't stop, but I'm very far off feeling the laughter.

'This is mental,' I say. 'What happened?'

Apparently, Hookem, who is a bit of an old boy, but a grizzled ex-forces type, started getting into it with Woolfe over rumours he was defecting to the Tories.

Woolfe, who is from the rough side of Manchester, offers him a fight 'outside' – schoolboy stuff, and unfortunately his pugilistic spirit is a bad match from his pint-sized frame. It's not clear who threw the first punch – if there was one – but everyone saw Woolfe fly through the door and crack his head on the fixtures.

Moments after storming out, he collapsed very theatrically on the floor.

Nigel is still shaken when I call back – Woolfe is not dead, so he's calmed down a bit, but clearly despairs at his party: Michael Schumacher at the wheel of a clown car.

Woolfe recovers and goes on to sell his story to the *Mail on Sunday* – no lasting damage, thank goodness.

Mr Brexit

Duty calls, so I'll be in South Africa during the Trump/Clinton showdown in St Louis. Nigel has been asked to work the spin room with the Trump team afterwards, because the establishment RINOS (Republicans in Name Only) have bought into the media's narrative of a blue landslide. Wiggy's going too, to keep an eye on him.

The Trump team's plan is to have Nigel – Mr Brexit, slayer of the insider status quo – as their man on Fox, giving a running commentary on the debate.

They've been on the air less than an hour when the Trump 'pussy tape' hits the press – SHIIT.

It looks and sounds awful, and Trump is forced to make a late-night apology – he sounds defensive, but doesn't miss a chance to hit back at the Clintons' decidedly patchy record when it comes to women. Still, I'm worried this could finish him off.

Truth is, men do speak like this, as do women – locker room banter, and all that – but it hardly matters: the liberal media have gone nuclear.

Wiggy has a less than sanguine take on the situation ('FUCK FUCK FUCK') when I tell him he needs to brief Nigel, who is oblivious due to his stone-age phone being out of commission.

If the Republicans were keeping their distance from Trump before, they're openly deserting him now – piling into him, even.

Wiggy calls the Trump team, who are obviously in panic mode – their man needs all the help we can give them. Wiggy assures them we are fully behind them and will do what we can, but convincing Nigel not to board the first flight to Heathrow is no easy task.

The two of them spend the next three hours going over the options. Nigel is cautious – he's no stranger to putting his neck on the line, but this looks more like a chopping block at this point.

He takes a deep breath.

'We stay.'

Due to go on Fox News at the top of the hour what feels like minutes later, he's acutely aware of how big the stakes are.

'What the fuck am I going to say?' he asks Wiggy. 'How earth do I defend this?'

He smokes frantically.

Trying to bring some levity to the situation, Wiggy goes into overdrive cooking up increasingly absurd sound bites. Nigel does not appreciate this at first but, Wiggy being Wiggy, he persists, and Nigel finally cracks, going from stony-faced disdain to collapsing in laughter.

Wiggy tries to press his one genuine line on Farage, but he dismisses it as useless in no uncertain terms, branding poor Wiggy 'the most useless cunt on the planet'.

Wiggy is not a sensitive soul when it comes to abuse (how could he be?) and scolds Nigel, sure he's on to a winner: 'Fucking use it!'

'Bollocks,' Nigel responds tetchily.

Before long, he's up, and presenter Sean Hannity goes straight to the point: how does Trump get out of this one?

'Well,' says Farage. He pauses briefly… then out comes Wiggy's line.

'The American electorate are not voting for a Pope.'

Boom, it's brilliant and the line is replayed on all the networks: 'Farage says Americans not voting for a Pope.'

Our man is soon on a roll; we double down and repeat the line on every network we visit. It starts to add some semblance of perspective to the feeding frenzy, and Trump's team call Wiggy to thank Nigel.

Later, the pair are presented with a whole panel of women who say they have been victimised by the Clintons – Trump has invited them to the debate. Nigel is in disbelief, but Trump is clearly playing for keeps.

They all end up in a hall together at one point: the Clinton victims on one side, the Clinton family on the other – with Nigel and

Wiggy smack in the middle. They're cringing so hard they feel they might sink into the floor at any moment. Wiggy tells me the whole thing was like a slow-motion car crash, and he's not wrong.

I was an ocean away and I still wanted to hide behind the sofa, but, a bit like a car crash, it was mesmerising, and Trump was on fire.

Nigel was back on Fox for the top of the hour before the dust had so much as settled. Wiggy comes up with another blinder – Farage, bouncing, gives him another reminder that he is shit, as I listen in over the phone. It's gold.

'Trump was like a big silverback gorilla, prowling the studio,' Nigel observes – BOOM, this line lands even harder. The American networks run it, the British networks run it, it's all over the papers the next day – Wiggy has excelled himself, and he and Farage squabble about who *really* came up with the lines

Nigel tells Wiggy off again, but is secretly pleased – though he'd never ever tell him. Our Belizean bombshell is the best man to have in a trench when the shit hits the fan.

They're back in those trenches soon enough: only Jeff Sessions, Rudy Giuliani and Kellyanne Conway are ready to defend Trump, and they need that Farage Disney dust in the spin room. It's packed, Wiggy tells me, calling in with a running commentary.

Three hours later, Nigel sees off his last gig – CNN, the Clinton News Network – leaving Wiggy free to start flirting with Judge Jeanine, a popular Fox presenter. They sit alongside Kellyanne Conway, eating cold pizza and drinking red wine (classy), waiting for Nigel to join them.

Kellyanne winks at Nigel and Wiggy as they part ways – job well done. Trump is still in the game.

What happens in Vegas

Back in the UK, we finally finish the first draft of *The Bad Boys of Brexit*, the title for my diary of the referendum. We've roped in Isabel Oakeshott, who wrote *Call Me Dave* with Lord Ashcroft. She is brilliant, funny, witnessed some of our adventures first-hand and is as much a rebel as we are, so it's a perfect fit.

She's shocked and clearly can't quite get her head around how bad we are – she despairs constantly but we love her and know our book will upset the establishment and the Vote Leave crew – which is the main thing!

In Vegas for the next American debate, we are picked up in a stretch limo. Thankfully no surprises this time, and the debate is actually a bit of a damp squib. Trump is still on form, though, and we still believe he will win.

Nigel is in high demand after last time and does wall-to-wall media, and we spend debate night with Judge Jeanine and the Fox gang again. Brilliant trip – but the media still have their blinkers on, and think we are mad and deluded to be associating ourselves with a clearly doomed cause. They can't taste the energy at the Trump rallies like we can.

The Trump team are clearly sensing victory, and the parallels between their campaign and Brexit are not lost on Trump, who is not shy about invoking its example.

Nigel's status as Mr Brexit and place in the Trump team are not lost on the Americans. The British media and the chinless Tory boys of the Vote Leave cartel clearly hate this, the former still struggling to accept that Brexit happened at all and the latter determined to push the fantasy that it was all down to their dreary little campaign.

They never miss a chance to dismiss Trump and to pretend that his campaign has nothing in common with the Brexit movement. The rest of the Tories are even more virulently anti-Trump, to say nothing of the media, where even the constitutionally impartial public broadcasters drop any pretence of neutrality.

None of this is escaping the notice of the Trump team, however, who are keeping tabs via Wiggy on all the vicious tweets and the any-way-the-wind-blows 'conservatives' behind a lot of them. This can only help our motley crew when he takes the White House…

NOVEMBER 2016

Plus Plus Plus

We decided we would watch the election results roll in from our office in Westminster. Trump's team seemed bullish last time we spoke with them, but a lot of the commentators have gone all in on Clinton: this election is already over, it's going to be a landslide, Texas might flip for the first time since Jimmy Carter, etc. etc.

'They're going to have egg on their faces when it all goes pear-shaped,' I tell Wiggy cheerily.

If Farage was wall to wall before, now he's now ceiling to floor as well. The rallies are electric and the crowds have clearly drawn inspiration from Nigel's triumph in the face of seemingly insurmountable odds. 'It's going to be Brexit Plus Plus Plus', Trump has promised them.

Breaking America hasn't come without a cost, however; we seem to be the only supporters Trump has in Britain. Everyone else is terrified to stick their head above the parapet, and the flak we're getting is ferocious.

Racists, sexists, closet fascists – it's Brexit Plus Plus Plus, right enough! Nigel lets the smears dash themselves to pieces like he's a rock standing against the tide, of course, but he's been battle-hardened by years of abuse. Wiggy and I are still taken aback by the viciousness of the attacks; at least from time to time.

We kick off election night at a book launch for Lord Ashcroft – an excellent event, made more so by the fact that our hosts took their eyes off the ball long enough for us to sneak six bottles of His Lordship's excellent Gusbourne fizz to celebrate with back in the office (we hope).

Mr Brexit is off to Florida first thing, so it's going to be an all-nighter – he's not sleeping and neither are we.

We watch as the results start trickling in and fire off a few tweets to the Trump team and our old friend the Mississippi governor

– he's following the proceedings from his man-cave in the governor's mansion.

CNN are giving Madam Crooked a 98 per cent chance of victory (cue laughter in our office) and the Clintonistas are cocky, but our spirits are – with some justification, as it turns out – high.

The results start coming in, and our grins spread wider the lower the news anchors' faces droop. The Dems' so-called 'blue wall' has been kicked over like an old picket fence and the Rust Belt is coming up Trump – he's going to smash it.

'It's Brexit all over again!' I declare triumphantly.

Still, as more and more states turn red, the US and UK media can't quite bring themselves to accept the inevitable, concocting ever more elaborate scenarios in which the electoral arithmetic could still return Hillary to the White House. One of Wiggy's sources tells him that she's already cancelled the planned celebration fireworks display, and he earns a rapid (and rabid) response from the 'Never Trump' trolls when he tweets this out.

Finally, the results come in from Florida – there's a suspicious delay while the tally is finalised in a few fraud-prone Democrat strongholds, but there's nothing to fear. Trump's team get in touch to confirm the impossible, and we're on our feet and dancing: we've won!

President-elect Trump – holy shit. Nigel can't quite believe it and neither can we – nor the rest of the world, come to that! The mainstream media is being laid low by an epidemic of face-like-a-smacked-arse-itis, and it's absolutely brilliant.

The Man with the Golden Lift

Wiggy and I like a drink, but truth be told we're not very good at it. Unfortunately, time waits for no hangover, no matter how monumental, and we were turfed out of bed unceremoniously and given our marching orders for New York – the President-elect had summoned us!

Nigel, who as usual seemed unaffected by our heavy night, was told he'd be making a slight detour, and we possed up with Gerry Gunster and Raheem Kassam, Breitbart's man in London and still close to Bannon.

The call soon came in: Trump Tower, 1 p.m. sharp.

A short flight and a few Alka-Seltzers later, we found ourselves walking down Fifth Avenue towards the famous skyscraper which the liberal cry-bullies had officially designated as America's answer to Barad-dûr.

To our not inconsiderable concern, thousands of these people were descending on the place just as we were coming up to the entrance – and when they realised Mr Brexit was among them, things started to get ugly. Fortunately, a very alert policeman recognised our plight and hurried us through before the crowd could find us all matching lampposts. Abuse filled the air behind us and we made a beeline to the bar (where else?) to regroup.

Nigel saw Bannon privately first, and then we got called up as well. The team greeted us with huge enthusiasm and laughter when they saw us, amazed that we had managed to come strolling into the mob right as the Secret Service were putting the building on lockdown. Thirty thousand people were now demonstrating outside, they told us – a narrow escape.

We were able to observe the meltdown from Kellyanne Conway's office for a while, eating crisps and popcorn and drinking beer like visitors to some sort of bizarre leftist aquarium. The scene was surprisingly calm, with various high-profile visitors to Trump taking the time to come to Nigel, thank him for his support and shake his hand – hoping a little of that Brexit magic would rub off, I think.

Bannon came to see us and we had a good discussion about the campaign, revisiting old battles and laughing at the high and low points.

Wiggy was desperate to see Kellyanne Conway, whose office we were occupying, having nursed a massive crush on her for some time since they first met. Sure enough, when she saw us she greeted him with a huge hug and he immediately turned crimson, uncharacteristically tongue-tied and struggling to get his words out.

Sod meeting Trump – the world's worst press officer had already gotten everything he wanted out of this trip!

They gossiped and joked with each other for a while, after he managed to pull himself together, and eventually she said the fateful words: 'Shall we go and see the President?'

Up we went in several shimmering lifts, before finding ourselves at those extraordinary golden doors leading into his apartment. Nigel added a touch of the surreal by ringing the bell, and the door soon swung open to reveal a relaxed and smiling President-elect.

'There he is!' he said, grasping Nigel by the hand. It was a brief but clearly personal moment – here were two men who knew what it was like to fight a brutal, no-holds-barred campaign in the face of overwhelming opposition, and come out on top at the other end. They were genuinely pleased to see each other, I sensed, and Trump invited us all to sit down.

He was obviously tired – his schedule had been brutal during the last leg of the campaign – but had a profound air of satisfaction. Our discussion ranged over dozens of subjects, and he was thoughtful and reflective throughout. It was perfectly clear he had every intention of acting on the promises made to the electorate, however hard the establishment might dig its heels in, and we shared some of our own war stories.

We were surprised at how open and friendly he was, remembering how mercilessly he had skewered Clinton and his lyin', low-energy rivals for the Republican nomination. He gave every impression of being genuinely happy to see us and genuinely interested in our opinions, and, corny as it might seem, we felt special.

One topic which stood out surprisingly was the issue of wind farms in Scotland – a blight on Britain's beautiful landscape which I hate as much as he seemed to.

After a very full ninety minutes, affairs of state couldn't be put off any longer. I'm sure Trump would have been happy for us to stay all night if it was possible – he and Nigel had forged an unbreakable bond, and it was clear he wouldn't forget how we had stuck by him while his own party had run for the hills. Loyalty counts.

Before we went, he asked if there was anything else we thought he should consider, and Raheem Kassam chimed in straight away: he should restore the bust of Churchill to its proper place in the Oval Office.

'Yes, I love that,' he beamed. 'Where is it, Kellyanne?' She said she would find out.

Now it was Wiggy's turn to pipe up – could we have a picture...?

'Yes, sure, of course!' he replied easily, and in a flash Wiggy's trusty iPhone was in hand, snapping Nigel and the President-elect right in front of those golden doors. Kellyanne took a group shot and we then said our goodbyes, Wiggy admiring the new crown jewel in an already very extensive selfie collection on his way down.

'Fuck me,' he beamed. 'These are brilliant!'

He showed Farage the shot of him and the President-elect – relaxed, happy.

'Bloody hell,' he said. 'That is the picture of 2016. Sums up the most extraordinary political year ever, don't you think?'

Wiggy tweeted the picture out to his small group of followers proudly, not thinking much of it, and paid his phone little attention after that. He was knackered, not expecting anything pressing and just could not be bothered to look at it – it was well past midnight in the UK, and who the fuck would be watching what we were doing with the political world in turmoil anyway?

As we sat down for dinner and ordered a celebratory bottle of red later on, however, we saw him switch it back on and turn ashen-faced.

'FUCK FUCK FUCK FUCK,' he said – which wasn't any great cause for alarm at first, just another day in the life. 'Have you seen this?'

Over 170 missed calls – Nigel's 'Picture of 2016' was everywhere; a global headline.

Nigel was silent. We all were, at first – and then we all burst out laughing. Britain's press were going bananas, and Wiggy's poor iPhone was groaning under the strain of the world's press trying to be first out of the traps with the story behind the photo.

We looked over at the TV screen. Sure enough, there it was: Trump and Farage, looking for all the world like the cats who had got the cream.

'Fuck,' said Nigel, with just a touch of self-satisfaction, I thought. 'I think the PM is going to hate me even more now.'

Nigel Farage, the first British politician to meet the new leader of the free world – and, much like Brexit, it was going down like a cup of cold sick with the British establishment. You have to laugh!

Monsieur Ambassadeur, with these tweets you are really spoiling us!

The fallout from the picture when we got home was just extraordinary. Our old friend Governor Bryant was soon on the phone from Mississippi – amazed and really pleased that we had seen Trump.

Only a handful of Republicans really stood by Trump through thick and thin, and the governor was one of them. A great and loyal man, and the President-elect is lucky to have him, as far as we're concerned.

Early efforts by Wiggy and I to get back to a normal life have been pretty hopeless, so we've decided to ride the wave until it drowns us. Planning a big party at the Ritz to thank Nigel for everything he's done over the last quarter-century; Freddie Barclay is hosting us and Ashcroft is supplying the booze. It's going to be great and we've made sure all of Nigel's friends and allies received an invite – I hope.

Wiggy managed a little taste of normality – by Wiggy standards – with a trip to Buckingham Palace for a Royal Commonwealth Society event.

Not quite persona non grata yet, then, but an official told him in no uncertain terms that he was not to discuss his weekend at Trump Tower or THAT picture with Her Majesty.

I think they tried to shuffle him off into a corner for decency's sake (quite right, to be fair to them) but, not to be denied, the Queen tracked him down and asked – and was that a knowing glint in her eye? – if he had had 'a good weekend?'

Wiggy saw that as his cue to tell all, I imagine, and I'm sure he did. When I pressed him for info, he was surprisingly tight-lipped, though, and refused to give me anything beyond a cryptic 'The Queen sees all!'

It's generally not too difficult to drag some gossip out of him, but the old fop takes the Palace surprisingly seriously.

That seriousness went right out the window a few days later, however, when he woke me 3 a.m. with an excitable phone call: 'Have you seen what Trump has done, Banksy?' he yelled down the line, to nobody's great pleasure. 'I can't believe the madman actually did it! Fucking nuts!' he kept repeating.

Groggily, I told him to a) get a grip, and b) fuck off – it's the middle of the bloody night.

'No, no, no!' he answered cheerily. 'Check your Twitter. Trump has just said that Farage should be British ambassador.'

That didn't seem very likely, I told him, perhaps a bit more grumpily than Wiggy deserved – but there it was, in black and white.

'What?!' I laughed, suddenly wide awake. 'He can't do that, can he?' Trump was pushing the envelope so far even we were beginning to sound like the Vote Leave mob.

'The press have gone mad,' Wiggy crooned. You could feel the cat-like grin spreading across his face through the receiver. 'The Foreign Office will be apoplectic.'

'Have you told Farage?' I asked.

'No – he's in Strasbourg, sound asleep.'

Wiggy had found out himself from none other than Governor Bryant, whose team called him up to pass on their apologies.

'What for?' he asked.

They explained that Trump and the governor had been talking about Nigel and musing about what they could do with him – apparently, the President-elect joked that he would make a fine ambassador to the White House, and said he would tweet his feelings on the subject accordingly!

Governor Bryant laughed, thinking how popular that idea would be with Downing Street – perhaps not realising that Trump was serious.

The President-elect's team were next on the phone, tipping Wiggy off that the fateful tweet had indeed been sent. Wiggy thought they were all having him on until his phone exploded into life at 1 a.m. UK time.

Trying my best to put a serious face on things, I told Wiggy he had better let Nigel know he was sleeping through a minor diplomatic incident and he was at the centre of it.

Predictably, Nigel did not appreciate the late-night call, did not believe Wiggy for a second, and didn't have much more to say on the subject other than 'Fuck off, Andy.'

Raheem was next up, trying to convince him it wasn't a wind-up, and eventually the penny dropped. He was in shock – we all were – and meanwhile the rest of the world was going into overdrive getting their heads around the tweet.

'I suppose this is where the "Plus Plus Plus" comes in,' I laughed. We had pulled off a revolution with Brexit, sure, but the old guard were still in charge, and they'd be carrying out the people's instructions reluctantly, if at all. The Trump revolution was different – the old guard had been cleanly decapitated, and the rules of the game had clearly changed.

No. 10 were pulling their hair out trying to bury the story. Wiggy received a ferocious call from some press officer calling him a cunt, and was told politely (but firmly) to fuck off.

'You're not in an episode of *The Thick of It*, you twerp,' Wiggy told him. 'And if you think you or I have any control over what Trump does with his thumbs, you'll be more use to the PM sat at home sniffing your armpits than stomping around the press office making a fool of yourself.'

Advantage: Wigmore.

The next morning, the question of Nigel's ambassadorship was being raised in Parliament, never mind the press. The commentariat were in an absolute lather trying to figure out why the world was being collectively trolled by a reality TV star. Nigel bloody Farage.

The whole thing was hilarious. Nigel was revelling in it, and his party swiftly acquired a new twist. Wiggy sent the brilliant and ever-patient Victoria Hughes, who had been our Boneglove wrangler-in-chief and voice of sanity through much of the referendum, but had decided against all sense to stay on with us, for some reason, out into London to buy as many Ferrero Rocher as possible.

'You know, like the old advert,' he explained. 'Monsieur Ambassadeur, you are really spoiling us!'

It's easy to forget that he really is an accredited diplomat at times like these.

True to form, Victoria rose to the occasion, and I was able to hand a plate of 200 chocolates to Farage when he arrived at the Ritz – it made an absolutely perfect picture, and I'm sure Downing Street were crying bloody murder when they saw it.

Britain's actual ambassador to Washington DC was none too pleased either, from we could gather – but he hadn't made the best of impressions on the President-elect, who knew exactly what he was doing. All the naysaying rhetoric from before the election was coming home to roost – for the ambassador, for May's team, and for all the smug little Eurocrats in Brussels who thought Clinton, the insider's insider, had his number.

We all knew the PM could never bring herself to actually make use of Nigel, of course – even though it was the most obvious thing in the world to do, given Britain's need to strengthen ties with America after Brexit and the clear personal rapport between the President-elect and Mr Brexit himself.

Still, better to stick with people who have zero contacts and a less-than-stellar reputation with the new administration than risk some bruised egos by making use of an obvious national asset – that's the establishment way!

Paul Nuttall was named the new leader of UKIP in late November, relieving Nigel of his interim leadership duties and allowing him to get his life back – or indulge in mischief on a full-time basis, at any rate – once again. He soon landed a weekly radio show on LBC and slots on Fox News, and was inundated with requests for speeches. Many were in the US, and Wiggy and I were happy to tag along and drop by Trump Tower on a regular basis.

Always fun; always surreal.

The press now had their teeth into us as the hardback of the referendum book was out, and the usual suspects had teamed up with Friends of Matthew Elliott Incorporated to try to be as rude as possible.

Wiggy and I didn't give a shit: we had set a new bar for rudeness in politics, and we didn't have much to fear from these amateurs. The book is honest about all our mistakes as well as our successes, including how we dismissed the Tufton Street cosy club behind Vote Leave.

It was Nigel that people heard on the radio, saw organising rallies, and going head to head with Cameron in the referendum; the bedwetters in the (now dissolved) Johnson–Gove fan club could pretend that the Electoral Commission designation made us vanish in a puff of smoke all they like, but proper analysts like Matthew Goodman knew who really won the referendum.

The fact that the public and the wider world all acknowledged Nigel as Mr Brexit was making their blood boil. ('I think you'll find we won designation; it's Douglas Carswell and Gisela Stuart who are the real household names in Britain' – yeah right!)

This was clearly illustrated when Lord Pearson nominated Nigel for a richly deserved knighthood – he only needed UKIP's sole MP to sign off on it, but the slanty-jawed, boggle-eyed bellend was convinced the man who brought him into UKIP didn't deserve so much as 'the order of the bottletop', and killed the whole thing.

Petty, childish and a great shame, but the political establishment will never forgive Nigel for taking their beloved EU away from them. Still, I'm convinced the Queen secretly loves him and would welcome him as a knight of the realm – some day.

JANUARY 2017

Long live the king

We've been invited to attend Trump's inauguration as guests of Governor Bryant, and we've decided to hold the mother of all parties at the historic Hay-Adams hotel in Washington DC to celebrate.

We'll be hosting 400 of our closest friends and allies, plus Gerry Gunster's team are making sure all the big movers and shakers are invited. Ashcroft is supplying us with some Gusbourne fizz for the event, so we can do our bit for British sparkling winemakers while we're out there.

We have tickets to the ball as well, so we're bringing the wives along to act as a bit of a moderating influence. It meant forking out a fortune for dresses, but this is an American coronation, I suppose!

The world still can't come to terms with the new king, however, and the hysteria is huge. Half a million representatives of 'The Tolerant Left' are planning a march for Saturday and tension is high.

First port of call is Arlington Cemetery with Ashcroft and Nigel, though, so we can lay a wreath for the only British soldier buried there. Very moving to see the thousands of neatly manicured graves stretched out as far as the eye can see.

It's a welcome pause for reflection for Nigel, whose media schedule is chock-a-block. We join him for the Fox interviews with our new favourite presenter Judge Jeanine. Brilliant, we think, and reminds us of Joan Rivers – unfiltered and great fun. She's coming to our party and bringing some more Fox friends.

We also have meetings with some mad Hollywood types about a *Bad Boys of Brexit* film. Wiggy is like a kid at Christmas, playing up to the assembled producers. He's always fancied himself as film star and it shows – but thankfully he's exactly what they want, and a big discussion about who will play us gets funnier and funnier.

The question of who will play the handsome, Bond-like Mr Tice occupies a large portion of the meeting, as does who is going to play Farage. Anyway, they are up for it and we invite them to stay for the party – they agree – and Wiggy promptly tips off the British press about our impending big-screen debut.

More headlines – thankfully not that bad! – and Elliott and Cummings are no doubt spluttering into their Duchy Originals organic cornflakes.

The party itself is nuts; anyone and everyone in Washington cuts loose and we all have a blast. Nigel gives a tub-thumping speech alongside Governor Bryant: three cheers for Brexit, and three cheers for Trump!

Inauguration Day itself is pretty special. We have the BBC following us preparing a documentary while we take our place among the throngs of Trump supporters to watch our man sworn in as the next POTUS.

It's a barnstorming, first-of-its-kind speech, and we're grateful to have a front-row seat for this historic event.

It's a challenge making our way back, and we hear 'Not My President' crybabies are kicking off. We have two Secret Service agents looking after us for a while and we decide to lie low in – where better? – an Irish pub.

Nigel is greeted like a hero and for the next three hours we raise our glasses to Trump.

Nuttall gets crèmed

We make our way to the ball along with another 10,000 guests, dressed up to the nines. It's as massive as the attendance figures would suggest, but we soon find ourselves in the VIP room with our old comrades in the Trump team, who are naturally on cloud nine.

We ask if Trump has put the Churchill bust back in the White House. Out comes the first official photo, and there it is – our man was as good as his word. Nigel raises yet another glass to the President.

Back home for the Stoke by-election, it's a different world. Paul Nuttall throws his hat in the ring, hoping to make a statement by winning 'the Brexit capital of Britain'. Can't see it, but Wiggy, Tice and I make the trip out to support him at Easter.

Nigel tries to keep a relatively low profile so as not to steal Paul's thunder, but inevitably he draws in big crowds at the campaign's main rally – and plenty of protestors, too.

Soon enough, the eggs are flying – but these are not ordinary eggs. Just for once, Wiggy lives up to his Olympic potential and manages to snag one out of the air: they're chocolate crème eggs!

Brilliant – he snaps a shot of me tucking into one for Twitter. Clearly our protestors have a better sense of humour than the Never Trumpsters.

Sadly, our photo op does not turn the tide for Nuttall – it's a strong second but he doesn't make it over the line, having been caught being 'economical with the truth' on his extensive CV. I call him the Purple Pinocchio, but Nigel doesn't see the funny side!

FEBRUARY 2017

Calexit

Across the pond again, Nigel is speaking at the Conservative Political Action Conference (CPAC) alongside Trump. Of course he nails it – 10,000 cheering conservatives all loving the dynamic duo!

Next stop is California, where we have a bit of a special meeting with a few super-rich people interested in splitting up California so the conservative hinterland don't stay prisoners of the Hollywood elites – Calexit, we call it.

What was supposed to be a small gathering ends up being well over a thousand people, all cheering Nigel and Brexit.

'We must say nothing to the press,' Nigel instructs us soberly. Fat chance that a thousand activists are going to be keeping this one quiet, and as predicted it makes the headlines: 'Farage to Break up California', screams the *LA Times*.

Nigel lays into Wiggy with his best Malcolm Tucker impression: 'Who the fuck leaked that, then?' he scolds.

'Fuck off,' Wiggy replies – gently. 'There were a thousand people in that meeting – of course it was going to get out.'

Nigel grumbles something about going for a smoke – seeing sense but not best pleased about it, we think.

Anyway, the meeting ends up raising $1 million to get the ball rolling. It's a tall order, but it's been done before – just as we thought we were coming to the end of the madness, we've ended up jumping right back in!

I put Wiggy in charge at our end – what could possibly go wrong?

Wigexit

I fly back while Nigel and Wiggy stop over at the Trump hotel to rendezvous with Ashcroft about an event in Ethiopia.

The gang decide to drink until departure time is on them, when suddenly there's chaos. Trump has just come in, spots Nigel and invites them over to dinner.

Naturally, Wiggy has a picture up on Twitter as soon as possible – headline news again! The establishment are reeling – but this time they fire back.

Watching CNN at home, I suddenly see they're accusing me of being a 'Russian actor'. An old meme in Blighty, but 'the resistance' are giving it a new lease of life stateside.

The Atlantic Council release a report concluding that Brexit was funded by the Russians and that Wiggy and I were the central players – absolutely mad, but suddenly that diary entry about us quaffing Stalin's booze with the ambassador isn't quite as funny as it used to be. Wiggy gets Mishcon de Reya on the case.

Then comes the follow-up punch – Cameron's old Attorney-General Dominic Grieve has made a formal complaint to the Foreign Office about Wiggy's diplomatic status.

Apparently, what with Brexit, Trump and all the rest, he's broken the Vienna Convention. He's summoned by the Foreign Office and expelled from the Court of St James by Boris, like some sort of Cold War-era KGB spy.

He's furious at the pettiness of it, but the truth is he's hardly been acting diplomatically of late, so he takes it on the chin.

The Prime Minister in Belize is sympathetic and tells him not to worry: he's going to Washington instead! Fuck you, Boris.

The British ambassador is naturally upset by the idea of our alternative British Embassy, so of course we do nothing whatsoever to smooth things over. We quickly secure an office in Georgetown for our little trips to DC.

The Foreign Office try to save their dignity by leaking the letters bollocking Wiggy for undermining the British state from the comfort of Chipping Norton, but he isn't too bothered – he gets all sorts of surprisingly supportive calls from all sorts of surprising places.

'Fuck them,' he tells me cheerily. He'll have to live without his diplomatic status in Britain now, but doesn't seem too put out by it.

It's Leave.EU wot won it

Wiggy has spoken with *The Guardian* about our use of data and AI during the Brexit campaign.

The lefties still can't get their heads around how we outplayed them, both at home and in the States.

Wiggy gave a good account of what we did, and for once played it with a pretty straight bat, describing how we outmanoeuvred the Tory cartel at Vote Leave and hijacked the referendum even after the crooked Electoral Commission awarded them designation.

It was Nigel and Leave.EU wot won it, we explained. Cummings has gone off the deep end, naturally, slagging us off and repeating that our mad antics prove that things would have gone south if Vote Leave hadn't been running the show – as if they were!

Trying to deny Nigel and UKIP were front and centre as far as the public were concerned only makes his lot look more delusional. Mark Wallace has called them out on it, and they're clearly furious, making all sorts of stupid mistakes to try to snatch up some crumbs of glory. They even claimed they were the ones who used our data!

The Remoaners have been working themselves into a lather with marches, petitions and Russian conspiracy theories while we've been off enjoying ourselves in America, clinging to the hope they can somehow overturn the result, like those grey-haired Japanese holdouts who were still fighting the Second World War from the jungles of forgotten islands into the '50s and '60s.

Three investigations have been thrown at us by the Electoral Commission – who haven't taken kindly to our appraisal of their abilities – and Liz has hit the roof with their incompetence (which is a nice change of pace).

They're being very officious about it, and I think it's put their noses out of joint a bit that we've just told them to fuck off – this is political, and they're welcome to do their worst.

Nigel was emotional on Article 50 day – the richly deserved culmination of a life's work. We decide to celebrate – at the local pub, for once.

Fuck doing the rounds on College Green with the world's press; if Cummings and Elliott really believe they were as instrumental as they say then they can carry the heavy water – if half the journos can even recognise them!

They didn't, of course, so all the journos descended on Nigel at the pub. He'd never looked more relaxed, sitting there in his Union Jack socks, holding court.

It had been a strange twelve months and, while I've been surprised before, I finished up this entry sure that nothing else could possibly happen to make it any stranger.

Then the word came in to me from the press office: Theresa May has called an election. You've got to be kidding me!

If you're looking for the index, there isn't one.
Deliberately. Read the bloody book!